THE MANCHESTER COLLEGE

D0319066

STAa Th

On Being a
Comedian

STAND UP!

On Being a
Comedian

Oliver Double

Methuen Drama

RECEIVED

15 MAY 2015

9.48

First published in Great Britain in 1997
by Methuen Drama

www.methuendrama.co.uk

Oliver Double has asserted his right under the
Copyright, Designs and Patents Act, 1988
to be identified as the author of this work.

A CIP catalogue record for this book
is available at the British Library.

ISBN 0 413 70320 7

Typeset by Palimpsest Book Production Limited,
Polmont, Stirlingshire
Transferred to digital printing 2002.

This paperback edition is sold subject to the condition that it
shall not, by way of trade or otherwise, be lent, resold, hired
out, or otherwise circulated in any form of binding or cover
other than that in which it is published and without a similar
condition, including this condition, being imposed on the
subsequent purchaser.

Contents

Acknowledgements

Writing this book has only been possible with the co-operation and support of a large number of people, and I would like to offer my sincerest thanks to anybody who has helped in any way, even if it has only involved listening to me blathering on boringly about the latest bit I've been working on.

I would like to thank all those who gave interviews, which were a vital source of background information: Terry Alderton; Malcolm Bailey; Arnold Bolt; Johnny Casson; Martin Coyote; Keith Dover; Leslie Frost (whose help was invaluable in giving me an insight into what it was actually like to see a show in a variety theatre); Phil Gasson; Steve Gribbin; Master Ruxton Hayward; Mandy Knight; Ian MacPherson; Kevin McCarthy, the Man with the Beard; Dylan Moran; Henry Normal; Gina Ryan; Kevin Seisay; Mrs Settle; Anvil Springstien; Ian Stone; Nick Toczek; Nick Wilty.

For the extracts from stand-up comedy acts which are included in the text (except for very short 'review-type' quotes), all rights of reproduction and performance remain with the copyright holders, to whom I am most grateful for permission to use their material. My thanks are due to the following, who gave permission to quote from material from comedy routines, interview material, or written sources: Tony Allen; Jim Barclay; Eva Reichman, for Max Beerbohm; Max Boyce; Jo Brand; Arnold Brown; Tony Burgess; Rhona Cameron; Jasper Carrott (and Steven Hutt at Highfield Productions), for Jasper Carrott; Frank Carson; Johnny Casson; Julian Clary; Bernie Clifton; Gwen Cooper, for Tommy Cooper; Martin Condell, AKA Martin

Coyote; Hunter Davies; Andy de la Tour; the late Florence Desmond, for extracts from *Florence Desmond by Herself* (Harrap, 1953); Bob Dillinger; Lisa Dixon, for Reg Dixon; Ken Dodd; Claire Dowie (and Colin Watkeys), for Claire Dowie; Adrian Edmondson; Ben Elton (and McIntyre Management Ltd.), for Ben Elton; Terry English, for Arthur English; Simon Fanshawe; Stu Francis; Routledge, for extracts from Sigmund Freud, *Jokes and Their Relation to the Unconscious* (Pelican edition, 1981), p.144; Leslie Frost; Phil Gasson; Tony Gerrard; Ronald Langevin and H.I. Day ('Physiological correlates of humor'), and Howard R.Pollio, Rodney Mers and William Lucchesi ('Humor, laughter and smiling: some preliminary observations of funny behaviour') (and Academic Press), for extracts from Jeffrey H. Goldstein and Paul E. McGhee (eds.), *The Psychology of Humor* (Academic Press, 1972); Edward E. Gray, for 'Monsewer' Eddie Gray; Stephen Gribbin; Mike Harding (and Larry Redmond), for Mike Harding; Jeremy Hardy; Master Ruxton Hayward; Lenny Henry (and Helen Constantinides), for Lenny Henry; D.T.S. King (and Tessa Le Bars), for Frankie Howerd; Claire Anderson at Virgin Books, for extracts from Frankie Howerd, *On the Way I Lost it*, (Star Books, 1976); Barry Took and the late Marty Feldman, for material written for Frankie Howerd; Mark Hurst; Jimmy Jones (and Brian N. Shaw at Empire Management), for Jimmy Jones; Jenny Lecoat; Norman Lovett; Ian MacPherson; Rik Mayall; Pauline Melville; Eric Midwinter, for extracts from *Make 'Em Laugh* (George Allen and Unwin, 1979); Gary Morecambe, for Eric Morecambe; A.W. Evans AKA Rory Motion; Tom O'Connor; Nigel Planer; Marion Peggy Baldwin, for Sandy Powell; Sybil Ray, for Ted Ray; Elizabeth Cherry, for Al Read; Michael Redmond; N. Piney at Barclays Bank Trust Company Ltd., for Beryl Reid; Nick Revell; Gina Ryan; Alexei Sayle; Anvil Springstien; Ian Stone; A. Stephenson, for extracts from Jimmy Tarbuck, *Tarbuck on Showbiz*, (Fontana, 1986); Mark Thomas; N. Bratley at Our Clubs

(Sheffield) Ltd., for Eric Thomas; Frank Wappat, for Bobby Thompson; Tim Vine; Johnny Wager; the estate of Max Wall (and Michael Pointon), for Max Wall; Charlie Williams; Charlie Williams (and Michelle O'Connell), for extracts from Charlie Williams, *Ee – I've Had Some Laughs*, (Wolfe Publishing Ltd., 1973); Nick Wilty; Victoria Wood (and Vivienne Clore at The Richard Stone Partnership), for Victoria Wood.

Thanks also to the following for kind permission to reproduce the photographs included in this book, whose copyrights remain with them: Getty Images Ltd., copyright © for Dan Leno, Max Miller, Frankie Howerd, Billy Connolly, Bernard Manning/The Comedians; McKenzie/Hulton Deutsch copyright © Doug McKenzie for Les Dawson; BBC Photograph Library, copyright © BBC for Bobby Thompson, Victoria Wood, Alexei Sayle, Ben Elton, Lenny Henry; The Richard Stone Partnership for Mark Thomas, copyright © F Sanjar; Channel 4 Stills Department copyright © for Jo Brand and to Jane Morgan for Eddie Izzard and Sheffield City Libraries for The Empire Palace Variety Theatre.

Every effort has been made to trace copyright holders, but in some cases this has not been possible; apologies are due for any errors or omissions in the credits which, if more information comes to light, will be corrected in future editions.

I would like to offer my sincerest thanks to all those who helped me in the vast and arduous task of tracing copyright holders of material which, in some cases, dates back to the early part of this century: Barry Took; Roger Wilmut; Jack Seaton at the British Music Hall Society; the British Broadcasting Corporation; Equity; the Grand Order of Water Rats; B.B.C. Radio Newcastle; The Society of Authors. What made this difficult job far more enjoyable than it might have been was the number of people who took time to talk to me on the telephone, passing on fascinating stories about their own work, or their late relatives' experiences, particularly Edward E. Gray, Will Fyffe Junior, Ted

Ray's son (whose name, I'm afraid, I can't remember), and Pauline Melville.

I would also like to thank: Clive Barker, who helped me to get this project started, showing immense generosity, and without whom this book would not have been possible; Michael Earley at Methuen, whose guidance and encouragement have been consistently excellent; Liz Hornby for her careful copy-editing and Helena Beynon and David Salmo at Methuen; my wife, Jacqui, who has read through various drafts and made useful comments, as well as offering loving support; my son, Joe, who has kept me laughing through the final stages of preparation; Adam Caveleri and Roger Monkhouse, with whom I have shared many experiences of performing stand-up comedy, some of which are described in this book.

Chapter One

Standing Up

The experience

I hear the sound of my own name getting applause and a bit of cheering and I'm on. I walk over to the microphone, timing it so I get there before the applause runs out. The expectation is bad enough as it is. Underneath the blurry glare of the lights there's a whole load of faces looking up at me, wanting to laugh but not knowing if I'm funny yet. I hit them with my first big gag, and bang! They laugh. I relax. The nerves drain away, and I'm a comedian again.

The good feeling that buoys me up and makes it feel like I'm floating can't be tied down with words. I'm giving the audience the pleasure of my company, and they're loving it. It's my thoughts, my pet theories, my idea of what's funny, and each time I give them the option, they laugh. Every punchline gets another life-enhancing woof which pumps me up with more and more energy. Even the bar staff are laughing. I'm surfing on a wave of goodwill.

Everything falls into place. The new material works perfectly. It's such a joy to do new stuff when it works. It's a bit like feeling my way in the dark, and when the laughs come, whoom!, the lights come on, revealing a surprise party in my honour. Somehow, I manage to breathe new life into those tired old gags that are limping a bit and really should have been sent off to the Old Jokes' Home a few gigs ago. I find a new way of putting them over, twist the delivery slightly, and suddenly they're as fresh as the day I first cracked them.

Better than that though, I'm improvising. New punchlines for old routines suddenly strike me. The idea comes into my head, and without a second thought it tumbles out of my mouth, and there's a laugh. I say things about what's going on in the room, how the jokes are going down, people in the audience, and the things I say get laughs. This is instant comedy, with a butterfly lifespan. These jokes exist for a moment, then they're gone. If you repeated them to somebody outside of the gig, you'd just get a blank stare. The strange thing about improvised stuff is that it just comes to me. It pops into my head unbidden. It is like the comedy god speaking through me. Somebody heckles, and there's a put-down coming out of my mouth before I can think about it. The audience cheers.

Before I know it, I'm into my last routine. There's something almost trance-like about a good gig, because time goes so quickly. I completely lose any sense that I'm in the odd situation of being stared at by a hundred strangers. It's like being deeply engrossed in a conversation. Things that I say onstage on the spur of the moment are quickly forgotten. Only when somebody comes up to me afterwards and refers to them do I remember having said them at all.

There's a huge roar when I leave the stage, and I feel triumphant. For the rest of the evening, people smile at me as I pass. Somebody buys me a drink. Somebody shakes my hand and tells me I'm great. Sometimes audience approval gets a bit ridiculous. I once did a gig in a tiny room above a Central London pub, and went down so well that when the final act failed to show up, the audience spontaneously started shouting for me to come back onto the stage. I had no material left to give them, so I impressed them by doing ten press-ups, then left the stage to another cheer.

Best of all, I get paid. I've just had the best night of my life, and now someone's counting ten-pound notes into my hand. I feed my wallet until it's satisfyingly fat, and leave the venue lighting up the night with my glow.

Sadly, it's not always like that, though. Sometimes it's like this –

The sound of my name being announced is like the order for the firing squad to go ahead and pull the trigger. The faces looking up at me are oddly disconcerting. I'm getting the sort of looks I got when I dropped my lunch down myself in the school dinner hall and everybody turned and stared. My first big joke comes and goes with little more than a bemused chuckle. I start to panic: that was one of my strongest gags. If they didn't like that, what are they going to make of some of the rubbish that's coming up?

Instantly my mouth is as dry as a desert. My brain goes numb. As the responses get weaker and more irritated, I begin to feel like the unfunniest man in the world. My jokes are like a list of casualties after a horrific terrorist bombing. I try to cling onto a scrap of hope. There's a couple of strong jokes coming up which might just drag the audience onto my side. This could be the turning point, but instead, the strong jokes come out sad and limp, getting not so much as a chortle. Now there's no chance. It's downhill all the way.

Nothing works. My poor, dry mouth is losing the capacity to speak English, translating the last three words of every punchline into some obscure Eastern European dialect. I can't move properly. In my mandolin song, my fingers turn into great useless, blobby pork sausages that actively search for the wrong notes. My props run away and hide in the darkest corners of the stage. Once, at a university gig in Salford, I made the mistake of putting all my props on a table at the side of the stage. I found myself increasingly unable to click with the audience, and stopped being able to move properly. In one routine, I had to bend down suddenly, and, sure enough, I smacked nose-first into the table and blood started gushing from both nostrils.

The fact that I'm stuck to this rotten script seems inescapable, because my brain is too numb to try and improvise.

Finally, in desperation, I try to force out some spontaneous comments, but they're stiff and shaky. Somebody heckles and gets a bigger laugh than I've had all night. I reel out an instant heckle put-down, but all I get is a sea of sneers and the odd pitying snigger.

Time goes so very slowly. I'm acutely aware of myself and of the difficult situation I am in. Every mistake, every garbled line hits me like a slap around the face. I try to hold myself together so the whole thing doesn't visibly fall apart. All I want is for this to be over. The audience looks at me as if they're a bank queue, and I'm at the counter trying to pay in a hundred pounds in small change. They're impatient, they're irritated, they just want me to finish what I'm doing as quickly as possible, then get lost.

After a lifetime's struggle, I get off the stage to a damp smattering of lame claps. Offstage, people avoid eye contact. The promoter tries to be supportive, but you can see his brain ticking away as he hands over the cash: 'That's the last time I'll be booking *him*, thank you very much.' I walk out into the cold, harsh night to the sound of the fulsome laughter which the next act is getting. For the rest of the night, my brain gives me increasingly intense flashbacks of some of the worst moments.

The challenge

This is what my best and worst experiences of doing stand-up comedy have been like. Usually, it's somewhere between these two poles, a little worse than the first but a lot better than the second. Whatever happens, stand-up is an intense form of entertainment for the comic. I would define stand-up comedy as *a single performer standing in front of an audience, talking to them with the specific intention of making them laugh.* The two key features in this definition present a hefty challenge:

1. *A single performer* As a stand-up, you're very much on your own. You can't rely on anybody else to help you out if

things get sticky. If you triumph, you can hog all the praise for yourself, but if you fail, that great, stinking pile of shame falls on your head and your head alone.

2. *The specific intention of making them laugh* Your job is to make the audience laugh. What you do is defined by your ability to create a specific response in a roomful of people. The challenge you set yourself is so difficult, it requires a degree of arrogance. If you call yourself a stand-up comic, what you are saying is, 'I can go into a room full of randomly assorted strangers and make them react exactly how I want them to.' If the audience doesn't laugh, you've quite simply failed. The content of your act is irrelevant. You may have been inventive, imaginative, intelligent, but if they didn't laugh, you're a failure. In this sense, stand-up is harder than stage acting, because a quiet audience in the theatre doesn't necessarily mean that individual members of the audience haven't enjoyed the play. If a stand-up comic goes down to silence, you can be fairly sure that not a single person in the room has had a good time. The stand-up's problems are also compounded by the fact that the job is dynamic and interactive. If a comedy film isn't getting the laughs in the cinema, the celluloid will keep rolling through the projector completely unaffected by its failure. The stand-up feeds on audience response, and if the laughs don't come, he or she will tense up, the delivery will lose its edge, the whole performance will get worse, and so the audience will laugh less and less.

The ego

Given all this, it is no surprise that stand-up comedy is an ego-ridden profession. When I first started, a good gig would send me floating off on a warm cloud of delirious happiness for at least a week. A bad gig would give me an eye-stinging feeling of being alone and unloved, which would last for about the same length of time. With experience, the intensity of these reactions has faded, although the bad ones have retained some of their emotional kick. I will celebrate a good gig with nothing more extravagant than an upwards tweak of the volume knob on my car stereo on the way home. As I've described, time zooms by when I'm doing well on stage, and the laughs and the applause and everything I did that was good quickly evaporate from my memory. The bad gigs still stay around to haunt me, sometimes for a couple of days. I mull over all mistakes, and work out ways of avoiding those pitfalls in the future. The idea that everybody who saw me that night has gone away with the idea that I am a no-hoper sometimes pops into my head and refuses to leave.

The least pleasant side of the ego problems that go with the job of stand-up is the competitiveness. Stand-ups don't just want to go down well, they want to go down better than anybody else on the bill. I've never been a particularly competitive person, but stand-up forces you to watch the opposition. This is a terrible admission, and I may be the only comic to think like this, but there's something fantastic about watching another act going down badly. Part of me is sympathetic, but deep down there's a bit of evil glee. There's a lump of pure selfishness in me that is thinking, 'Ha! I went down really well, and he's dying on his arse! I'm brilliant and he's rubbish!' At its least heinous, this is the product of insecurity, the need for reassurance, the need to know that I'm not the only person in the world capable of going down that badly. At worst, it is pure, insane egomania, the desire to be enthroned as absolute dictator of the comedy universe, and to see all my challengers viciously struck down.

The boring bits

Being a stand-up isn't just a seething mass of ego-trips and jealousy, though. There's also a lot of boredom involved. Whether on public transport (battling against late trains and overpriced refreshments) or in a car (hurtling down endless stretches of bland, grey motorway) getting to the gig always means a struggle against tedium. It's not much better when you get to the venue, as there's inevitably time to kill before the show starts. Usually, this involves a bit of small talk with the person who runs the club. This comes in two flavours. There's conversations with the promoters I've already worked for, which might go something like this:

PROMOTER: Oh hi there, how's it going? (*Translation: How have the gigs been going recently? Not been dying too much, have you?*)

ME: Not bad, not bad. Yeah, things've been going pretty well recently, actually. (*What, don't you trust me or something? I'm a good act, you don't need to worry on my account.*)

PROMOTER: Have you been busy? (*I'm not the only one stupid enough to book you, am I?*)

ME: Reasonably, yeah. Yeah, actually I had a really hectic week last week, 'cos I was in Leicester on Wednesday, my own club on Thursday, Manchester on Friday and Saturday, then I had to go down to Bath on Sunday. (*Look, I told you, you can trust me. I do get other gigs, and I run my own as well.*)

PROMOTER: So are you still in . . . Sheffield, is it? (*The only thing I really know about you is where you live . . . and I'm not even one-hundred-per-cent sure about that.*)

ME: Oh yeah. I don't really have any plans to move in the near future. (*Why are you asking me these stupid questions?*)

Then there's the conversations with promoters I've never met before, usually people who have never seen me work. They might go something more like this:

ME: Hi, I'm Oliver Double, I'm supposed to be doing a gig for you tonight. (*Translation: Hi, I'm really funny, believe you me!*)

PROMOTER: Oh right, nice to meet you. Do you want

somewhere to dump your bags? *(Oh, thank God for that, at least one of the acts has turned up on time.)*

ME: Yeah, that'd be great. *(I'm glad you asked that, my arms are killing me.)*

PROMOTER: Just put them through here. So, do you make a living doing this, or do you have a day job as well? *(You can make people laugh, can you? Tell me you can. Please tell me you can.)*

ME: No, this is my main thing, this is all I do really. *(Hey, trust me, I'm a professional.)*

PROMOTER: And does it normally go pretty well? *(Are you sure you're not just completely hopeless?)*

ME: Well it seems to, yeah. *(Oh for God's sake! Look, I'm going to be good tonight, OK? Probably.)*

One of the questions that promoters I haven't worked for before tend to ask me is, 'Have you been doing this long?' I usually keep things a bit vague when they ask this. On the one hand, I want to reassure them, but on the other, I don't want them to think I've been around too long to be still doing gigs on this level. Sometimes, it's best to deliberately wind them up. On one occasion, when a promoter asked me, 'Have you been doing this long?' I feigned wide-eyed innocence and came back with, 'Well actually, this is the first gig I've ever done.'

After the show, if you've got there by train, there is the prospect of staying the night on somebody's couch, and a good night's sleep is by no means guaranteed. I once found myself without a bed for the night after a show in Chester, and one of the other acts kindly offered to help me out. Just as we got to his door, he turned around and said, 'How are you with dogs?'

'Oh, well . . . not terribly keen actually,' I replied, a bit sheepishly.

'I'd just better go and lock Benny in the back room then, or he'll be all over you,' he said.

It turned out that Benny was a Staffordshire bull terrier,

and as I settled down, fully clothed, under the blanket on the sofa, I started to read the local newspaper that'd been left lying across the floor. The main headline was about a local girl who had been mauled by such a dog that very day. I tried to settle down for the night, but the noise of Benny hurling himself against the door was curiously unsettling. It sounded like somebody was trying to batter their way in with a sack of potatoes. The fact that I needed to go to the lavatory didn't help much, but a full bladder was far less threatening than an encounter with Benny on the way to the toilet.

Then there are the times when there isn't even a couch to bed down on. On one occasion, I missed the last train from Derby by a minute, and had to spend the night on a bench in the waiting room. Luckily there was some heating on, but my night's sleep was not improved by the fact that somebody else had already bedded down on the other bench. All night, he kept making scary strangled-chicken noises in his sleep.

Another time, in Walsall, the venue I was playing at had sorted out a bed and breakfast for me, but when I turned up at the place where it was supposed to be, it was nowhere to be seen. After desperately wandering the streets for a couple of hours trying to find somewhere that was open, I eventually went to the police station to ask for advice, and luckily, they managed to find a B&B that would take me in for the night. The next morning, without prompting, the landlady served me up a massive breakfast of bacon, eggs, liver, mushrooms, beans and lard-rich fried bread. Being a vegetarian, this posed a bit of a dilemma. I was the only guest there that morning, so it would have been conspicuously rude to push half of the food to the side of the plate, but on the other hand, I have a moral objection to eating meat. As it turned out, the bacon was really nice.

In any event, whether you spend the night away or manage to make it home, the chances are that you won't be able to get to sleep straight away. The adrenalin continues to pump around your body long after the show is over, and gives you plenty of time for watching some mind-rotting late-night television. I remember coming across *American Gladiators* and *World Wrestling Federation* for the first time, and slouching there with slack-jawed amazement that TV could be so brainless. There's also an ultra-low budget cookery show called *Get Stuffed*, in which student types make recipes in their own kitchens, filmed on a hand-held domestic camcorder. It lasts about five minutes, and they show several episodes per night. You know you've got a serious late-night TV habit when you start waiting up for the last episode.

Another post-gig hazard is the friendly punter. The classic unwanted friendly punter experience is when somebody comes up to you after a show and says, 'Here's a joke you could use, mate.' The joke that follows is always something completely depraved, usually involving two naked nuns and a Nazi stormtrooper. What amazes me is the idea that I can have given the impression that I would want to hear such a joke, let alone consider telling it. Then again, the capacity people have to misunderstand comedy is extraordinary. I used to do a routine which looked at why we are disgusted by menstrual blood, getting a few gross laughs along the way. In it, I specifically said that the taboos which surround menstruation are 'stupid', because 'they make women embarrassed about the normal functions of their bodies'. In spite of this, I've had grinning lads come up to me after a gig and say, 'The periods stuff was really good, 'cos you really embarrassed some of the girls.'

Sometimes people make comments which bring home to me just how little they understand of the whole business of stand-up. One is: 'When you're up there on the stage, how do you think of things to say?' The idea that a comic stands in front of the microphone without any kind of prepared material and just says the first thing that comes into his or her head is touchingly naive. Then there are comments which damn with faint praise. People will say things like, 'You're so brave, I don't know how you can stand up there in front of all those people,' or, 'I don't know how you remember all those things you have to say.' Personally, I would much rather people praised me for being funny, than for being brave or having a good memory.

In the end though, these people are only trying to be friendly, and there are times when a cheery-faced punter is the one glimmer of light in a dark and savage evening. After a hellish gig, in which your chances of being funny are torn asunder by barrages of hate-filled heckling, it is almost inevitable that a couple of people will come up to you and say, 'Sorry about the rest of the audience, mate, *we* thought you were brilliant anyway.'

This sort of comment is always welcome, although sadly, there are the exceptional cases when you don't even get that. There was one occasion when I was called in at the last moment to do a show at a big nightclub in Middlesbrough. Originally, it was supposed to be a one-man show by a hypnotist, but he had pulled out and had been replaced by a couple of other acts and myself. The evening started with a magic act with plastic grins, who performed tedious tricks to a backing tape. The audience was not amused. They were followed by a middle-aged balancing act, whose genuine skill was masked by ridiculous stage costumes. After the initial laughs of derision at the sight of a middle-aged man in a toupee and a yellow stretch nylon bodysuit had died down, the audience began to get restive.

By the time I went on, they were baying for blood. The compere said, 'You'll be pleased to hear that the next act is a comedian,' and somebody shouted, 'He'd better be fucking good.' There was real violence in the threat. I was so tense I thought I was going to implode, and the mass of menacing faces glaring at me didn't help. Nothing worked, and the background chatter was quick to start. I could hear murderous oaths being muttered loudly. One table of lads started heckling, but every time I tried to interact with them, they'd instantly shut up. Then, as soon as I got back into my material, they'd start heckling again. It took no more than ten minutes for the antagonism in the audience to be vented on me and I came off thoroughly defeated. After the show, there were no kindly comments by well-meaning punters, there were no 'Well, I thought you were good's. The only reaction I got from individual members of the audience was when a couple of twenty-year-old women walked over to me and very deliberately, one at a time, kicked my props bag.

My peculiar career

My own perspective on the joys and hazards of being a stand-up is a very particular one. I don't know what the job is like for a famous and successful stand-up comic, as I am still clinging onto the very bottom rung of the showbiz ladder. The nearest I have got to being rich and famous is appearing on Radio 4's *Kaleidoscope* a few times and a three-minute spot on the snoozeworthy daytime TV show *Pebble Mill*. I should also point out that my way into the world of stand-up comedy was unusual. I first got interested in it whilst I was studying drama at Exeter University in the mid-1980s. The Arts Committee at the Guild of Students used to organise termly cabarets, in which anybody could get up and perform in return for the payment of a can of beer. The first time I went, it was the first time I'd ever seen anything approaching a variety show, and I was dying to get up and try my hand. Only cowardice prevented me. The next time they organised a cabaret I came prepared, and earned three cans of beer.

From there, I began to perform sporadically, and became involved in Exeter's political benefit circuit. Anti Apartheid, Devon Labour Briefing and the Exeter Safe Energy campaign were just some of the causes that benefited from my developing comic skills. Most of the shows went on in a room above a pub just outside the town centre. They were dominated by anarchist punks and followers of Class War, and doing routines between ear-splitting bands with names like The Waste and The Garbage Grinders was a tough start to a stand-up career. My fellow performers on the Exeter anarcho-vegan cabaret scene included two Scots lads in a band called Nyah Fearties who went on to get a bit of attention in the music press, and a fat poet called Jon Beast who later gained a cult following through performing with the indie band Carter USM.

When I moved to Sheffield in 1987, I started organising shows of my own at the university under the title Red Grape Cabaret. The name was taken with unselfconscious pretentiousness from a cabaret run by the communist German playwright Bertolt Brecht, which had been shut down by the Nazis. From running termly shows in which anybody who wanted could perform a whole set of all-new material, we quickly evolved into a hardcore of four performers with a mission to unleash our emerging comic genius onto the world. As well as myself, there was Roger Monkhouse, now making a modest name for himself on the alternative comedy circuit; Adam Caveleri, now a medical physicist, but who took time out of researching the human heart valve to do comedy shows until comparatively recently; and Phil D. Rogers, who left the group when his performing nerve snapped. (After a few bad shows, he began to resent the audience, chastising them when they didn't give him the laughs he thought he deserved. Disillusioned with stand-up, he now works in the book retail trade.)

Selling ourselves as a package of individual acts, we began to trek around the arts centres, student unions and provincial comedy clubs of the land. Our travels took us all over the Midlands and further afield, up to pubs in the North East and down to hippy festivals in Cornwall. We became worryingly familiar with motorway service stations up and down the country, and got used to the idea of an after-gig meal being no more than a microwaved pasty, a can of coke and a chocolate bar. We learned our trade as we went along. Some nights we were nothing more than a parade of laughless wonders, our rawness and inexperience all too glaringly obvious. Other times everything clicked into place, and we came away feeling like proper grown-up comedians.

Meanwhile, we also worked on our solo careers. In April 1989, I went to London for the first time to do a series of open-mic. spots in established comedy clubs. My London debut was in a tiny pub room in Hampton Wick, and the regular compere was Eddie Izzard. I'd only heard of him because he had been at university with Adam, but I was immediately impressed. He came on to a shower of goodwilled heckles, which immediately made me panic: I didn't know if I'd be able to handle that. I needn't have worried, though. The heckles were just for him, and they stopped dead as soon as the other acts came on. He played that audience like a conductor controls an orchestra. The heckles were carelessly swished aside. In his fruity posh voice, he slurred and muttered as he dredged out bits of whimsical nonsense straight from his subconscious, and his audience immediately converted them into laughs.

Later that week I had the misfortune to do an open-mic. spot at the club which Malcolm Hardee ran just after his notorious Tunnel Club had shut down. Gerry Sadowitz, then at the height of his infamy, was there just to watch the show. One of the acts was Jack Dee, whose snarling cynicism fitted in with the mood of the audience. It was the day after the Hillsborough disaster, and that fact was used as a jokey way of introducing me, what with me being from Sheffield. By the time I reached the stage, the audience were chanting 'Fuck off' in unison, at full volume. My proudest achievement was that I managed to silence them a couple of times, and actually made it through my five-minute spot, but my habitual signing-off line, 'My name's Oliver Double and showbusiness is my life', sounded particularly absurd that night.

In the summer of 1989, Red Grape Cabaret took a show called 'Comedy Abattoir' up to the Edinburgh Fringe Festival. It was a classic Edinburgh good-luck story. In the first week, we found ourselves playing to as few as three punters, but consistently glowing reviews allowed us to sell out by the end of our last week. On the back of this success, the number of gigs I got, both with and without the group, increased, so that by 1991 I was ready to go full time, with the help of the government's Enterprise Allowance Scheme. Then in 1992, I helped to set up Sheffield's Last Laugh Comedy Club in a pub called the Lescar. I became the resident compere there, and later took over the running of the gig.

What is unusual about my career pattern is that I have worked mainly outside London. Most of the alternative comedy circuit is still concentrated in the capital, and although I have gone through phases of going down to work the London clubs every couple of months, I have concentrated most of my efforts on the ramshackle provincial circuit. Working in the provinces makes for an interesting life, because the gigs tend to vary so much from one to the other. This is partly because the idea of pub-based alternative cabaret is less well-established outside London, so the people running the shows sometimes make mistakes; and partly, it's because there's less work around, so I tend to accept anything I can get.

I've found myself performing to three hundred students at Lampeter University one night, and twelve people in an art gallery in Bradford the next. I've turned up to venues and found that the only publicity for the show is a single piece of felt-tip-scrawled paper stuck to the wall. I have worked in discos, trying to get laughs out of hordes of dancers shouting with puzzlement and annoyance because the music has gone off. I have been put on the same bill as acoustic guitar-wielding singer-songwriters, jugglers and tedious performance poets. To give an idea of the chaos I encounter, here's my Top Five hit parade of bizarre gigs –

Number 5! In October 1995 I went down to Oxford to do the first night of a new comedy club. As I struggled to find a parking space, the act I had driven down with got a call on his mobile phone from a nervous promoter wondering where we had got to. When we walked into the venue, we found out the reason for his nerves. The gig was due to start in half an hour, and so far, the audience consisted of a table of elderly people finishing their meal in a distant corner, and two thirtysomethings propping up the bar.

The promoter dashed out to do some desperate last-minute leafletting, and we waited for an audience to arrive, glumly sizing up the venue. It was an arts centre bar with nightclub trappings, all split levels and brass railings: not a particularly comedy-friendly environment. We eventually started at about eleven o'clock, an hour after the advertised starting time. There were just twelve people in the room, including a tableful of the promoter's friends.

In spite of the circumstances, the show was tremendous fun. Members of the audience regularly threw in comments, and some of them became part of the act. Every time a new punter walked in, I got everybody to turn around, grin blankly and say, 'Hi! Have you ever thought of bringing Jesus Christ into your life?' in unison. There's an old gag on the alternative circuit which most comics have probably used at one time or another: when somebody goes to the toilet, you say to the audience, 'Let's all hide!' On this occasion, the whole audience went ahead with the plan, hiding behind the speaker stack at the side of the stage. I only did about half of the material in my usual twenty-five-minute set, but I was on the stage for more than forty minutes.

Number 4! In 1991, I compered a show at UMIST in Manchester. Not having had much experience of compering, I did all of my material right at the beginning, thinking I could get through the rest of the show by doing little more than introducing the acts and throwing in the odd off-the-cuff gag. It was a well-organised gig, with a proper stage, a decent public address system and a hundred or so students sitting round tables and listening and laughing obligingly. Everything ran to plan at the start of the show, and my act was respectably received, but as the evening went on, my off-the-cuff skills were tested to the limit.

The first act was a mildly crazy American juggler and, at one point, he was setting up a trick in which he would juggle fire-clubs whilst riding a unicycle. Somebody shouted out that he should watch out what he was doing with his blazing clubs, as he was getting a bit close to the smoke detector. Rising to the challenge, he put the flames directly under the detector. Almost instantly the whole place sprang to life with bleeping alarms and flashing lights, and the building was evacuated. Three fire engines turned up and people started murmuring angrily that the false alarm would cost the students' union hundreds of pounds.

Half an hour later, we were allowed back into the building, and it was my job as compere to turn this bemused mob back into an audience, and put the show back together. When everybody had finally traipsed back in and settled down, I walked onto the stage and delivered the obvious line for the circumstances: 'It's amazing the lengths some people will go to to get a laugh, isn't it?' There was a big laugh, and the gig was back on course.

Number 3! One of Red Grape Cabaret's first bookings, in 1988, was to entertain a roomful of students after a protest march about student grant cuts. We turned up at Aston University, ready to start at the unpromising time of 11 am. We were going to start our show with a comedy song, so at five to eleven, I walked onto the stage wearing a gas mask, my electric guitar at the ready.

As it turned out, the meeting was packed with Socialist Worker students who decided that comedy was inappropriate at such an important event, and started shouting that they wanted a debate instead. As the guttural political slogans got louder and the tension reached fever pitch, I began to feel a bit stupid sitting there with my electric guitar and my gas mask, so I walked off the stage. The student union hacks who had booked us obviously decided that now was the time for a face-off with the SWP. They told us not to worry, our show would definitely be going

17

ahead, not least because the guest speaker, Clare Short, had not turned up yet. So I went back on there, still with my electric guitar and my gas mask. The howls of protest had not died down.

Eventually, I decided enough was enough, and I came off again. Reluctantly, they agreed that we would not be performing that day. Amazingly, when Clare Short eventually arrived, she went out and faced them without any kind of prepared speech. If she was intimidated, she certainly didn't show it, and she launched into her speech without breaking into a sweat. Something about her absolute confidence struck a chord with the howling politicos, and they shut up and listened obediently. Her voice resounded with absolute authority, silencing the revolutionary hecklers and turning them into appreciative punters. It has often occurred to me that with steel nerves like that, if her political career falls apart, she could do worse than try her hand at stand-up.

Number 2! In December 1989, I was called in at the last minute to do a show in Barrow-in-Furness. The journey up to this remote Cumbrian town involved changing trains twice, and as signs of civilisation grew fewer and further apart, I got the impression that I was travelling back into the Middle Ages. After a bite to eat at what proudly proclaimed itself to be 'Barrow-in-Furness's first American theme restaurant' (in reality a pizza joint with half a Cadillac stuck to the wall), I went to the venue. It turned out to be a disused disco. The 'community cabaret' I had been booked to appear in was one of the last events there before it was due to close for good, and the place was gloomy and shabby. The carpets were sticky, the walls were starting to peel, and the dangling glitterballs were tarnished. It was the disco of the living dead.

The show started with a very English country and western band and a performance poet, and then, just before I went on, there was a pantomime featuring prominent members of the community. My curiosity was aroused when the booing started. I peeked out from backstage and saw that it was the wicked witch who was on the receiving end of the catcalls, which seemed much too heartfelt to be just a bit of pantomime fun. My instincts had served me well. The wicked witch was being played by a Labour councillor, who was involved in a prolonged and bitter dispute with the local trade unions. The trade unionists gave full voice to their grievances as the panto limped lamely to its conclusion. Then it was my turn to go out and knock 'em dead. It's showtime!

As it turned out, it wasn't too painful. Not everybody was listening by this time, but a few enthusiastic youngsters sitting at the front created the illusion of being an audience. They listened and laughed as I rushed through my fifteen minutes, and gave me a kind round of applause at the end. Afterwards, I went to the hotel that was provided by the organisers and drank in the bar until the early hours. On the train on the way back, I rejoiced as civilisation slowly came back into view.

And finally, at Number 1! In June 1993, Red Grape Cabaret were booked for a student ball in a large block of student accommodation called Mason Hall, in Birmingham. We were due on in the early hours, so we didn't bother turning up until after midnight. None of us was looking forward to the show. Student balls normally involve going on after a hypnotist who has the audience in stitches by making volunteers take off their shirts and pretend to be Tarzan or something. By the time you go on, the audience has turned nasty, and you usually perform to a hail of paper cups filled with the last droplets of cheap wine.

Student balls also tend to run behind schedule, and this was no exception. Our starting time came and went, and by the time we went on, the PA hire firm had packed up and gone home, taking with them not only the PA, but also the stage lighting. As it turned out, the lack of lighting was not a problem, as it was now 5.30 am and the summer sun was streaming through the massive windows. The student sound engineers hastily rigged up an impromptu PA system. From their schoolboy physics, they knew that, in theory, you can use headphones as a microphone if you plug them into an input channel. No sooner said than done! They hastily rigged up a set of speakers to an amplifier, plugged in the headphones, and – hey presto! – an instant public address system!

By now, most of the students had stumbled drunkenly back to their rooms. Through the windows, we could see newly consummated couples lying down together on the grass, sharing bottles of wine and basking in the dawn sunshine. Their faces were covered with postcoital idiot grins. The forty-or-so students who still had a taste for merrymaking assembled in front of the stage, and Roger went on to start his compering. The impromptu headphone-microphone unit gave him the voice of a British Rail platform announcer, so he quickly cast it aside. Amazingly, the idyllic, peaceful atmosphere of the summer morning didn't stop the audience quickly descending into a mob of belligerent hecklers, and Roger's unamplified voice fought a losing battle to be heard over the din. Eventually he gave up, and with incredulous amusement, introduced me onto the stage.

I was steeled and ready for a fight, so the first laugh rather threw me. I kept my guard up but moved onto the next punchline, and sure enough, there was another laugh. Never leaving myself open for an instant, I ploughed on through the set, and the laughs kept coming. I even managed to fend off a drunken shouter in a dinner jacket, much to the delight of his fellow punters. I came off to a rousing cheer. I was pleased with my victory, but it felt very odd to have been engaged in a Titanic comedy struggle so early on a beautiful summer's morning.

Chapter Two

Variety

Not really songs at all

I've just listened to a record called 'Mrs Kelly' by Dan Leno. It's one of those ancient, mechanically recorded things that sounds like you've got a chunk of fluff the size of a mothball on your stylus. It starts with a bit of a song: an unmemorable tune, accompanied by the sort of piano you associate with a traditional pub sing-song. Then the song stops, and Leno *speaks*. His voice is thin. It sounds as if his Cockney accent has been poshed out by elocution lessons, but there are still those old-fashioned inflections that you hear when you see chirpy Londoners on old newsreel footage. 'A's are pronounced as 'e's, so that 'Spaniard' becomes 'Spenniard', and the 'r's are slightly rolled making them more like 'd's – 'very' sounds almost like 'veddy'. In the speech, Leno is playing a woman who is unlucky in love:

'My first husband, he was a Spaniard. Said he was a Spanish Count in his own country. He didn't count for much in this. But oh, girls, a Spanish Count, do be careful of um . . . well of counterfeits! He told me that in his own country, he was a bullfighter. I found out he worked at a slaughterhouse. And he said that the olive complexion was the colour of the people in his country. I found out it was dirt! But you know, Jim, Jim's a totally different man.

Jim loves me. You know, and he's lodging now with Mrs Kelly. You know, Mrs Kelly? You know Mrs Kelly, but, b. . . Don't you know Mrs Kelly? Her husband's that little stout man with the . . . always at the corner of the street with the greasy waistcoat. Good life, don't look so stupid, don't you must know Mrs Kelly. Don't you know Mrs Kelly?? Well of course if you don't, you don't, but I thought you did, because I thought everybody knew Mrs Kelly. Oh and what a woman, perhaps it's as well you don't know her. Oh, she's a mean woman. Greedy. I know for a fact, her little boy who's got the sore eyes, he came over and told me. She had half a dozen oysters, and she ate them in front of a looking glass to make them look a dozen.'

The song ends with the piano coming back in while Leno sings the final verse. What's fascinating about this is that it dates from the time when stand-up comedy came into being in this country. This lump of character comedy monologue, the meat in the middle of a musical sandwich, represents the point at which this new form of spoken comedy crawled from the primeval swamp of Victorian music hall song. Here's a rough and ready three-point guide to the evolutionary process.

1. The Victorian music hall
Music hall entertainment was largely made up of songs, usually comic ones. They had relentlessly jolly little plinky-plonky tunes, most of them sounding exactly the same to the modern ear. Think of some of the more famous songs – 'Any Old Iron', 'Down At The Old Bull And Bush', 'Roamin' In The Gloamin', 'Two Lovely Black Eyes', 'My Old Man Said Follow The Van' (real title: 'The Cock Linnet') – and you have a pretty good idea of the musical style. The music hall comic was a forerunner of both the pop singer (songs, hedonism, chance for working-class people to become rich and famous and die young) and the stand-up comedian

(solo performer working directly to an audience to get laughs). A typical act would be made up of a string of songs performed in character, with quick costume changes between numbers, and the odd bit of dancing or strolling up and down the stage thrown in for good measure.

2. Embryonic stand-up

By the beginning of this century, the mutation of comic singer into stand-up comedian was well under way. It started with the odd gag being thrown in between the verses, and this developed into the 'Mrs Kelly' format, with a big chunk of patter inserted into the middle of the song. The concept of stand-up, spoken comedy directed straight out at the audience, was so new and novel that it didn't yet have a name. In 1905, J. Hickory Wood described Leno's style in his book *Dan Leno* (Methuen):

> 'One calls his performances on the hall "songs" for want of a pithy word that is better; but they were not really songs at all. They were diverting monologues in a style of which he was undoubtedly the originator as he was its finest exponent. With him the character was the first consideration; the amusing wealth of monologue or "patter" was the means whereby he gave his audience an insight into that character, whilst the verses struck one as being, in most cases, a somewhat unnecessary interlude.'

3. Stand-up Comedy

By the 1930s, the transformation of funny singing into funny talking was complete, but singing and even dancing remained an important part of the art of stand-up comedy right up until the variety circuit collapsed in the early 1960s.

It's hard to believe that the kind of performance that Leno

23

has left us engraved on this scratchy record really is the single-cell organism that eventually evolved into stand-up comedy. Stand-up is vibrant, immediate, dynamic and, crucially, funny. I'd have to inhale a lot of nitrous oxide before I could get a laugh out of Leno's records, and as a comic, I'd hate to face an audience with the Mrs Kelly monologue as my only laughtermaking equipment. Dan Leno was the king of music hall comedians, but he's left no trace of a laugh on his records. Listening to him and his contemporaries from the other end of the century is a bewildering experience.

Mark Sheridan's comedy, for example, stands out as being particularly weird. Sheridan became famous for songs like 'I Do Like To Be Beside The Seaside', and went on to shoot himself in a Glasgow Park after a nervous breakdown in 1918. His patter was delivered at breakneck speed, in a bizarre accent with carefully rolled 'r's, which sounds like a cross between Scots and W.C. Fields. Any jokes I've managed to pick out from the verbal blur are painfully thin. Things like: 'They're all wild in our regiment, even the cigarettes they smoke are wild, Wild Woodbines.' Or: 'We've got the finest bugler in the world in our regiment, I've known him to blow a blast in Dublin, if you'd been in Plymouth you'd have seen the Sound. Ha ha!' What his audiences found funny about this kind of thing is an almost unfathomable mystery.

The passage of time has taken its toll on the battered vinyl legacy of these embryonic stand-up comics, a problem worsened by their poor sound quality. In 1901, when Dan Leno recorded 'Mrs Kelly', recording techniques were extremely primitive. Listening to it is rather like overhearing a conversation in the next room during torrential rain. It can't have been easy for music hall artistes to adapt to the newfangled recording process. Instead of working to a live audience in a theatre, they had to perform their routines into a large metal horn. Dan Leno's frustrated reaction was, 'How the hell can I be funny into a funnel?' while his contemporary, George Robey, said in one of his recorded routines: 'I am asked to come here and sing into a tube. Yes. I know, it's all very well. I'm asked if I will kindly oblige by putting my face here and making myself ludicrous.' There's a story about another music hall comic, Tom Leamore, who insisted on moving away from the microphone to do his stage walk between every verse while he was recording. The problem was that he wasn't getting back to the mike in time to sing the next bit. In the end, the recording engineer had to put the cellist in his way to stop him moving about.

What really cripples the recordings is the lack of audience reaction. The comics had nobody to work to, and so their performances are oddly stiff and formal. The excitement and joy they could generate on stage has been completely drained by the recording process. The lack of audience laughs also makes the jokes inaudible to modern ears. When I listen to old recordings of comics, an audience laugh tells me the comic has just told a joke, even if the passage of time has made the joke incomprehensible to me. Leno was doing his Mrs Kelly routine in the vacuum of a recording studio, so it's anybody's guess which bits made his music hall audience laugh, and how loudly.

Just at the time when Leno and his contemporaries were getting their audience rolling in the aisles with their mutant hybrid of song and stand-up, another great transition was taking place: music hall was changing into variety. Music hall grew out of tavern sing-songs in the middle of the nineteenth century. As they grew in popularity, they became more of a commercialised form of entertainment than an informal gathering. The generally agreed birth date for music hall proper is 1852, when Charles Morton opened the Canterbury Hall, and after that, it spread like wildfire. By 1868, there were five hundred halls across the country, two hundred of them in London alone.

It's difficult to think of music hall without thinking of the BBC's recreation of it in *The Good Old Days* on television in the 1970s, with men in striped blazers and ladies in large hats singing along as some celebrity of the day sang 'Boiled Beef And Carrots' or whatever. This was a sanitised, rose-tinted, soft-focus picture. In reality, music hall was the product of a different world, of a Victorian London awash with poverty and grey, filthy slums, with horse-drawn carriages trundling along cobbled streets swirling with smoke and fog. The first music halls were little more than large rooms built onto the back of taverns. Inside, working-class men would have a hedonistic good time, sitting round wooden tables, eating pies and pickles and swilling ale whilst listening to songs and jokes from the stage. Many of the songs were about food or drink or sex, and all three would be on sale in the auditorium. Booze and food were sold by the management, and sex was available on a less official basis, from the prostitutes who used the halls to increase their trade.

As the halls became more popular, there was a conscious effort to move upmarket. The newer halls were bigger and more palatial. Inside, they reeked of luxury and splendour, with plush carpets and chandeliers, balconies and proscenium arches, gilded plaster mouldings and red velvet curtains. They were given names like the 'Palace', 'Empire' or 'Coliseum'. Champagne was sold along with the ales. The audiences broadened out. As the men-only policies were dropped, women began to attend, and the plusher halls were frequented by stylish upper-class funseekers or 'swells'.

A night out at the music hall offered a hefty slice of entertainment. A chairman would introduce up to thirty acts in a show which could last up to four hours. It might include songs, comic patter, clog dancing or acrobatics. Cross-dressing was a big part of music hall culture, and not just with men impersonating women. 'Male impersonators' like Vesta Tilley were hugely successful, and actually influenced men's fashions with their stage costumes. This is the root of the 'principal boy' and the 'dame' in modern pantomimes. Towards the end of the nineteenth century, music hall stars started appearing in pantos, often bringing whole chunks of their act with them, including gender reversal.

At the beginning of the 1900s, the music hall circuit started to restructure itself. Under pressure from moral campaigners, the halls made a play for respectability. Alcohol, food and prostitutes disappeared from the auditorium. The first Royal Variety Show in 1912 gave the halls an official seal of approval which encouraged the middle classes to start swelling the audiences. The entertainment itself also changed. The mammoth thirty-act shows were replaced by shorter bills, presented twice nightly. The music began to change after a British tour by the Original Dixieland Jazz Band in 1919, becoming more influenced by American popular styles. All these changes meant that music hall was pronounced dead, and the new form of entertainment it had evolved into was christened Variety.

Variety was different from music hall partly because it had to co-exist with other attractions like cinema, radio and eventually television, as well as rival live forms like concert party and revue. This meant cross-fertilisation as well as competition. George Formby and Gracie Fields went from being big variety stars to being big movie stars, and their cinematic success boosted attendances when they played in variety theatres. Al Read made his name as a radio comic after the second world war, and his radio star status allowed him to top the bill when he played the variety circuit. However, competition with other forms of entertainment meant that the variety circuit was in a state of continuous, slow decline. In 1920, there were sixty-nine variety theatres in London and six hundred in the rest of the country, but that number would continuously fall over the next few decades. At the beginning of the 1930s the General Theatres Corporation (GTC) and Moss circuits (which were owned by the same company, but run as separate circuits) boasted fifty-three theatres. When

27

the circuits were finally merged, there were just twenty-four left.

A night out

For somebody like me, born in the 1960s after it had all disappeared, it's easy to see variety as a dusty folk-memory of shabby, faded glamour: a parade of inadequate acts with false smiles. In fact, the variety circuit was part of a vibrant entertainment scene a million miles away from the out-of-town multiplex cinema style of today. I live in Sheffield, and if I could jump back in time to the 1950s for a good night out, I'd be faced with an enormous number of options. I could hop on a bus or a tram and go and see a play or a variety show at one of the theatres, or I could see a film at one of the fifty cinemas that were spread all over the city.

If I wanted to see a variety show, I could go upmarket or downmarket. There was a hierarchy among variety theatres from the number ones run by Stoll or Moss Empires, to the number twos and threes on the MacNaghten, Broadhead or Barrasford circuits. In Sheffield, that would mean a choice between expensive places like the Lyceum, cheaper but well-kept places like the Empire, and shabby joints like the Attercliffe Palace, where I might find myself surrounded by mums with kiddies in pushchairs, laden with shopping bags. The theatre building might be grand and ornate with domes and pillars and balustrades. There might be picture frames attached to the wall around boards announcing the week's acts. Inside, there'd be stalls, balconies and boxes, maybe a pit, possibly a gallery. The bills would change every week, running twice nightly from Monday to Saturday. I might find myself sitting next to a regular: some people would sit in the same seat in the same theatre at the same showing on the same day every week.

Before the show started, the orchestra would play. Maybe they'd be good and maybe they'd be ear-jangling but, in either case, they'd probably be part-timers: milkmen or factory workers in the day, musicians in the evening. On either side of the stage there'd be an indicator board made up of electric bulbs which would light up to form numbers showing which act was on stage, as listed in the programme. The first half would probably start with dancers, and then there'd be a series of acts: greenhorn comedians, acrobats, magicians, performing animals, paper-tearers or contortionists, none of them lasting more than about twelve minutes. In the latter years of variety when they were struggling for audiences, there were also nude acts, in which women were allowed to appear naked for the pleasure of the male members of the audience, but were forbidden by law to move. They just stood there like statues.

In the interval, the orchestra would play again. If I was in a Moss theatre, they might play a selection of numbers from the current musical they were putting on in one of their West End venues. Down would come the safety curtain, onto which they'd project next week's bill and adverts for local businesses. I could go to the bar for a drink, or maybe buy some sweets. I could have some Smarties or a choc ice, but anywhere posher and my choice might be restricted to something more expensive like a box of Terry's All Gold.

After the interval, the dancers would kick off the second half whilst the rest of the audience straggled back from the bar. There'd be a couple more acts, maybe a singer and a speciality act, and then there'd be the top of the bill, probably a comedian or a singer. By the 1950s, when the variety circuit was on its last legs, you might have got the top of the bill doing the entire second half of the show. A '50s bill-topper might be a comic like Frankie Howerd, a singer like Alma Cogan, or perhaps a band led by the likes of Joe Loss or Harry Roy. The musical style would be big band jazz with stiff British rhythms, dance hall music for a seated audience. There'd be guest vocalists, singing with wobble-voiced earnestness in *Brief Encounter*-style stage-school accents. The band leader might crack a few gags between numbers, and get embroiled in some wacky crosstalk with some of the musicians. The audience might be asked to join in with some community singing, harking back to the music hall days when the punters used to join in with the choruses. By the late 1950s, the music changed as singers like Cliff Richard and even Buddy Holly introduced rock'n'roll to the dying variety circuit.

All-round entertainers

The comedians who populated the variety circuit hit the audience with an all-singing, all-dancing style a million miles from the just-stand-there-behind-a-mike-and-tell-gags approach of today. Stand-up grew out of singing, and music remained a big part of it for decades. Take apart a performance by Max Miller, the epitome of variety comics, and you'll see that the songs, the poems, and the soft-shoe dancing are as much a part of his peacock appeal as the string of saucy gags he came out with. It was important for the stand-up to be a showman, not least to ensure that the audience would applaud, as Max Wall pointed out in a radio interview in 1990: 'In those days we had to learn an instrument or dance or sing or do something to get off the stage to a hand. This is what was unforgivable, if you got off without a hand.'

In the 1920s and 1930s, stand-up comedy was still new enough for people to invent their own variants of it, refusing to restrict themselves to just standing there and reeling out gags. Billy Bennett, for instance, would sing songs and declaim monstrous monologues parodying popular poets like Kipling. Harry Hemsley replaced the single voice of the stand-up with sketches in which he would play a whole family of characters. He sat on the stage as the father, and voiced the conversations between the imaginary offstage characters, concealing his lip movements by hiding behind a newspaper which he pretended to read.

Florence Desmond pretty much invented the modern form of stand-up's close relation, comedy impersonation.

Impressionism already existed, but Desmond's innovation was to do impressions of more than one character at once and make them interact. This came about when she wrote a piece called 'The Hollywood Party' for a BBC broadcast in 1932, in which she played a whole string of movie stars, including Marlene Dietrich, Greta Garbo, Jimmy Durante and Gracie Fields. The piece was turned into a best-selling HMV record and was subsequently included in her stage act. All those present-day impressionists who do fast-cut conversations between Sean Connery and Roger Moore, or whoever, hark back to Desmond's 'Hollywood Party' routine.

Colourful costumes, colourful characters

Today, there is an idea that the stand-up should present him or herself to the audience undisguised by theatrical artifice, wearing everyday clothes instead of a stage costume. Variety comics took the opposite approach, dressing in a way which left the audience in no doubt that they were supposed to be funny. Looking back to his days as a child performer in the 1930s, Eric Morecambe put it this way in a 1976 radio interview: 'In those days it was a northern trait that a comic had to be dressed funny to tell everybody that, "Look folks, I'm a comic."'

This trend went all the way back to the music hall, when Dan Leno and his contemporaries delivered their half-sung, half-spoken routines in bizarre, theatrical costumes, looking more like circus clowns than modern stand-ups. Some had their own trademark look, making them as instantly recognisable as Charlie Chaplin, who was himself a product of the music hall. Mark Sheridan, for example, carried a battered umbrella and wore a tight raincoat, an elongated bowler hat, and the biggest, silliest pair of bell-bottomed trousers I've ever seen – he looked as if he had a megaphone wrapped around each knee. Wilkie Bard had a big, bald, Mekon-like forehead, and his trademark was a large spot of greasepaint just above either eyebrow. George Robey also enhanced his eyebrows with greasepaint, painting them into thick, black crescents. His costume was completed with a bowler hat, a frock coat and a walking cane.

Silly stage clothes were still big in the 1930s and 1940s. Max Miller's wife provided him with a series of gaudy suits, insanely baggy creations splashed with bold floral patterns or swirls of dazzling primary colours, worn with a lurid kipper tie and a white trilby. Sometimes he would complement his costume with a jewel-encrusted cane. A comic called Stainless Stephen celebrated his Sheffield origins by commissioning a local firm, Firth Vickers Ltd., to make him a stainless steel waistcoat, which he wore with a matching steel hatband, illuminated buttons and a revolving bow tie.

The other option was to wear an evening suit, and the straight two-way choice between fool's clothes and formal clothes was so ingrained that when comics like Ted Ray and Frankie Howerd started playing the theatres in ordinary man-in-the-street suits, it was considered quite an innovation. Ray had started off as a 'gypsy violinist' act in the late 1920s working under the name Nedlo, and when he started out as a stand-up in the early 1930s, he wore a typically cartoonish costume of a white suit and an enamelled white bowler hat. Then, inspiration struck: 'As clearly as though a voice had spoken the words aloud, I found myself thinking: You've been wrong all along. Why keep yourself aloof from the audience? Why not be *one* of them? Forget all about comic make-up, the white bowler hat, those fantastic, ridiculous props. Why, there's no need even to bother about a dinner jacket. Just be human. Stroll on the stage in an ordinary suit, just as if you'd walked in from the street.'

Plain-dressing comics like Ray and Howerd remained the exception, and even the last generation of variety comics, who outlived the circuit itself, wore silly costumes. Think of Max Wall as Professor Wallofski, in big boots, tights and scruffy dinner jacket, with that absurd long black pageboy haircut topped with a bald pate. Think of Ken Dodd, bucktoothed and spike-haired with his tickling stick in his hand. Think of Tommy Cooper, his huge figure wrapped in a dinner suit, a fez jammed on top of his head, with daft flaps of hair escaping from either side. The funny outfit is crucial to their comic identity. When Tommy Cooper appeared fez-less in sketches on television, he looked worryingly incomplete, like Mickey Mouse without the ears.

In the music hall, some comedians would play a whole series of comic characters. Dan Leno, for example, played brides-to-be, beefeaters, shopkeepers and henpecked husbands, among other things. As with much later comedians like Dick Emery or Harry Enfield, the comic would be clearly visible behind the character.

There were also performers who presented a single comic character. A popular single-character type was the northern halfwit character adopted by the likes of Tom Foy, Jack Pleasants (best known for the song 'I'm Twenty-One Today') and George Formby senior. Formby senior's stage character was pathetic and lovable, with a voice uncannily similar to that of his son, the ukelele-playing George Formby. His humour totally relied on his character, the main joke being that he thinks he's fashionable and streetwise, but is actually too dim to realise that he hasn't got a clue. In his song, 'Playing The Game In The West', he says:

'Do I look like George Lashwood? Huh huh! Huh huh! Aye, it's a funny thing, I were told that this morning. Very funny. He gets his clothes made at t'same place as me. Funny how they all copy my style, isn't it?'

The joke here is that George Lashwood was a rival music hall star, famous for dressing in the height of fashion, whereas Formby was pathetically scruffy, in a battered bowler hat, with his too-long scarf sticking out from the bottom of his too-tight jacket. There was genuine pathos in Formby's comedy: the chest disease which eventually killed him made him cough so badly that he worked it into the act with the catchphrase 'Coughing better tonight.' The northern nitwit character lived on in George Formby junior who, like his father, was more a comic singer than a stand-up. There were differences between them, though, and not just the fact that Formby junior played the ukelele. In his early career, he included a second character in his act, playing a cloak-swirling, bomb-wielding anarchist, as well as the Lancashire simpleton.

The single-character comedian set the tone for subsequent generations of variety acts, who adopted larger-than-life stage personas: Max Miller's sex-crazed libertine, for example, or Frankie Howerd's outraged gossip, or Tommy Cooper's accident-prone nervous wreck.

Working the theatres

If the crazy costumes and outlandish stage personas of the variety comics sprang from their music hall origins, other aspects of their acts were influenced more by the working conditions they enjoyed or endured. They lived a week-by-week existence. Sundays would be spent travelling to the next town on their itinerary and finding lodgings for the week. This could be a thankless task, as theatrical landladies were a force to be reckoned with, often ruling their guest houses with an iron fist. They might take a keen interest in their guests' morals, ensuring they didn't entertain visitors after a certain hour. At worst, they might simply refuse to take you in. Florence Desmond, who worked the circuit in the 1920s and 1930s, has recalled the snobbery she encountered: 'One Sunday it was raining, just to make things worse. I was worn out with trying to find rooms. In despair I tried an address I had been given. The landlady came to the door, looked me over, and said, "Where are you from?" "The Hippodrome," I replied. With a sniff she said, "I'm sorry, but I only take 'em from the Theatre Royal."'

The digs varied from spick-and-span houses with crisp,

fresh bedding and generous helpings of bacon for breakfast to filthy, flea-infested hovels with damp sheets and meagre platefuls of vile food. Ernie Wise has described how the acts used to leave coded messages in the visitors' books to warn future guests: the phrase 'I shall certainly tell my friends' meant that the place was lousy, even if it was preceded by polite comments.

Having sorted out the accommodation on Sundays, Monday mornings would be spent doing the bandcall, in other words rehearsing with the theatre orchestra. The show would open on Monday night, and would run twice nightly until Saturday. Unlike dancers or acrobats, comics would not have to rehearse in the daytime for the rest of the week. This meant finding ways of killing time, perhaps reading the newspaper in the park, or placing a bet. Going to the afternoon showings in the local cinemas was a popular choice, particularly given that the acts were sometimes given a free pass.

The variety circuit was a system of rigid hierarchies. Firstly, there were different grades of theatre, with acts having to build up their experience slogging around the number twos and threes before they were good enough for the number one venues. Secondly, there were hierarchies within the bills. A comic, for example, could eventually become a bill-topper, whereas a speciality act would never play more than a supporting role. That's why Max Wall gave up his dance act to take up comedy: 'As a comedian, I could go up the long gradient into a bit of stardom, perhaps, later in life.' Even amongst comics, there was a rigid pecking order. The first-spot comedian was far lowlier than the second top (who closed the first half of the show), and the second top was lowlier than the bill-topper.

It was important to learn the backstage etiquette, to know which of the theatre staff should be tipped at the end of the week and how much you should give them. The stage door keeper, the electrician and the stage manager would all have different rates, and failure to tip them might make them uncooperative next time you played at their theatre.

Variety theatres were often big and cavernous, and could be cold and hostile places for a comic to play. Standing there on the stage looking out across the chasm of the orchestra pit to the rows of people in red velvet seats in the stalls and the balconies must have been a daunting experience for the beginner. The first problem to overcome was audibility, particularly before the theatres were installed with public address systems in the 1930s: the acts had to learn to project their voices, and this was sheer hard work. Ronnie Tate, son and stooge of pioneering sketch comic Harry Tate, has described the physical strain: 'You had to learn to throw it out so everybody could hear, but you had to shout your guts out to do it. We used to come off wringing wet, after shouting for twenty minutes.'

Another problem was visibility. The grandiose palaces that had been built at the end of the music hall era might have looked like a million dollars, but their sightlines could be very poor. Variety historian Leslie Frost remembers Hull comic Bunny Doyle turning this problem into a gag when he played at the Sheffield Lyceum: 'He used to make a point of lying full-length on the stage, and he used to joke, saying: "Now them in t'gallery can see what I look like."'

Inevitably, the size and shape of the theatres influenced the style of the comics who worked them. First of all, you had to learn how to play to all parts of the auditorium, down to the stalls and up to the gallery, taking everybody in. Frankie Howerd's sister Betty helped him learn the technique when he started out on the circuit in the mid-1940s. She would move about the theatre and watch him from all angles, checking that he wasn't ignoring any particular area, making sure his facial expressions were visible to all.

Ruxton Hayward, who toured the dying variety circuit in the 1950s in the revue *Crazy Days*, told me his standard heckle put-down, which I think gives an idea of what it might have been like to play those big theatres. If someone shouted something derogatory at him, he would reply: ' "I know that. You know that." And then I'd point in the wings. "And he knows that. But what's our opinion amongst two thousand others?" '

It's the sort of gag that could only work in a large auditorium. In the sort of club I play, it would sound a bit ridiculous, because saying 'What's our opinion among a hundred others' isn't as impressive as being able to boast the support of two thousand other punters. There's also the length of the put-down. In an alternative comedy club, the heckler would probably shout you down before you could get to the punchline, but with the kind of focus that a big, raked theatre space creates, I can imagine the three-line build-up would provide just the right kind of tension needed for the eventual joke.

A good heckle put-down would be a valuable tool for the variety comic, because the theatres weren't just big, they could also be frightening. Arthur Askey started out as an after-dinner speaker and a concert party comic, and was terrified about the idea of trying to move on to the variety circuit. It was only after the radio series *Bandwaggon* made him a star in the 1930s that he dared to work in variety.

Variety audiences have always had a reputation for being difficult. In 1923, T.S. Eliot wrote of Nellie Wallace being 'interrupted by jeering or hostile comment from a boxful of Eastenders'. Heckling was still being endured by the likes of Jimmy Tarbuck right at the end of the variety era: 'Some audiences, especially in the old music hall theatres, were never noted anyway for their patience, and when I made my debut in 1959 at the Met in the Edgware Road the barrackers were well on their toes. After a particularly poor joke from me, a voice from the gods bellowed: "Get off!" Another voice from the audience countered with: "Give the kid a chance." Back came the voice from the gods: "I'd give him eighteen months!" '

The centre of the heckling universe was the Glasgow Empire, known as the graveyard of English comics. Most comedians had their own horror stories to tell about variety's most feared venue, and it seems its reputation was deserved. It was traditional to throw bottletops at the acts on Saturday night, and on one particular occasion the theatre was cleared by the police after the orchestra leader's head was cut open.

Heckling wasn't the only problem; audiences could be difficult in many other ways. Harry Secombe used to do a shaving routine, in which he did impressions of how different people shaved. One night in Bolton, the audience got the wrong end of the stick, assuming he hadn't had time to shave before the show and was just getting ready for his act. Total silence was gradually replaced by noisy disapproval. Fellow Goon Peter Sellers, who started his career as a comedy impressionist, got so fed up of getting no laughs at a theatre in Coventry that he jettisoned his act and instead played the audience some records of traditional Scottish music. He claimed to have got more applause when he solemnly took a bow at the end than he did when he'd done his normal routine.

Perhaps the most terrifying example of audience hostility is an incident involving Frankie Howerd. He was completely thrown whilst performing in a Sunderland variety theatre on his debut tour in the 1940s, when something hit the stage with an ear-splitting crack. A shipyard worker in the gods had thrown a ship's rivet at him. If it had been on target, it could have killed him.

Friendly comedians

The way most comics tackled the difficult problem of winning over big, unfriendly theatre audiences was to try and come across like an old mate. They started making themselves familiar to the punters before they even came on stage, with the bill matter that was printed on the poster and in the programme: This was a little phrase which appeared under their name and gave an idea of what the act was like. Nellie Wallace, for example, was 'The Essence of Eccentricity', Frankie Howerd was 'The Borderline Case', and Max Miller was 'The Cheeky Chappie'. The bill matter would start to make the comic feel familiar to the audience by letting them know what kind of comedy to expect. Billy Bennett was billed as 'Almost a Gentleman', which set the tone perfectly for his raucously pompous stage character, standing there in a terrible dinner suit and army boots, with slicked-back hair and a big, black moustache.

The familiar relationship was also helped by the use of signature tunes. Each comic had their own unique tune which the orchestra would play to welcome them onto the stage. Dick Henderson's was 'Tiptoe Through The Tulips', for example; Reg Dixon's was 'Confidentially', and Jimmy Wheeler's was 'Let The Sun Be Your Umbrella'. Comedians' signature tunes worked just like television theme music. Just as surely as *EastEnders* will follow the *EastEnders* theme, when the band struck up with 'Mary From The Dairy', the audience knew Max Miller was about to strut onto the stage. They cheered in anticipation.

Once on the stage, the variety comic had the perfect device for cementing a matey relationship with the audience: the catchphrase. Think back to the last generation of variety comics who survived into the television age, and instantly their catchphrases spring into your head. Think of Tommy Cooper, and you think: 'Just like that!' Think of Ken Dodd, and you think: 'How tickled I am!' Think of Larry Grayson, and you think, 'Shut that door!' Frankie Howerd conjures up a whole host of catchphrases, because he was a genuine catchphrase factory, his masterpieces including: 'Ladies and gentle-*men*!'; 'I was a-*mazed*!'; 'Not on your Nellie'; 'Nay, nay, thrice nay'; and perhaps most famously. 'Oo no, missus!' He even added a saying to the English language: 'And the best of British luck' started out as a Howerd catchphrase.

Different comics used these verbal trademarks in different ways. Sometimes they were just a way of squeezing extra laughs out of a gag. Dick Henderson, a tubby northern comic in a bowler hat who made his first London appearance in 1918 and continued to play the circuit until shortly before his death in the late 1950s, would follow up a good punchline by saying, 'Ha! Ha! Joke over!' In other cases, catchphrases were used to reinforce the comic's stage character. The self-satisfied Max Miller, for example, would tell the audience, 'There'll never be another', while Albert Modley, a comic who played the circuit from the 1930s onwards with a variation of the George Formby northern halfwit style, would sporadically comment, 'Ain't it grand to be daft?'

Catchphrases only actually become catchphrases by being repeated, and, unless the audience knows them, they have no effect. Once established, they help to cement the friendship between comic and audience by making them all part of the gang. Tommy Trinder was a contemporary and rival of Max Miller. Born in 1909, Trinder slogged round the variety theatres as a second-spot comic in the 1930s, eventually working his way to the top of the bill. Wearing a trademark narrow-brimmed black trilby and making the most of his lengthy chin, he followed Miller's example of being as cocky and boastful as possible, banging the gags home in a gleeful Cockney accent. His catchphrase was 'You lucky people!', and as well as putting it in his stage routines, in the early 1940s, he paid for it to be plastered over advertising hoardings all over London. It became so familiar that when he said it on stage, the audience would actually join in and say it with him.

Reg Dixon provides us with a classic example of the catchphrase in action, making the audience part of the comic's conspiracy and maximising the laughs. Dixon played the variety circuit after appearing in an RAF show during the second world war, and found fame by winning the job of resident comedian on *Variety Bandbox*. Peculiarly, he adopted a northern accent on stage, despite actually coming from the West Midlands city of Coventry. His stage character was the pathetic victim, constantly picked on by others, always suffering ill-health. His catchphrase was 'I'm proper poorly', delivered with a delightful laugh-triggering leap into falsetto on the word 'proper'. He used it with impressive efficiency: 'And then something happened. I don't know what it was, but I didn't feel well. (*Giggle from audience*) I didn't. I felt poorly. (*Laughter*) I felt *proper* poorly.' (*Laughter*)

Here, he gets two and a half laughs from its build up and execution. His poise, and the audience's anticipation, are impressive. There's a giggle as they think the catchphrase is coming. He uses the word 'poorly', so now they're sure it's coming, and they laugh properly. Then he gives it to them, and they laugh again. By holding back from giving it to them straight away, he gets the maximum possible number of laughs.

Predictability

If bill matter, theme tunes and catchphrases all helped to create a familiar rapport, the flipside was predictability. If you went to see an established comic in a variety theatre, you'd know exactly what to expect, because new material was a rare treat. Comedians worked all over the country and wouldn't return to a theatre for at least a year, so there was no pressure to come up with new stuff. There were acts who didn't change their material for decades, who'd be thrown if they had to change a single word.

Having said that, the widely held belief that variety comics never changed their acts is not entirely true. On 24 October 1938, Max Miller was recorded live at the Holborn Empire, and the recordings show that he even changed material between houses: his material for the first house is almost entirely different from the material he delivers to the second house. Whether he completely changed his songs and routines between performances simply for the benefit of the recording is unclear, but he was recorded live a number of times throughout his career, and over that period his material changes constantly. On the fringes of the variety circuit, there were even wilder deviations from the idea of doing the same material throughout a career. Comics who worked summer seasons in Scottish seaside resorts, for example, had to come up with an entirely new act as often as twice a week.

Generally though, most comedians stuck to the material that they knew. They'd also stick to a limited set of stock subjects, a tendency which dates back to the music hall. Max Beerbohm wrote of the 'quaint monotony' of music hall comedy, and listed the stock subjects which most of the jokes were about: 'Mothers-in-law; hen-pecked husbands; twins; old maids; Jews; Frenchmen, Germans, Italians, Negroes (not Russians or other foreigners of any denomination); fatness; thinness; long hair (worn by a man); baldness; sea-sickness; stuttering; bad cheese; "shooting the moon" (slang expression for leaving a lodging house without paying the bill).' Many of these subjects survived into the variety era, with comedians still regularly telling gags about mothers-in-law, hen-pecked husbands, old maids, Jews, fatness, and thinness. There were also new stock subjects, like doctors and commercial travellers.

Then there was the question of copying. Variety comics had no qualms about ripping each other off, and a standard way of starting out as a stand-up was to fill your act with tributes to the big names of the day as a way of finding your own style. Will Fyffe, for example, a Scots comic who played the variety theatres in the early part of this century, started off by doing impressions of Billy Merson, George Formby senior and Jack Pleasants. Formby senior and Pleasants were also impersonated by Sandy Powell when he started out in the 1920s, and in turn, Powell would himself become one of the impressions that Harry Secombe did as a beginner in the late 1940s.

There was also the question of stealing material. There's a well-known joke which Max Wall used to use in his act, which he remembered in a radio interview: 'In one room I found nine people together, talking. One said, "Twenty-four," and the others went, "Ha ha ha ha." "Eighteen." "Oh ho ho ho ho." I said to the waiter, "What's the idea?" He said, "They've been together so long, they know each other's jokes, so they just call them by numbers." (*Laughter*) I thought I'd have a go, so I called out, "Ten!" Not a laugh. "Fifteen!" Not a laugh. I said, "What's the matter?" He said, "They don't like the way you tell 'em."' *(Laughter)*

The situation this gag describes is a perfect metaphor for variety comedy. Nowadays on the alternative comedy circuit, where the idea is that if a comedian tells a joke on stage, it is a joke that he or she has written, stealing material is a cardinal sin. There was no such squeamishness in the variety theatres. Stealing jokes was not only forgivable, it was positively celebrated. In 1932, a critic of the early radio comedy scene wrote in the *Radio Times*:

'I do not complain because many of the jokes are old. All jokes are old, and all jokes are fresh. The most depressing bore in the world is the gloomy fellow who says: "I've heard that one before!" He ought to be bumped off. Are nine persons to be deprived of a jest because the tenth has heard it? The most familiar joke in the world is new to millions of people, for millions of people are born every year, and there must be a period in their lives when any joke, however blue-mouldy with age it may be, must be fresh and sparkling. I will not grumble, therefore, when I hear a chestnut.'

The same joke would appear time and time again, coming from the mouths of different comedians. There was a joke (which was used by sketch comics rather than stand-ups) that went something like this:

FEED: Where do you live?
COMIC: London.

43

FEED: And have you lived there all your life?
COMIC: Not yet.

This same gag appears in sketches by Albert Burdon in 1925, Sandy Powell in 1929, and Collinson and Dean in 1932.

Another example spans a much greater number of years. The first version of the gag is from a wartime routine by Billy Russell, a character comic who played a grizzled old man, with a furiously rasping, screechy voice: 'Aye, eh, you can't read nowt about it in the 'paper, it's this Ministry of Inflammation, they won't allow it to print nowt. Tell me they're going to allow it to print some pictures of the Siege of Mafeking.' *(Laughter)*

The joke is that because of wartime reporting restrictions, the newspaper is hideously out of date: the siege of Mafeking was during the Boer War at the end of the nineteenth century. In a 1973 television show, Tommy Cooper told a variation of the same joke, in which he read about the sinking of the *Titanic* in a magazine in a dentist's waiting room. The point of the gag is slightly different, making fun of the fact that the magazines in waiting rooms tend to be rather elderly, but the basic comic concept is exactly the same. The same gag cropped up again in Ken Dodd's show at the London Palladium in 1990, this time with him reading about the death of the Kaiser in a doctor's waiting room. Given that the joke pokes fun at things that are out of date, it's ironic that it's been around for so long.

Rampant gag-pilfering inevitably led to the occasional problem. When Eric Morecambe and Ernie Wise were starting out as a double act whilst touring as youth discoveries just before the second world war, a comic called Scott Saunders accused them of stealing one of his jokes, but then gave them permission to use it when they told him they'd actually stolen it from somebody else. When they came to the gag in question in that evening's show, the joke was greeted with a yawning silence. Saunders had double-crossed them and used it himself in the first half.

Comics didn't just steal from each other, though, they had certain common sources to loot for jokes. One of these was the American comedians who broadcast on British radio and appeared in the London variety theatres. Ted Ray even had a gag about it: 'Bob Hope's opening night, every comedian in London was in the audience. Bob Hope walked on the stage. Oh they . . . the noise was deafening – two thousand pencils being sharpened. *(Laughter)* I had my notebook out too, ha ha! I wasn't knocking them off, I was getting them back.' *(Laughter and applause)*

Another common source was the huge anthologies of jokes which were published at the time, like Lewis and Fay Copeland's *Ten Thousand Jokes, Toasts and Stories* which came out in 1939. It wasn't just a question of taking the odd joke from one of these books – some would transfer whole routines from page to stage with hardly an alteration. Because different comics mined the same books for material, the same jokes would crop up again and again. The way that jokes bounced about from comic to comic down through the decades, you could almost have replaced them with numbers as they did in Max Wall's gag. The only question is, where did Wall pilfer *that* joke from?

Regulation and control

If comedians tended to stick to tried and tested material, and steal other people's gags rather than write their own, they had good reason for it. Facing a large, cold theatre audience who might throw metal rivets at you if they didn't like you would be reason enough to play it safe, but there were other factors as well. One was that sometimes audiences would positively demand old material. Leslie Frost, who used to go to see the variety shows at the Sheffield Empire every week, remembers: 'In them days, people didn't demand new material. In fact, when Norman Evans used to come ("Over the Garden Wall" – he dressed as an old washerwoman), he used to slip and hit hisself on a brick. Now they waited for that. And if he'd've missed it out, they'd've been very miffed.'

Something else that encouraged predictability was the fact that the comedians were rigidly regimented and controlled by management. The timing of the acts was strictly regulated. Every act on the bill would be allowed a certain number of minutes, and would be expected to keep to that exactly. Overrunning in the first house would delay the start of the second house, and overrunning in the second house could mean that people in the audience would miss the last bus or tram home. Variety acts were indecently short by today's standards. A comic might be allowed only seven or eight minutes on stage. Even the top of the bill would get only twenty, although after the war this grew to thirty or forty, the precedent being set by visiting American performers. Ruxton Hayward, touring the variety circuit in a revue in the 1950s, was given a spot which lasted just three minutes. A Yorkshire comic called Joe King used to time his act by lighting a cigarette as soon as he got on stage: he started his closing song when it burned out.

In the short space of time allowed, the comedians would have to win over a potentially hostile audience not just for the glory of getting laughs, but also to satisfy the theatre manager. Each manager would have a comments book, in which remarks about how well each act went down would be written. Reports would also be sent back to the theatre chain's booking agent. If an act went down badly, it could mean that work would start to dry up.

Management didn't just judge how well a comic was doing, they also had some control over the content of the act. The theatre chain's booking agent wielded fearsome levels of power. One of the most infamous was Cissie Williams, who booked for the largest chain, the combined GTC and Moss circuits, from the 1930s to the 1950s. In his book *The Grades*, Hunter Davies describes her in action:

'Alongside her, on either side of the aisle, would sit a clutch of anxious agents, watching her every move. Every so often an agent whose performer happened to be on stage would be summoned to the great lady's side where he would crouch while judgement was passed. "This act is going on too long." "This has got to come out." At the interval it was a race for the pass-door between the agents and Cissie's assistants to see who could get to the artiste first to pass on the good/bad news. "Her word was law," says one agent. "If it didn't go well, that could be a whole year's work up the spout. You often felt your whole career was on the line."'

There was also regulation through demarcation. Because of the way a variety bill was constructed, acts had to do what they were booked to do. Each act had a defined role, and they couldn't deviate very far from it. If you were a dancer, you had to dance; and not tell jokes. This caused Max Wall a spot of trouble with the manager of the Victoria Palace: 'I was booked as a dancer and I was not allowed to speak. When I put a joke in one night, he came whizzing round and he says, "What was that you said? You said something there." "Well mister," I said, "I tried one joke out." He said, "You, you can't, we've got people on the bill," he says, "that tell jokes," he says, "that are top of the bill, that speak." He says, "You're a dumb act."'

Breaking the rules

If this kind of regulation encouraged some comics to take a predictable approach, others kicked against it by ridiculing the rigid conventions. In one of Sandy Powell's most famous routines, he sent up ventriloquism in a sketch about a wheezing Chelsea Pensioner with an appalling vent act. Struggling with his uniformed dummy and against the scepticism of his elderly female assistant, he desperately tried to maintain his pride in spite of a total inability to ventriloquise:

SANDY POWELL (TO DUMMY): Now tell me, sonny – where do you live, and where were you born? (*as dummy, his lips very visibly moving:*) I was gorn . . . in Wolvergganktonn! (*Laughter*) (*Drops dummy, puts hand to forehead in despair.*)

KAY WHITE: Where was he born?

SANDY POWELL: Wolverhampton!! (*Laughter*) Ooh, I wish I'd've said, 'Leeds'! (*Laughter*) I'm glad it wasn't 'Czechoslovakia'! (*Laughter*) (*Prepares to put sword back in scabbard.*) The finest blade in the world! (*Pushes sword in, pretending to cut hand.*) (*Laughter*) (*Picks up dummy's body, places it on his knee upside down, so its bottom is where its head should be.*) Now tell me, when your father . . . (*notices dummy's bottom*) I know his face and I just can't place it. (*Laughter*) (*Kay White hands him the dummy's head.*) Oh, thank you. (*Puts it on top of dummy's bottom.*) Now tell me, when . . . (*drops body again – picks it up – then throws it away again*) I don't need that any more. (*Laughter*) Well, everybody knows how it's done! (*Laughter*)

Watching archive footage of this sketch from 1973, towards the end of Powell's career, what impresses me is not just the laughs he gets at the expense of bad ventriloquists, but also that he constantly teeters on the edge of tragedy. His gravel-voiced despair at his own uselessness is heart-rending as well as hilarious. The way he puts his head in his hands after failing to get the dummy to say 'Wolverhampton' genuinely tugs at the heartstrings.

What Powell did for ventriloquists, Tommy Cooper did for magicians. An enormous hulk of a man with a silly hat on, his desperate facial expressions suggested he was in the throes of a major life crisis. He would break out into a madly relieved, deep-throated chuckle when the audience laughed at his string of weird gags and failed magic tricks. An appearance on a TV variety show in the 1960s gives a good idea of his destructive approach to the art of stage magic.

Walking on with a saw in his hand and an inane grin on his face, he starts by saying, 'Now you've all no doubt seen that wonderful trick where I saw a lady in half? You have? Well to heck with it then.' He throws the saw away as he completes the punchline. The audience laughs, and his silly chuckle resounds around the stage. He does a disappearing handkerchief trick, making silly noises as he does it, and warning the audience. 'If you see any suspicious moves, don't say anything.' Another laugh. When he tries to make the hankie reappear from a tin, instead rubber snakes spring out, and he cries out a shocked 'Ayaa!' The audience laughs again. Then he tries to make a cane disappear by rolling it up in a sheet of newspaper. When he unrolls the paper, the cane clatters disappointingly onto the stage, stubbornly refusing to disappear. He laughs nervously and tries again, with the same result. Without any fuss, he snaps the cane across his knee, throws it away and moves swiftly on to the next item. Every stage of his failure and discomfort has the audience hooting with laughter.

Horace Kenney was a sketch comic of the 1930s who applied the same basic concept to stand-up comedy. In his sketch 'The Music Hall Trial Turn', he played a doddery old Cockney with a death-rattle voice. With a look of pathetic hope on his pasty little face, he looked like a very small portion of death warmed up as he mangled his jokes beyond recognition. His stooge, playing the theatre manager, looked on with appalled disbelief:

HORACE KENNEY: A Scotchman and an Irishman were one day havin' a walk along a street, side by side, together, it was on a Monday they were walking, no Wednesday, no Saturday . . .
THEATRE MANAGER: It was during the week.
HORACE KENNEY: Yes, it was. One day of the week. And as they was walking along, they suddenly came to a big shop window with glass all over it, and the Scotchman, 'e turned to 'ave a look in the window, as 'e . . . wanted to

see in it. And the Irishman, 'e looked on the other side of the road. And on the other side of the road, was a very big tree, very high and tall, with leaves and branches sticking out all over it, it was growing there. And er, when 'e saw the tree, 'e turned to the Scotchman and 'e said, ''Ere, Murphy,' 'e said, 'if that big tree was to fall into that big window and break it, as it would, if it did,' 'e said, 'what would the window say to the tree?' Yes, oh yes, this is good. Then said the Scotchman to the Irishman, 'Well I don't know Sandy, tell me, what would it say?' Then said the Irishman, 'Why, the window'd go and say, "Enormous."'

THEATRE MANAGER: 'Enormous'?

HORACE KENNEY: Yes sir, that's what it'd . . . No, no, take that back, 'Tree-mendous.' Yes, 'Tree-mendous.' It wouldn't say, 'Enormous.' Well, that's the end of that one. (no audience)

Powell, Cooper and Kenney satirised certain types of variety act by feigning incompetence, but others took a more subversive approach. Frankie Howerd, for example, would break the rules of stand-up comedy by actually telling the audience off when they laughed: 'And before I could argue . . . Cease! *(Laughter)* . . . before I could arg . . . Cease! *(Laughter)* Oo, you make me mad!' *(Laughter)*. This is a wonderful invention. The job of the stand-up is to make the audience laugh, so telling them off for it is obviously absurd. By doing it, he gets them to do exactly what he is telling them not to. However, Howerd wasn't the first to do this. The technique actually dates back to the end of the music hall era, when stand-up comedy was just coming into being. George Robey would come over all pompous when his audience laughed: 'Oh, it's no laughing matter, my friends. I say it's no laughing matter. Look here I say, before we . . . go any farther we may as well understand one another, I say, here. I, I, I've not come here to be made a laughing stock of. No, it's hardly fair to me. I don't think

I know what you're doing really. I'm sorry to have to chide you, but I'm afraid I must put it down to ignorance on your part. "Ha ha ha ha," yes, it's all very well.' (no audience)

Another comic who got laughs by tearing up the stand-up comedy rule book was Beryl Reid, who started out as an impressionist with the North Regional Follies in Bridlington in 1936, and went on to be a successful comic after the war before eventually becoming a respected character actor. Her innovation was to lay bare the stand-up comic's techniques. She started out at a time when consummate professionals like Ted Ray had got to the top by slickly serving up strings of unrelated gags, garnished with lashings of charm. Ray had no particular persona or underlying theme. What marked him out was the shiny professionalism with which he doled out the jokes. This Ted Ray routine dates from about 1950, and was written by Denis Goodwin and by Bob Monkhouse, who would go on to become a comic very much in the same vein:

'While I was in hospital, they treated me with the latest wonder drug. Phenolacetate rictopholicide antibottigitamabataphol. *(Giggle)* "Wonder drug" they call it, honestly . . . it's just good old Epsom salts with a publicity agent. *(Laughter)* You know I . . . I'll always remember a few months after our, our little boy Andrew arrived. My elder son, Robin, was due to go into hospital to lose his tonsils. And he was very brave, he said to his mother, he said, "I'm not afraid of going into hospital, mum. I'll take my medicine, but I'll tell you one thing – I'm not gonna let them palm off a baby on me like they did to you." *(Laughter)* He said, "I'm gonna hold out for a puppy," and talking of *(Laughter)* animals . . .'

This is about gags, pure and simple, without any trimmings. Ray isn't giving us his comic view of the world, he's just going from punchline to punchline by the shortest possible route. When he finishes the joke about his son, he's started

51

the link to the next gag before the audience even has time to laugh.

Beryl Reid gave this stand-up style a novel twist in one of her routines as the character Marlene. Marlene was a parody of the youth culture that was just starting to emerge in the early postwar years, and she wore the most garish versions of the teenage fashions of the time, complete with enormous earrings. Reid used a thick Brummie twang for the character, becoming the first to use the Birmingham accent for comic effect. In this routine, from a 1951 edition of the BBC radio show *Music Hall*, she parodies the punchline-to-punchline approach by admitting that the basic premise for each joke isn't true, and laying bare the techniques of the stand-up comic:

'Well now, I start off by saying my mother's not very well. She's all right, see, but I have to say that because it's part of the joke. This morning she swallowed an egg, whole. Now she's afraid to move in case she breaks it, and she's afraid to sit still in case she hatches it. You couldn't help laughing at that, now, could you? Now I say, "Any road up," like, a sign that I'm going to say another joke. Any road up – you know I said my mother's not very well? It's making her very irritable, 'cos just before I came here she hit me with an oak leaf. The one out of the centre of the dining room table. Didn't 'alf 'urt my 'ead. I like rub my head, see – acting like she hit me. She never touch me. Nice woman, my mother. Now I'm going to say it again . . . any road up, my boyfriend took me down to Devon last year. I never been there, see – Birmingham, I come from. I never been abroad till I came here on the coach. He'd never been to Devon before. It's a lot of lies – he lives there.' (no audience)

This kind of joking about the process of joking is way ahead of its time: it would become very popular with the alternative comedians that came along decades later.

Surrealism

One of the inherent contradictions of variety comedy was that while it could be samey and predictable, there was also a streak of wild absurdity running through it. Variety comedians sometimes strayed into territory somewhere between whimsy and pure surrealism. There was a line of jokes, for example, which conjured up bizarre images of the human body. At its tamest this meant jokes about fatness or thinness, but other gags were genuinely odd. Billy Bennett, for example, would talk about the physical peculiarities in his family: 'My wife's father has a long beard, he looks as though he has eaten a horse and left the tail sticking out. My brother had a single hair on the end of his nose. It was so long that every time he sneezed it cracked like a whip. One night he took a pinch of snuff and flogged himself to death.' (no audience) There are many other examples of this kind of thing, like Max Wall explaining that he is standing behind the microphone because if he stood in front of it, he'd have to talk through a little hole in the back of his neck; or Beryl Reid worrying about her soya flour and egg make-up, because if she gets too near the fire, she breaks out in crispy noodles. Ken Dodd has brought the concept right up to date, exploring the comic possibilities of organ transplants: 'You could have another ear under your arm. Fancy another ear . . . frighten the life out of people. *(Lifts arm up.)* Say, 'I beg your pardon, how dare you talk to me like that?' *(Laughter)* You could have another mouth on the top of your head, another mouth. When you're late for work in the morning, stick a bacon sandwich under your cap and eat it on the way to the bus. *(Laughter)* Don't burp, or you'll blow your hat off.' *(Laughter)*

Why variety comics were so obsessed with jokes about grotesquely distorted bodies is anybody's guess. One advantage is that they have universal appeal. The root of comedy is incongruity, deviation from the expected norm, and the human body is an expected norm familiar to all. Everybody has a body, and everybody knows what a normal one looks like. It's easy for anybody to understand that talking through a hole in the back of your neck or whipping yourself to death with a hair on the end of your nose is a funny state of affairs. Often, jokes work by conjuring up a vivid absurd image in the mind of the listener, and the images conjured up by these jokes couldn't be more vivid.

It could be that the gags about distorted bodies also tap into subconscious fears about ill-health and disease. In real life, Tommy Cooper was an obsessive hypochondriac with a passion for off-the-shelf medicines, and this showed in his comedy. His routines were scattered with jokes about doctors and dentists. Some of these were simple throwaway gags, like, 'I went to see my doctor, I had to – he's ill.' Others were genuinely surreal: *(Scratches tooth.)* 'My teeth itch. *(Laughter)* I went to the dentist, he said my teeth are all right, but my gums have got to come out.' *(Laughter)* Given Cooper's comic obsession with pain and illness, and his habit of clutching his chest in mock panic during his act, it's not surprising that when he died of a heart attack in the middle of a live television performance, the audience assumed his collapse was just part of the show.

The surreal strand runs right through the entire variety era, from the time when stand-up first started to evolve out of comic song, to the generation of comics who worked the circuit as the last theatres were closing. It was there in Dan Leno's work. In one routine, for example, he wittered on insanely about eggs: 'Then comes *the* egg. That is the egg I am talking about. That is the egg that causes all the trouble. It's only a little round white thing, but you can't tell what it's thinking about. You daren't kick it and you daren't drop it. It has got no face. You can't get it to laugh. You simply look at it and say, "Egg!"' (no audience)

It's still very much in evidence in the work of Ken Dodd, who started out in variety in the mid-1950s. Dodd's act is entirely built on whimsy and strangeness. He looks bizarre, with his enormously spiked hair and his bucktoothed grin, his hats, his big, bright furry coats, and his tickling stick in his hand. Without relenting for a moment, he shovels out bucketloads of quirky one-liners, piling absurdity upon absurdity, and occasionally coming out with completely off-the-wall comments, like: 'Are you ready backstage?' *(Reply comes back: 'Yes.')* 'Release the goats!' *(Laughter)*

One of variety's most brilliant pieces of surrealism came from a sketch comic, rather than a stand-up. Jimmy James started out in the 1920s, and his career stretched right through the rest of the variety era. Wearing a trilby and a lumpy pinstriped jacket, his hangdog face drooped with care as he conversed with two strange-looking stooges, one tall and lanky, the other too short for his overcoat. In his most famous sketch, one of the stooges claims to have an increasing number of large jungle animals in the box he is holding under his arm. James stays calm, and gracefully manipulates his cigarette as he tries to control his disbelief, an almost sane man caught between two lunatics. The minimal physical action combined with the escalating lunacy of the conversation anticipates both Samuel Beckett and *Monty Python*. The mad absurdism of *The Goon Show* also makes more sense when you remember that the Goons served their showbiz apprenticeships on the variety circuit.

Weird wordplay

Just as inventive as the surreal gags was the way variety comics twisted and maimed the English language. Two of the wackiest wordsmiths were Stainless Stephen and 'Monsewer' Eddie Gray. Stainless Stephen worked the circuit from the 1920s onwards and enjoyed some radio success. His biggest comic invention was to speak his punctuation out loud: 'Somebody once said inverted commas comedians are born not made full stop. Well, slight pause to heighten dramatic effect, let me tell my dense public innuendo that I was born of honest but disappointed parents in anno domini eighteen ninety something full stop. Owing to my female fan following the final two digits must be left to the imagination, end of paragraph and fresh line.' (no audience)

'Monsewer' Eddie Gray was a juggling comedian-cum-magician with glasses, a bowler hat and a big, black, handle-bar moustache. Years before Miles Kington dreamed up Franglais, Gray was delivering routines in a bastard hybrid of French and Cockney: 'Now, ce soir – that's foreign for this afternoon – moi's gonna travailler la packet of cards – *une* packet of cards, not deux, *une*. Now I have 'ere an ordinaire packet of playing cards – cinquante-deux in numero – fifty-two in number – ein, swine, twine, and every card parla la même chose.' (no audience)

Inventive originals

The comics who took a more inventive approach shone out among the ranks of lesser comics with their stolen gags on over-used themes. Take Max Wall, for example, who found fame as a comic through appearances on *Variety Bandbox* after the war. Wall had a face moulded from clownish melancholy. His jokes were often surreal, and there was a dark underbelly to his humour. The more sinister side of his comedy must have sat very uncomfortably in the jollity and glamour of a variety show, which he specifically attacked in a joke about the old showbiz expression 'born in a trunk': 'Nobody's born in a trunk. *(Giggle)* No no no, ridiculous. *(Giggle)* It's good showmanship, good salesmanship, but I mean, well . . . *(Giggle)* Oh no. As far as I'm concerned, I was born at home, quite normally. Yes. It wasn't until after they saw me they put me in a trunk.' *(Laughter)*

Wall cut a morose figure on the stage, his voice deep, rich and soaked in gloom as he followed up failed punchlines with a weary grimace and commented, 'How desperate can a comedian be?' There was a kind of cruelty underlying some of his strange jokes: 'At the age of six, I lost both my parents. Yeah. What a card game that was. *(Laughter)*

Never played cards since. Was afraid of winning them back.'
(Laughter)

Another inventive original was Frankie Howerd, whose career began in a slot for ex-Services performers in a 1946 touring variety show called *For The Fun Of It*, and continued right up to his death in 1992, taking in radio, television and film work on the way. Howerd came over like a neighbourhood gossip who'd wandered onto the stage by mistake. Wearing a scruffy brown suit, he had one of the best-loved faces in British comedy, with bushy eyebrows and long, rubber features that were perfect for expressing outrage as he regaled the audience with tales of the indignities he claimed to have suffered. The misadventures he described in his routines were whimsical and far-fetched. Perhaps he'd describe riding a camel in the Sahara desert, getting a job as a lion tamer, or delivering a couple of elephants across London via tube train.

His approach to comedy was new and daring. Max Bygraves, a fellow ex-Services act on his first variety tour, remembers him baiting the audience, insulting them and pretending to forget his lines. Sometimes the theatres would rock with laughter; on other occasions he'd go down to silence, or worse. His trademark was his extraordinary way with language. His voice was gruff and gravelly with a hint of Cockney, but it seemed camp and effeminate because of the way it frequently lapsed into a falsetto shriek. His style of delivery was a million miles from the word-perfect slickness that most other comics adopted, as he pointed out in his autobiography, *On The Way I Lost It*: 'The real secret of whatever success I had was my delivery. In those days comics were very precise: they were word-perfect, as though reading their jokes from a script, and to fluff a line was something of a major disaster. My nervous, stammering, jabbering delivery was a bit different. Then apparently, it had never been heard of before.'

His sloppy, stop-start, stammering delivery reached its peak in his radio work. A 1960s routine, written by Barry

Took and Marty Feldman, told the tale of how a trip to the doctor led him to take a ten-guinea cruise to Tokyo on a coke trawler, and the way it starts is extraordinary:

'Uhh . . . *(Giggle)* How are you, you all right? I . . . no I don't feel . . . you know, I'm usually sort of . . . you know, but . . . I don't know, I suppose it must be . . . you know, I don't feel the . . . I don't know. *(Giggle)* Mind you, no, I think it's thisss . . . don't you? *(Laughter)* Mmm. And of course, I mean . . . I . . . Mind, you haven't come here to hear my troubles, I mean I don't, no, you've got troubles of your own, I mean you haven't come here to hear my troubles, but I mean . . . all this . . . ah, tell you what, ah, tell you how it started, tell you how it started, now . . . *(Laughter)* No listen, no, no listen! No. You see, I went . . . I was . . . I went to the doctor's, what's today? Sunday, no, Tuesday . . . week. I went to this doctor's, I went to the doctor's, and I wasn't, I thought, I went in the evening to the doctor's, you see. I go, I go in the evening, 'cos it gives 'is, gives 'is 'ands a chance to warm up, and umm . . . *(Big laugh)* So, well, I mean you know . . . *(Laughter)* So no, first, eh? *(Laughter)* First thing in the morning, *(high-pitched:)* WOOO!!! So anyway . . .' *(Big laugh)*

By the time he's told and milked his first real gag, which exploits the comic potential of cold hands touching intimate parts, he's used 192 words, got eight discernible laughs, and 58 seconds have elapsed. Remarkably, he doesn't start making sense, let alone get into his first joke, until about three-quarters of the way through this excerpt, yet the spluttering nonsense is enough to get four laughs by itself.

King and country

If most variety comics were safer and less imaginative than the likes of Max Wall and Frankie Howerd, this was reflected in the politics of their material. Variety championed a kind of cosy conservatism, built on the bedrock of music hall's tub-thumping, right-wing populism. Music hall singers were chest-beating, flag-waving patriots, who cheered the Tories and bashed the Liberals. They gave the world the word 'jingoism', which originates in a song called 'We Don't Want To Fight', sung by G.H. Macdermott in 1877, which forcefully told the government to get stuck into the Russo-Turkish war. It became an anthem of the Right, being sung by parades of Young Conservatives smashing up radical assemblies, and mobs which broke the windows of Gladstone's house. Jingoism was part of the very bricks and mortar of the music halls – they weren't called 'Empires' by accident, and Oswald Stoll even used the slogan 'Support the EMPIRE' to promote his theatre chain.

Over the years, this jingoism softened into a cosier, less abrasive brand of nationalism. It was still at full strength during the first world war, as the music halls resounded with patriotic songs encouraging young men to sign up and fight for their country. Harry Lauder was knighted for his efforts as a kind of unofficial recruiting sergeant, and Siegfried Sassoon wrote the poem 'Blighters' in disgust at this kind of thing. By the time the second world war broke out, however, the position had subtly shifted. Billy Russell, for example, might finish his routines with a defiant message for 'Mr 'Itler and Goebbels and the other Nasties', telling them: 'We're still laughing, we're still smiling, and we shall do till the whole damn lot's finished!'; but most of his time was spent moaning about wartime restrictions, perhaps ridiculing the ARP wardens: 'And, er, to make matters worse, that R.I.P. lot, 'e come again last Saturday night, I said, "Now don't tell me, there's no light shinin' through the windows," 'e says, "I know. There's a light shinin' under your door." I says, "Well blimey, you don't expect they're coming on their 'ands and knees do you??"' *(Laughter)*

More provocatively, Tommy Trinder told a gag about a man walking down Whitehall, who asks a passer-by which side the War Office is on. 'Ours, I hope,' replies the passer-by. This was dangerous enough to be banned by the BBC in 1943. But while Trinder cracked gags about the government, he wasn't actually trying to bring it down. He certainly did his bit for the war effort, tirelessly travelling around to entertain the troops.

Ridiculous radicals

As well as waving the flag, music hall had also stuck its boot into the Left. The Liberal Party in general, and Gladstone in particular, had been figures of fun, and it was reasonably common to find comics sending up the rhetorical style of the soapbox socialist. Perhaps the best example is Dan Leno's 'Midnight March': 'Now is the time and the only time. When time is time, you can't get away from the facts. What did Mr Gladstone say the other day? I again ask you, working men of England, what did he say? You know some people see things when they look at 'em; you can't eat soap and wash with it.' (no audience)

This simple comic concept survived into the variety era. Billy Bennett's declamatory style was perfect for it, and in among the silly songs and poetic parodies, he'd do a ridiculous political speaker, demanding 'social reform, tariff reform and more than likely chloroform.' Edwin Lawrence can be seen doing pretty much the same thing in a 1930s low-budget film called *Stars on Parade*, appearing as a member of the Window Box Weeders' Union. A variant on the same theme was the patter section in the middle of Will Fyffe's song 'I Belong To Scotland', in which he played a drunken orator speaking on behalf of the British working man, and complaining about the 'capu-tilists' who begrudge his getting drunk on a Saturday night.

Another kind of radical that acted as a handy joke-target was the suffragette. Billy Bennett quipped: 'The trouble today is that women are trying to rule the country. They say their place is at the poll. I think so meself. They can go either to the South or the North Pole – I don't care which.' (no audience)

This kind of fun-poking became less common over the years, and another music hall obsession which faded away was the preoccupation with class. Music hall singers got a lot of laughs out of poverty, spattering their acts with gags about debt and pawnbrokers, but this wasn't something they passed on to their descendants in variety. However, there were some remnants, the most obvious being Billy Russell. He began his career as a solo comic just after the first world war, with a grizzled, bad-tempered labourer character (bill matter: 'On Behalf of the Working Classes'). Russell looked like a cartoon peasant, in his tatty tweed jacket, corduroy waistcoat, spotted neckerchief and battered trilby, with a false nose like a dimpled golf ball underlined by a walrus moustache, and a clay pipe dangling from his lips. His comic technique was to constantly bemoan his cartoonish poverty in a wheezing, high-pitched harangue: 'Walls are that thin you can 'ear the woman next door change 'er mind. *(Laughter)* Put a shovelful of coal on yer fire, you're cookin' somebody else's dinner. *(Laughter)* Every time they pull the chain next door, they empty our bath, now who's *(Loud laughter)* gonna live in a 'ouse like that and pay rent for it?'

Russell was by no means the authentic voice of the working class. In real life, he had a comfortable upbringing as the son of a Hertfordshire theatre proprietor, and his accent was as false as his over-the-top costume, distinctly proletarian but geographically non-specific. Whilst he claimed to speak on behalf of the working classes, his complaints weren't political. He was certainly no communist: 'Russia! And they brag o'the freedom! They're interferin' wi' the working man's innocent amusements! Takin' all the kings and queens out o' the packs o' playing cards! Now if you want to go "nap", you've got to have four town councillors and a sanitary inspector!' *(Laughter)*

Scotsmen and Jews

Another music hall obsession which faded away in the variety era was race. The flipside of the flag-waving support for the empire was a derogatory attitude towards other races, and the most obvious manifestation of this was the 'nigger minstrel' tradition, in which white performers smeared their faces with brown make-up to present grotesque parodies of black people. A residue of this survived in song-and-dance acts like G.H. Elliot's 'The Chocolate Coloured Coon', and could even be seen as late as the 1970s in *The Black and White Minstrel Show* on television. But there was little trace of it in stand-up comedy.

Variety comics were more likely to tell gags about regional rivalry than about race. This is not surprising, given that regional differences were much bigger in the variety era than they are today. According to showbiz folklore, the anarchic, drunken sketch comic Frank Randle never really won over London audiences in spite of being a comedy hero in his native Lancashire. In the same way, it is said that Max Miller never quite matched his dazzling success in the South when he played in the North of England. This might account for the gag he used to tell about the Yorkshireman who went to London and missed his Yorkshire pudding so much that he 'battered himself to death'.

Like racial jokes, regional gags tend to rely on stereotypes. 'The Irishman', for example, is always dim in jokes. Max Wall used to tell the one about the Irishman who sent an overcoat through the post: he cut the buttons off to reduce the weight, then put them in the inside pocket. Jokes about Scots could involve one of two stereotypes. The first was an addiction to whisky, as in the Billy Bennett gag about the Scotsman who was suffering from 'a gathering of the clans': the doctor painted whisky on his back, and he broke his neck trying to lick it off. The second was stinginess, a stereotype which the Scots shared with Jews.

The one strand of racial humour which continued to

flourish in the variety era was the Jewish joke. There were a number of Jewish comics who worked the theatres, like Julian Rose and Issy Bonn. The main difference between the two was that Rose used an Eastern European Yiddish accent, whereas Bonn spoke with a mannered, Hollywood-influenced American intonation. Their Jewishness added flavour to their comedy, their jokes being sprinkled with names like Levinsky and Finkelfeffer.

It also gave them the chance to exploit the stereotype of Jews as money-minded, business-obsessed people. Here's an Issy Bonn joke, which gets comic mileage out of applying business logic to the simple-arithmetic problem: 'They got a boy, Sammy, what a boy! Last week in school the teacher said, "Come here, I'll try you out in arithma . . . math . . . adding things up, yeah? *(Giggle)* Teacher said, "If one pair trousers costs ten shillings, how much would you pay for ten pairs?" Sammy said, "Ten pair, ten shillings a pair, four pound ten," the teacher said, "You're wrong, it's five pound." He said, "Ho no, four pound ten, it's my best offer, take it or leave it." ' *(Laughter)*

Bonn also traded on the stereotype of Jewish people being ridiculously wealthy. One of his characters has so many gold teeth, she sleeps with her head in a safe, for example. Dating from 1941, this gag might at first seem dangerously anti-Semitic. After all, the bogeyman of the rich Jew had helped sweep Hitler to power in the previous decade. It seems more likely, though, that this kind of Jewish joke was mainly benign, and that variety audiences felt affectionate towards comics like Rose and Bonn. Rose was billed as 'Our Hebrew Friend', and Bonn's most famous song was 'My Yiddishe Momme', a sentimental ballad which shamelessly plays on the audience's empathy. In any case, audiences in London's East End would be largely made up of Jewish punters.

My wife, my wife . . . (1)

The cornerstone of variety comedy's cosy conservatism was

the wife joke, which again originates in music hall. In music hall jokes, marriages were always made in hell. George Robey had a routine in which he played a newly-wed bride, who declares, 'There isn't a word for marriage – it's a sentence.' The devil in the hell of music hall-joke marriages was most definitely the wife. In 'The Grass Widower', Dan Leno played a man seeing his wife off at the station, who harbours murderous feelings towards his wife: 'She turned round and said, "You brute! You massive brute! I believe you wish I was dead!" Isn't it *funny* how wives guess your thoughts!' (no audience)

This kind of joke was just as popular with variety comics, and the imaginary wife that they conjured up provides a fascinating index of social attitudes, because in each of her hideous qualities, she was a reverse image of what was expected of real-life wives.

My wife, she's so bossy

In the 1930s, at the end of his career, the music hall comic Tom Leamore recorded a song called 'I Thought She Was So Shy', with a patter section about a fearsome wife. Through the crackles on the record, his wobbly Cockney voice pours out his woes:

'Well, I told him a bit about my family troubles, he said, "It's your own fault, you must put your foot down my boy!" I said, "Put it down? I've hardly got the strength to lift it up!" He said. "Come on, hurry up and have a drink before it's too late. Now," he said, "you must take a leaf out of my book. You must be boss of your own house. Never mind about your wife's family, do exactly the same as I do. Now, as soon as you go 'ome, start ordering your old woman about, and make her wait on you. She'll think the world of you for it." I said, "All right, I'll try it on in the morning." So this morning I made a start. Soon as she jumped out of bed, I said, "Now then Selena, get out

of bed, come on, 'urry up. Clean my boots, get a polish
on 'em!" I don't know what ever made me say it. Well,
I took her breath away for over a minute. Yes, and she
took mine away for an hour and three-quarters! Oh, what
a temper!' (no audience)

Thirty years later, in 1963, Al Read was still joking about
the same kind of wife:

'No, I mean to say, you've all had it, a night out with
the lads. A few over the eight, as you totter down those
stairs the morning after the night before, what greets you?
(Mimes wife.) (Laughter) All wives do that, don't they?
They all, they all do that don't they? *(Mimes wife again.)*
(Laughter) "I hope you know, you came to bed stripped
with your hat on." *(Laughter)* That's the wife from the
kitchen. "When was that, love?" "Well, if you think you're
gonna keep coming this trick three or four nights a week,
we're going to have a different arrangement. I 'eard you,
creeping up those stairs, and you'll be breaking your neck
one of these nights, hopping up and down that landing
trying to get your pants off. *(Laughter)* And I thought
you were never going to come out of that bathroom.
(Giggle) I don't know what the neighbours'll think
next door, I don't. *(Giggle)* That landing light was
never off. *(Giggle)* What with both taps full on, and
you moaning, "Oh never again, never . . ." *(Laughter)*
I mean you can't win with the wi . . ., now take my wife
– please.' *(Laughter)*

The interesting thing about this routine is that it stretches
both forwards and backwards through the decades. Sty-
listically, it is years ahead of its time, relying more on
observation, characterisation and mime skills than on simple
jokes. Those mime skills are particularly impressive given
that Read's fame was built on a career in radio. He conjures
up a sympathetic, timid husband, nervously straightening

his tie as the accusations begin to fly, and a terrifying wife, clasping his hands together and twitching his head and elbow like an epileptic chicken. He gets two laughs out of that mime alone.

In other ways, the routine is firmly rooted in the same domestic values as the Tom Leamore song. The audience laughs when he first mimes the wife, instantly recognising the character he is conjuring up. This is not necessarily because Read's mime skills are devastatingly accurate, but rather because the comic stereotype of the bossy wife had become completely ingrained. That's also why the audience remains sympathetic towards the husband, even though most of the laughs are at his expense, as the wife recalls his drunken antics of the night before. It is obvious that the wife is the villain of the piece from the way that the audience laughs at the plainly insulting final joke, the old chestnut: 'Take my wife – please.'

My wife, she talks so much . . .

Closely related to the bossy-wife joke is the talkative-wife joke. Max Miller, for example, had a gag about giving his wife a ride on the back of his motorbike. He gets irritated because 'She never stops talking! Yap yap yap, all the time!' He drives faster and faster to try and shut her up, and eventually gets pulled over by a policeman: 'Listen,' he said, 'I'm not going to pinch you for speeding,' he said, 'but I want to tell you,' he said, 'your wife has fallen off,' he said, 'about two miles back.' *(Laughter)* I said, "Thank God for that, I thought I'd gone stone deaf!"' *(Laughter and applause)*

My wife, she's so ugly . . .

As well as being bossy and garrulous, the joke-wife was also hideously ugly. Plain-speaking northern comic Dick Henderson, for example, conjured up a grotesque, Bride

66

of Frankenstein-type figure: 'She came right up to me and looked into both of my eyes. And I looked into her one. Mind you, I didn't mind her only having one eye. What I really took exception to was her teeth. Not that I do in the ordinary course of events, but I did to hers because they belonged to her sister, and her sister has a bigger mouth than her.' (no audience)

My wife, she's so fat . . .

A particular feature of the wife's ugliness was often her enormous size. Billy Russell's grizzled old working man was savage about his wife's fatness: 'What a boiling piece, what a size, what a figure! She's like a Venetian blind with the cord broke. *(Laughter)* It's remarkable 'ow far the 'uman skin'll stretch without burstin'.' *(Laughter)*

Her enormous size was related to a most unladylike propensity to shovel food down her neck: 'Says she's goin' on the 'Ay diet, that ought to suit 'er, she eats like a bloomin' 'orse. *(Laughter)* See 'er with the nose-bag on, it's an education, 'er stomach's got no mem'ry. *(Laughter)* She sat down today, she 'ad a beefsteak, if it'd been any bigger she could've milked it.' *(Laughter)*

And as for her cooking . . .

Although she could have quite an appetite, the joke-wife was a terrible cook, quite unable to provide her husband with proper meals. Dick Henderson's wife was typical in this respect: 'Ee, by gum, she can cook. She's what one would call a religious cook. Everything she sends up is either a sacrifice or a burnt offering.' (no audience)

The anti-wife

Put together, therefore, the joke-wife's features fit together in a repugnant Identikit portrait of the kind of woman

67

real wives were supposed to avoid becoming. Joke-wives were bossy, talking and nagging all the time, because real wives were supposed to respect their husbands, bowing to their authority. Joke-wives were terrible cooks, because real wives were supposed to have adequate culinary skills to provide meals for their families. Joke-wives were fat and ugly because real wives were supposed to be slim and beautiful, to serve their husbands sexually. There's a Max Miller joke which specifically shows the wife's obesity impairing her sexual function: 'She's the best wife in the world, and I really mean that, she weighs twenty stone. Twenty stone. What I go through. *(Laughter)* On our wedding night, on our wedding night, she woke me up, she woke me up. And she started shouting, "Here, here." I started shouting, "Where, where?"' *(Loud laughter)* The image conjured up here is surprisingly, grotesquely graphic: a vagina lost in vast swathes of fat, which her husband has to 'go through' to penetrate her.

As well as reinforcing the ideal of the perfect wife by ridiculing women who deviated from that model, wife jokes could also be more simply misogynistic. One of Max Miller's gags, for example, had sinister undertones: 'But we never row, the wife and I, never row, never 'ave a row. We get on nicely together, and d'you know why? Because I help her in everything. Everything. Yesterday I did the washing with her, yesterday. Today I did the ironing with her, today. Tomorrow I'm going to do the cooking with her, tomorrow. Then on Saturday, I'm gonna wipe the floor with her.' *(Laughter)*

This is domestic violence in joke form. Today, it seems distasteful or even shocking, but the first house at the Holborn Empire on 24 October 1938 laughed at it without thinking twice.

My mother-in-law . . .

Another variant of the wife joke is the mother-in-law gag,

which is older than stand-up comedy itself. The music hall singers who preceded the stand-up comics certainly gagged about mothers-in-law. George Leybourne, for example, who died in 1884, had a song called 'If I Ever Ceased To Love', which was a list of things which could never happen. Among them is the line, 'May a sane man adore his mother-in-law.'

The mother-in-law was a figure of fun because she sided with the wife against the husband, helping her to dominate him. Interestingly, while the mother-in-law joke survives to this day, there were also jokes about other members of the wife's family, which have now fallen into disuse. These worked exactly like mother-in-law jokes, with the other in-laws helping to keep the husband down. Billy Bennett, for instance, quipped: 'Of course, I walked into that wedding with both eyes shut. Her brother shut one and her father shut the other.' (no audience)

The old maid

Ninety per cent of the time, variety jokes held that marriage is hell, but when it came to women who opted out of married life, it was shown in a very different light. The old maid was a stock figure of fun, and in one of Max Miller's poems, she is described as 'a bundle of sour discontent' because she rejects 'sweet married bliss'. There's nothing in Miller's delivery that suggests that this sudden reversal – from marriage being unending domestic strife to being sweet bliss – is an ironic joke, and there's no audience laughter.

The key feature of the old maid was sexual frustration. Max Wall told a gag about a man who becomes the victim of two 'old dames': 'By the way, did you hear about the two old dames? Two old dames went for a tramp in the woods. Yes. But he got away.' *(Loud laughter and applause)*

Whilst she was a figure of fun, the old maid wasn't necessarily a hateful figure. Nellie Wallace was a survivor from the music hall era. Born in 1870, she made her stage debut as a clog dancer in a Birmingham hall in 1888, but was still working the variety circuit with a blend of songs and patter in the 1930s. She was the living embodiment of the old maid, with goofy teeth, round, black-rimmed glasses and painted-on crescent-shaped eyebrows. She wore tatty, furry, feathery costumes that managed to be outlandish and frumpy at the same time. Her basic gag was that she was desperate for a husband, and blissfully unaware that she was too ugly to get one: 'This is the third time that I've been jilted. Me first was a sailor, me second a soldier, and me last a baker. Oh what a nippy little bit of goods me sailor was! I can see him now. He used to pull me to him, sit me on his knee, and say, "Any old port in a storm." He hadn't had a storm lately. Ah, but he was the one. My soldier, my buxom, blue-eyed soldier. He never took me out in the light. He said I was best in the gloaming.' (no audience)

Wallace's old maid might have been laughable, but she was more pitied than hated. Maurice Willson Disher, a critic of the time, wrote of her ability to 'excite our sympathy' with her 'protruding teeth and a heart-rending squint'.

There was also another side to the domestic jokes that variety comics told. Just occasionally, you might find a routine that laughed at a bullying, domineering husband instead of a bullying, domineering wife. Al Read did one on a TV variety show in 1973, in which he plays two men having a conversation in a pub. The first is a boorish loudmouth, the second is essentially the same timid-voiced tie-straightener who we previously saw being bullied by his wife:

- You're not worried about your missus, are you?
- Well, well she will be wondering where I am.
- I wouldn't give 'er a second thought. Do you know where *she* is?
- Yes.
- Then what the 'eck are *you* worried about? *(Laughter)* Won't she 'ave your supper ready when you get 'ome?

– Oh, I, I, I shouldn't think so.

– I wouldn't stand for that, I say I wouldn't stand for that. See – you want to let 'er get to sleep, make 'er get up, and cook your supper. *(Laughter)* And then don't eat it. *(Laughter)*

The scene Read so vividly brings to life here is the same as the one referred to in Tom Leamore's 'I Thought She Was So Shy': a man advising his friend to assert his dominance over his wife. The big difference is that here, the man who offers the advice is the bully, not his friend's wife. When he tells his friend to wake his wife up and make her cook for him, there is a slightly shocked tone in the audience's laughter, suggesting that for once, their sympathies lie with her and not him.

One of the contradictions at the heart of variety comedy was that whilst it could be very cruel to women, keeping women in their place with its monstrous stereotypes of nagging wives and frustrated old maids, and even laughing about domestic violence, it didn't prevent women from becoming comedians themselves. There's an assumption today that the woman comic is a modern phenomenon. A recent *South Bank Show* specifically stated that 'Victoria Wood was Britain's first stand-up comedienne.' In fact, Wood was preceded by a variety circuit liberally strewn with funny women. There were comic singers like Nellie Wallace and Gracie Fields, sketch comedians like Hylda Baker and Doris and Elsie Waters, impressionists like Florence Desmond, as well as bona fide stand-ups like Jeanne de Casalis, Suzette Tarri and Beryl Reid. In the music hall era, singers like Marie Lloyd and Vesta Tilley had been some of the biggest stars. It is true that funny women were vastly outnumbered by funny men, but the proportion of women to men was probably every bit as good as it is in the modern alternative comedy circuit.

All la-di-da-di-da

Here's a quick quiz. Can you work out what on earth the audiences were laughing at in these three jokes?

1. *Frankie Howerd:* 'You know, and . . . so I said, "Excuse me," I said, "Could I see your brochures?' So she said . . . *(Loud laughter)* "I beg your pardon?" I said, "Your brochures, your *tours*." *(Laughter)* She said, "You're not touring over *my* brochures," *(Laughter)* she said, yes . . .'
2. *Max Miller:* 'So the soldier said, "Well," 'e said, "I, I met this girl," 'e said, "and er, she asked me to see 'er 'ome, she told me she lived out in the country. Well I took her the short way, across the field . . ."' *(Laughter)*
3. *Reg Dixon:* 'Some of them are genuine though, like that one which advertises pills – that make you jump over five-bar gates. *(Giggles build into laughter.)* D'you know, I cleared the gate with a foot to spare. *(Laughter)* No, I opened it coming back.' *(Laughter)*

Answers:

The first one is about breasts. Even though 'brochures' isn't an established euphemism, somehow the audience picks up on the idea that Howerd is talking about the woman's breasts, and this idea is reinforced when he refers to her 'tours' even though that isn't an established euphemism either.

The second one is slightly harder. This time the joke is about sex. When the soldier says that he took the girl home across the field, somehow the audience picks up on the idea that he did that so he could have sex with her there.

The third one is harder still. At first sight, the audience's laughter is inexplicable. The joke is that the pills in question are laxatives. They let Dixon jump over a five-bar gate because the effect they have on his bowels force him to

72

make an unholy dash for the lavatory in which a closed gate is no obstacle. When he says, 'I opened it coming back,' he means coming back from the toilet.

All three jokes rely on innuendo, obscene meanings hidden behind apparently innocent language. Innuendo was the variety comedian's favourite tool, even more popular than the wife joke. The second gag in the quiz is part of a longer Max Miller story, dating from 1957:

'Now there's a soldier, soldier standing in the dock. The judge is at the back, the jury over there, the defending counsel down here. The judge said to the soldier, "This is a very serious case. We shall have to hear this *in camera.*" And the soldier said, "What does that mean?" and the judge said, "It won't make any difference to you. The jury, they know what it means. The defending counsel, he knows what it means. And I know what it means. Clear the court." And he said to the soldier, "Tell me exactly what happened," so the soldier said, "Well," 'e said, "I, I met this girl," 'e said, "and er, she asked me to see 'er 'ome, she told me she lived out in the country. Well I took her the short way, across the field . . . *(Laughter)* And when I got to the centre of the field, I don't know what came over me. But I got 'old of 'er. No rough stuff, no, no rough stuff, that came later, see? *(Laughter)* And I started to kiss her and she passed out. She passed right out. Then after that, it was all la-di-da-di-da." *(Laughter)* And the judge said, "All what?" The soldier said, "All la-di-da-di-da," and the judge said, "What does that mean?" The soldier said, "Well, the jury, they know what it means. *(Laughter)* And the defending counsel, he knows what it means. And if you'd've been there with your camera – you'd've known!"' *(Laughter and applause)*

The first thing that stands out here is the level of misogyny. Although it's not explicitly stated, the implication is that the soldier is on trial for rape, but the audience finds it perfectly acceptable to laugh at the idea of him having 'rough stuff' with the woman. Looking beyond this, what stands out is that the joke is a perfect metaphor for the technique of comic innuendo. The point is that everybody except the judge knows that 'la-di-da-di-da' means sex. Like the jury and the defending counsel, variety audiences knew exactly what was meant by la-di-da-di-da, even though Miller couldn't talk about sex more openly. Audiences were razor-sharp at spotting hidden sexual meanings, because innuendo gags were so common. Now that sex can be more openly discussed, this sharp-eared ability to spot concealed smut has waned, and that's why you might have had problems working out what the gags in the quiz were all about.

What's so funny?

The forbidden subjects which variety audiences found funniest were sex and toilets, but particularly sex. The sex gags came in two types. There were those which made hidden references to sexual body parts, like Frankie Howerd's brochures/breasts gag, or a Max Miller joke about a woman who went to the chemist to get something to remove the hairs from her 'little Chihuahua' (i.e. her pudenda). Then there were gags about the actual sexual act, like this, yet another Max Miller gag:

'It's a little girl, she keeps biting her nails, her mother said, "Stop biting your nails, because you know what'll happen to you," said, "What'll happen to me?" she said, "You won't half get fat – if you bite your nails." She said, "Well I won't bite them any more, Mum." Her mother took her shopping, got on the bus, and there's a feller sitting in the corner of the bus, weighing about twenty stone. And she said. "Mum, I'll get like that, won't I?" She said, "You'll get worse than that – if you bite your nails." Said, "Well I won't bite them any more." And

74

after shopping they got on another bus, and there's a blonde sitting in the corner. She's carrying a bit of weight as well. *(Laughter)* That's what I like about you, you're so quick, you're quick. *(Laughter)* And the kiddie kept looking at the blonde and the blonde kept looking at the kiddie, and the blonde, she couldn't stand it any longer, so she said – to the kiddie, "Do you know me?" and the kiddie said, "No – but I know what you've been doing!"'
(Loud laughter and applause)

Again, the joke parallels the variety comic's innuendo technique, as the little girl subverts her mother's attempts at parental control by making a sexually suggestive comment while remaining totally innocent of what she has said. It's also interesting to note that even the idea of the woman on the bus being pregnant was naughty enough to have to be hidden behind the phrase 'She's carrying a bit of weight.'

At its best, the sexual innuendo gag was a genuine art form. Suzette Tarri worked in radio and in the theatres in the 1940s and 1950s, winning the *Sunday Chronicle*'s Number One Comedienne award in 1945. She put herself over as a working-class gossip, telling bawdy tales in a yodelling Cockney whine, with a confidential manner that made her instantly endearing. A routine about her relationship with her butcher in the years of postwar rationing sees her at the height of her powers:

'I said to 'im, "Now look 'ere Charlie. I 'ope you're gonna treat me nice for old times' sake." He says, "I will Suzie, but not in front of a shop full of customers." *(Laughter)* Kep' his word too. Eh? *(Laughter)* Oh yes. That evening while I was sittin' in me 'ome, like, I 'eard a flop in me 'all, see? And 'e pushed a pound of sausages through me letterbox. *(Extended laughter)* Yeah. *(Laughter)* They were, they were tied in a true lover's knot. *(Laughter)* Yes. With a, with a little card on them, "For old lang's syne." *(Laughter)* So of course, I went into him next morning to thank him, he said, "Don't thank me, thank the lady who left 'em on the counter three weeks ago." *(Laughter)* Yes. But you know, I 'ad to leave me old butcher, I couldn't stand it. And you know at one time, I thought there was going to be romance between us. Well any girl would, I'll tell you what 'appened. It was during the war it 'appened. I went into 'is shop you see, and slipped on a piece of gristle. *(Laughter)* There. When I came to, I was layin' across 'is chopping board. *(Big laugh)* Yeah. 'E was fannin' me with a piece of liver. *(Laughter)* 'E was lookin' down into me eyes and callin' me 'is Worker's Playtime. *(Laughter)* Yeah. And d'you know, when I got 'ome, I found 'e'd tucked a couple of kidneys underneath me four penn'orth o' scrag end.' *(Laughter)*

On every level, this is an exceptional piece of stand-up. Without any apparent effort. Tarri manipulates the audience's responses like a conductor controlling an orchestra. The audience takes a moment to get the follow-up gag to the 'treat me nice for old times' sake' joke ('Kep' his word too') so she throws in an 'Eh?' and they catch on immediately. The 'Eh?' isn't laboured, it is said with total confidence, as if she knows without doubt that that's all that will be needed to drive the joke home. Later, she gets a long laugh for the gag about pushing a pound of sausages through the letterbox, but manages to milk it further just by saying 'Yeah', which somehow brings the laugh back to life.

The routine uses rationed meat as a way of making sexual innuendo to conjure up some grotesque, almost poetic images. When she says something like ''E'd tucked a couple of kidneys under me four penn'orth o' scrag end,' it's not exactly clear what kind of sexual act she is hinting at, but the mind boggles at the possibilities. The image of being fanned with a piece of liver brilliantly subverts conventional romantic imagery. What is really clever, though, is that the jokes manage to be about both the meat and the sex. The sausages gag evokes the bizarre image of the butcher posting his genitals through the letterbox, but as it develops it becomes clear that Tarri really is talking about sausages. Suddenly the gag is back to being a topical jibe about the petty corruption that went on in the austerity of the late '40s and early '50s.

Toilet jokes were less common than sex gags, but went down just as well with audiences. Tarri sneaked a gag about her husband using his helmet as a chamberpot into a wartime radio routine. The laugh is big enough to allow her to keep it going, stoking it with 'ooh's and 'ooh yes's: 'Ooh! Ooh, what a washout! 'E goes to bed every night in 'is tin 'elmet. *(Giggle)* Says 'e needs to be ready for any emergency. *(Extended laugh)* Ooh yes . . . ooh . . . ooh . . . yes, you can laugh, oh what a washout!'

Nudge-nudge, wink-wink jokes about sex and lavatories may seem a little puerile today, but in the variety era they were absolutely hilarious. Max Miller made himself the king of variety comedy, and he built his kingdom on smut. Born in 1895, he started his showbiz career working in a concert party in his native Brighton shortly after the first world war, before moving into the variety theatres and working as a solo comic. By the end of the 1930s, he had climbed to the top of his profession, and he stayed there until the variety circuit fell apart in the early 1960s.

Whilst not blessed with perfect good looks, his twinkling blue eyes and cheeky, toothy grin compensated for the podgy roundness of his face, and his outrageously colourful costumes made him an extremely attractive figure before he even opened his mouth. His voice was coloured with a strong South-East accent, held in check by the stage professional's attention to diction, and he rattled out the gags in a fast, high-pitched voice, which gradually slowed and deepened over the years. Sometimes boasting, sometimes disapproving of the dirty meanings the audience took from the things he said, he was constantly overbrimming with self-confidence, audibly gleeful at the simple fact of being Max Miller. His charm was enormous, allowing him to conjure up laughs out of nowhere. He could start the laughter at the beginning of his act with a simple series of 'well's and 'no's and 'shuddup's.

But Miller's real passion was the dirty gag. Sex was his unrelenting topic, and his huge popularity meant he could mine that topic more thoroughly and exhaustively than anybody else. To show just how funny his audiences found his sex gags, witness this excerpt from one of his performances, at the Metropolitan Music Hall, Edgware Road, London, on 30 November 1957:

'I'm writing another one now, a sequel to "Annie and Fanny", and it's called . . . it's called, "A Fan Dancer Minus Her Fan". *(Laughter)* That's like "without", see? "A Fan Dancer Minus Her Fan". I 'aven't finished it yet, I 'aven't finished it, I'm working on it now. *(Laughter)* I've got the beginning, I've got the beginning. And I've got a part of the end, but what I'm after is that middle bit, that's what I want. *(Loud laughter)* If I get that I'll be all right, I'll be all right. *(Laughter)* I'll give you a rough idea what it's all about, I'm not gonna give you a lot. 'Cos I want it when I come back, you see. *(Laughter) (He sings, accompanying himself on the guitar, to the tune of 'Oh Dear, What Can The Matter Be?':)*

'I started courtin' a smashin' fan dancer,
To marry her, that was my plan.
Now it's all off with that smashin' fan dancer.
She fell down and damaged her fan . . . 'ere!' *(Extended loud laughter)*

That final laugh lasts for a full nineteen seconds, an extraordinary length of time. What makes it even more remarkable is that there are only two basic jokes in the whole routine, both hidden references to the female genitals: the first is that 'fan' sounds a bit like 'fanny', and the second is that when Miller says 'the middle bit' he really means the middle bit of a woman, not the middle bit of the song. He gets nineteen seconds of laughter out of the fan/fanny joke even though it's the second time he's cracked it, the first being when he announces the title of the song. Incredibly, as the routine continues after this excerpt, he manages to milk both jokes even further.

Censorship

One of the main reasons that variety audiences bellowed with laughter at this kind of thing was that it was forbidden. It was the ever-present shadow of the censor that made smut so popular. The censor hovered like a vulture over all comedy, live or broadcast. On the radio, the guidelines were laid down in a document called the *Green Book*, produced by the BBC in 1949. In some ways, it was years ahead of its time, for example banning derogatory references to miners, the working classes and 'coloured races'. It specifically forbade the use of the word 'nigger', and noted that, 'Chinese abhor the description "Chinaman" which should not be used.' It was not until thirty years later, with the birth of alternative comedy in 1979, that comedians would voluntarily adopt this kind of non-racist ethical code.

Most of the *Green Book*, though, was conservative and prudish. It allowed political jokes, but banned anything abusive towards politicians and political institutions. It also banned anything improper, like jokes about lavatories, underwear, lodgers, commercial travellers, marital infidelity, or 'immorality of any kind'. It gave a list of banned expletives: 'God, Good God, My God, Blast, Hell, Damn, Bloody, Gorblimey, Ruddy,' etc., etc.

In the theatres, censorship was strict but fuzzy. Stand-up comedy was beyond the grasp of the government's stage censor, the Lord Chamberlain. As there was only one person speaking, it didn't count as a play, and was therefore exempt. However, variety theatres were always under the beady eyes of the local Watch Committees. The Watch Committees existed to check safety precautions in the theatres, but they also looked out for any indecent content in the shows. Even though they had no legal right to do this, they did succeed in bringing cases to court. Sam Harbour, the manager of the Coliseum, was once taken to court over something Max Miller had said on stage in his theatre. Only by claiming that Miller had inserted the line without his knowledge did he escape being charged.

Possibly because of this kind of legal threat, theatre managers would censor shows themselves. As early as 1883, the Music Hall Proprietors' Society stated, 'it is the desire of every Music Hall proprietor to prevent songs of an objectionable character being sung.' Theatre managers continued to excise objectionable stuff throughout the variety era. When Frankie Howerd's career took a temporary nosedive in the late 1950s, he found himself low down the bill in a summer season show in Scarborough. The manager made him take whole chunks of material out of the show, including a sketch originally devised for a children's pantomime, because it was deemed too filthy. Even a joke about a woman called Yvonne was questioned, because the name was suspected of being a sexual innuendo – the manager thought that 'Yvonne' was supposed to sound like 'Heave on'.

Perhaps an even more ridiculous example of management censorship was an incident involving Arthur English. English was a Cockney comic, who made his name as a kind of 'spiv' character, before later going on to play Mr Harman in the 1970s sitcom *Are You Being Served?* His career began just after the second world war with an engagement at the Windmill Theatre. The Windmill put on nude shows, but booked comics to entertain the audience in between the displays of naked women. Many of the big names of postwar British comedy started out there. In spite of the fact that most of the Windmill's audience came to stare at bare female bodies, Arthur English's act was still censored by the manager: 'I used to finish up with this gag mentioning a chamber pot, you see. And he said to me. "I'm sorry son, but you're not allowed to do that, this is a clean show."' The irony of a comic being banned from making a toilet joke in a theatre where most of the audience couldn't clap because their hands were too busy is so great that it requires no further comment.

This kind of restriction cried out to be dodged and subverted. One radio comedian, Jack Warner, who went on to play the lead role in the long-running television series *Dixon of Dock Green*, had a catchphrase which specifically referred to censorship. He would replace any expletives in his monologues in *Garrison Theatre* with the phrase 'blue pencil'. This was a reference to the blue pencil which commanding officers used for scrubbing out anything naughty in letters home from the troops.

The comic who made most of the forbidden appeal of smut was, perhaps inevitably, Max Miller, who openly played on the thrill and danger of dodging the censor. Here's an example taken from a performance at the Holborn Empire in 1938:

'Now I've got to be very careful about this next number, because before I went away on a cruise, I said to Bertie, Bertie Adams, the manager, I said, "Bertie – I've got a little number that I want to sing here when I get back." So 'e said. "Let me hear it," because he hears all my songs, you see, and all my gags, because he tells me what to cut out, you see. He does, he tells me. I don't take any notice but he tells me, see? *(Laughter)* And he told me, says, "If you're gonna work it when you come back, be careful." Now I'd better have a look, he might be on the side, you see. *(Giggle)* He's there. *(Giggle)* I'll sing it dead quiet.' *(Giggle)*

By lowering his voice to escape the beady-eyed attention of the imaginary manager on the side of the stage, he could make the audience all part of his conspiracy, making it very much him and them against the powers-that-be. It must have been exciting to be like the jury and the defending counsel in the 'la-di-da-di-da' joke, knowing that you were in on a secret code which not everybody understood. Miller was capitalising on this when he told the audience, 'That's what I like about you, you're so quick, you're quick,' when they laughed at a hidden meaning. Sometimes he'd take a different approach, feigning innocence, and telling them off for reading something dirty into what he'd said: 'Oo you wicked lot! *(Laughter)* You're the kind of people who get me a bad name.' *(Laughter)*

Wish-fulfilment

Sex gags were often about marital infidelity, and audiences could pick up on the subtlest references to it. Here's an economical Suzette Tarri one-liner, for example: 'Only this morning I said to my 'usband, "Where were you last night?" 'E said, "It's a lie!"' *(Laughter)* A variant of this was the lodger joke, which always relied on the idea that a male lodger will always get up to sexual shenanigans with the lady of the house. Here's one of Max Miller's lodger gags: 'Did I tell you about the feller who came 'ome one night and his wife'd got two black eyes? He said. "Where did you get the black eyes?" She said, "The lodger gave them to me." He said. "The lodger?" She said, "Yes." He said, "Where's the lodger?" She said, "Upstairs." He shouted upstairs, he said, "Did you give my wife two black eyes?" He said, "Yes." He said, "What for?" He said, "I found out she was being unfaithful to us." Now listen . . .' *(Laughter)*

In a time when adherence to the institution of marriage, and sexual morality in general, were far stricter than they are today, infidelity gags may have provided a safety valve for the frustrations that people stuck in unhappy marriages must have felt. They were the flip-side of the wife joke. Wife jokes expressed the feeling that marriage is hell, putting the blame squarely on the wife's shoulders, and infidelity jokes were a form of wish-fulfilment for those who longed for a sexual freedom they could never attain.

This must have been a factor in Max Miller's vast popularity. Miller constantly portrayed himself as a sexual adventurer, moving from conquest to conquest without a care in the world. He could turn problems that the rest of the world endured into advantages, effortlessly swatting aside his audience's cares and woes with throwaway gags. Here's his response to wartime restrictions, in a routine delivered at the Finsbury Park Empire in 1939: 'All dark and no petrol. *(Laughter)* I don't want any petrol, I didn't ask for any. *(Laughter)* I don't! I used to take 'em out into the country. Any doorway now, 'ere!' *(Laughter)*

In a time of stricter sexual morality and greater repressed desires, this kind of carefree, sex-mad adulterer must have been an enormously attractive fantasy role model, particularly to the men in the audience. Miller's libidinous stage persona was as much a fantasy to the man himself as it was to his audience. He died in 1963, before the sexual revolution, and while he portrayed himself onstage as a sexual athlete with an ever-growing string of conquests, in fact he had just two lovers in the whole of his life, his wife and his long-term mistress.

An insidious trend

In his 1935 book, *The Story of Music Hall*, Archibald Haddon made a dire prophesy about the future of variety (which he still refers to as 'music hall'): 'The music hall of today retains to a considerable extent its inherited addiction to "smut", but the direction it is taking has a more insidious trend, and the possibilities are deadlier. The result, if no halt is now called, may be the ultimate extinction of the music halls; for how can they continue in a land of good repute if they definitely cease to be reputable?'

The fact that the variety circuit went on for almost three

decades after Haddon's doom-laden warning shows that his fears were a little over the top. Smutty gags weren't nearly as dangerous and subversive as he believed them to be, because whilst they dodged the censor, they also relied on censorship for their effect. The innuendo joke works by making a hidden reference to something that can't be mentioned openly. If it becomes acceptable to mention that thing openly, the joke becomes largely irrelevant. Max Miller included a poem in his act in 1938 which illustrates this point perfectly:

> 'She's a girl that's just built to my liking,
> A wonderful figure is Nelly. *(Laughter)*
> Two rosy lips, and very broad hips,
> And a nice little mole on her shoulder . . . Goodnight everybody!' *(Laughter)*

The technique he uses here is the suspended rhyme. He uses the name 'Nelly' at the end of the second line to plant the suggestion in the audience's mind that the fourth line will end with a rude word, namely 'belly'. The fact that the audience has picked up on this is indicated by the laughter of anticipation which the name 'Nelly' provokes. Then, at the last moment, he backs out of saying 'belly', substituting it with the innocuous 'shoulder'. The fact that the substitute word doesn't rhyme reinforces the idea that a last-minute substitution has been made. The audience laugh again at having their expectations confounded.

Today, the joke is meaningless, because 'belly' has lost its shock value, having become the kind of word a parent might use with a small child. Without the prohibition on the word, the poem has lost its comic point, and the only thing that is funny about it is that not daring to say 'belly' is amusingly quaint and old-fashioned.

Ultimately, innuendo humour wasn't about laying down a challenge to the censor, it was more about sneaking out dirty jokes behind his back. It certainly didn't challenge existing sexual values. What the variety joke had to say about sex was usually little more than puerile glee that it was being mentioned at all, like a small child shouting, 'Bum poo willy!'

Where the smutty joke did challenge social values was in its attitude to marital infidelity. Max Miller made promiscuity something to be admired, and not only did he spin yarns about his own extra-marital adventures, he also cracked jokes about his wife having a bit on the side: 'Here's a funny thing, now this *is* a funny thing. I went 'ome the other night, there's a funny thing. *(Laughter)* And I went in the back way, through the kitchen, through the dining room to the drawing room. And there's a feller standing there, not a stitch on. *(Giggle)* Can you imagine that, lady? *(Laughter)* How's your memory, gel? *(Laughter)* He hasn't got a stitch on, I called the wife in, I said, "Who's this?" She said, "Don't lose your temper Miller, don't go raving mad." I said, "I'm only asking a fair question, who is it?" She said, "He's a nudist – and he's coming to use the 'phone", there's a clever one from the wife, eh?' *(Laughter)* What's unusual here is the way he tolerates his wife's infidelity. He's more impressed at his wife's cunning than he is angry about her unfaithfulness. Given the rough treatment he gives her in other jokes, I'd have expected him to take a hypocritical stance, seeing his own extra-marital adventures as one thing and his wife's as quite another, but in fact he applies the same lack of sexual responsibility to his wife as he does to himself.

Another fly in the moralists' ointment was the ambiguous sexuality of camp comics like Frankie Howerd. Most variety comics treated gays as figures of fun. Tommy Trinder, for example, joked about a man called Rosie who lost his job as a lorry driver because every time he got to a traffic light, it turned lavender. Howerd's angle was different. His persona had many unmasculine qualities: his gossipy manner, his frequent leaps into a high-pitched falsetto, his old-womanish insistence on getting himself 'comfy' before he started. Crucially, he made no pretence of being married, thus denying himself the use of wife jokes.

By the 1960s, he was starting to make actual references to his homosexuality. In a 1966 edition of *The Frankie Howerd Show* he got a big laugh by recalling how his boss had told him he was 'neither one thing nor the other'. This ambiguity wasn't the main thrust of his act, though, and he certainly didn't present himself as some kind of monstrous gay parody. His suggested homosexuality was just part of his persona, to be accepted as part of the package. It would be ridiculous to paint him as a radical gay liberationist, given that he never came out of the closet, but the fact that such a popular public figure was making is-he-isn't-he? jokes before it was even legal to be homosexual is remarkable.

More openly gay was Larry Grayson, who had toured the variety circuit as a bottom-of-the-bill female impersonator in the 1950s before breaking through to stardom on television in the 1970s. His gossipy style was obviously influenced by Howerd's but his sexuality was far less ambiguous. His catchphrase was, 'What a gay day,' and he peppered his act with comments like. 'He's anybody's for a doughnut.' What made Grayson's angle less subversive than Howerd's was that his homosexuality was pretty much the whole basis of his act, and he could be enjoyed by a straight audience as little more than a gross gay stereotype.

Closing the theatres

By the late 1950s, the variety circuit was falling apart, and by the early 1960s the last theatres were closing down. In 1958, Morecambe and Wise left Britain for a working holiday in America and Australia. When they got back for the summer season of 1959, they found that most of the work had dried up, because there were so few theatres left. Many of Max Miller's last appearances were opening the bingo halls into which the closed-down variety theatres had been converted. Ironically, as the theatres closed, audiences turned up again, presumably to witness the end of an era. Ruxton Hayward remembers what it was like: 'Well, what it meant was you didn't have anywhere to go back to, you know, in six months' time. The houses were full on closing week, 'cos everyone was coming to see the last show. In fact, I went to see Liberace at the Chiswick Empire when it closed down. And it was crowded of course, standing room only and all that sort of thing. Not because of Liberace, because I don't think he was famous then, but because the theatre was closing everybody wanted to see their last chance.'

The death of variety has been blamed on many things. The main suspect is the increasing popularity of television. As more and more people bought their own sets, the need to go out to be entertained decreased, and so the number of punters going through the theatre doors decreased. To combat the decline, more nude shows and the emerging rock'n'rollers were brought in to boost audiences, but packing the theatres with dirty old men and teenage rockers just helped to turn away family audiences. Jimmy Tarbuck, whose career began as variety circuit was falling apart, has given his own explanation for its demise:

'A typical variety package in those days featured one hot star, maybe a singer with a hit record, surrounded by a load of rubbish. Audiences soon objected to having to sit around watching terrible acts for an hour and a half before their favourite came on. The rest was predictable. Profits turned into losses, and one after the other the old variety theatres closed, or were made over to some other kind of entertainment.'

So it was that the circuit which had nursed stand-up comedy through its infancy eventually keeled over and died. Variety comedy enjoyed an afterlife for years after the last theatres shut down, because those who had cut their teeth on the circuit, comics like Tommy Cooper, Max Wall,

Chapter Three
Funny in Theory

If the string of strange experiences that has been my career has given me a peculiar perspective on stand-up, something else that has had the same effect is my academic research into the subject. Delving into the quagmire of comic theory is not an especially rewarding experience. Since Plato, hundreds of philosophers, linguists, psychologists and sociologists have theorised about comedy, and in the whole of that two-thousand-year period, they have come up with no more than three basic theories. The first argues that jokes work by being aggressive towards a third party. The second argues that the root of humour is incongruity, and that all jokes involve some kind of mismatch of ideas or a confusion about meanings of words. The third, most famously put forward by Freud, argues that jokes exist to allow the harmless release of anti-social emotions.

Each of these ideas has a grain of truth in it. Take the following joke, for example, told by Max Miller at the Holborn Empire in 1938:

'And between you and I – my wife's the ugliest woman in the world. The ugliest woman in the world, I'd rather take her with me than kiss her goodbye.' *(Laughter)*

If you look at it in different ways, this gag can support each of the theories:

1. *Aggression:* The joke is aggressive towards the wife, and implicitly towards wives generally. The laughter is exclusively at her expense.

2. *Incongruity:* We know from other jokes that Miller doesn't enjoy spending time with his wife, so there is something illogical and incongruous about being with her constantly to avoid having to kiss her goodbye – rather like cutting off his nose to spite his face.

3. *Release:* By showing aggression towards wives, the joke harmlessly gives voice to the tensions and conflicts which threaten the social institution of marriage.

My favourite theory by far is the second of these, the incongruity theory. It seems to me that there is a clash of ideas or meanings at the heart of every joke, whereas there are some gags which have not a whiff of aggression or release about them. The following joke, for example, was told by the Irish alternative comic Michael Redmond on a 1988 edition of *Friday Night Live*:

'I like going into newsagent shops and saying, "Excuse me, is that Mars bar for sale?" When he says, "Yes," I say ... "OK, I might be back later, I still have a few other ones to see."' *(Laughter)*

There's nothing in this that suggests a breaking of social taboos or a Freudian release of repressed anti-social emotions. Nor does it work by being aggressive towards newsagents or Mars bars. The thing that makes the gag funny is the simple, incongruous silliness of buying something small and trivial like a chocolate bar as if it were a big, expensive item like a television or a computer, for which you'd need to shop around a bit.

Having said that, incongruity is not in itself enough to create laughter. When Oedipus kills his father, marries his mother and tears out his own eyeballs, his behaviour is about as incongruous as it could possibly be, but he doesn't get many laughs. There must be some added ingredient which turns incongruity into comedy, and I believe that that extra something is faith. Just as we suspend disbelief to get caught up in the plot of a film, so we must actively believe that a joke is funny to be able to laugh at it.

This is something we learn to do as we grow up. At a certain age, small children begin to recognise the structure of jokes before they actually understand them. In *Humour: Its Origin and Development*, Paul E. McGhee describes psychological tests which found that if you tell five-year-olds a joke, like 'Why did the farmer name his hog "Ink"?', they will find a completely meaningless punchline ('Because he kept getting away') every bit as funny as one which makes sense ('Because he kept getting out of the pen'). The only thing that can possibly have been making the children laugh is their belief that the joke is supposed to be funny, their faith in its funniness.

The same is true with adults. A joke may be clever, witty, well crafted and intelligent, but unless we have faith that it is funny, we will not laugh. I can remember times when I have watched a comedy film which I previously found hilarious in a roomful of people who were completely unamused by it. Their hatchet-faced mirthlessness has destroyed my faith in its funniness, and I have found myself sitting there as glumly as everybody else.

So, my theory of the secret formula for all jokes is this: *Joke = Incongruity + Faith*. Faith is the difficult part of being a stand-up comedian. It's relatively easy to think up incongruities: puns, sudden shifts of meaning, and unlikely combinations can all be produced by an averagely creative mind, without too much effort. What's difficult is putting these incongruities across in a way which makes the audience believe that they're actually funny, making them have faith that you really are a comedian and that it's OK to laugh.

Chapter Four

The Clubs

A night out in Sheffield

Before I'd ever set foot in a working men's club, my image of the average club comic was a fat, dinner-jacketed buffoon spewing out wrinkled stereotypes and prehistoric mother-in-law gags. I knew that this was in itself a stereotype, so when I first started going to watch comics working the clubs, I wanted to see how the reality matched with my preconception.

In many ways it was far worse than I had imagined. I remember a July evening in 1988, in a working men's club in the northern part of Sheffield. The club in question was a large brick building with ample parking space, situated in a district that is mainly white working-class, but with a big Asian community. It looked rather like a cross between a pub and a warehouse. It was quite a trek to get out there, and the evening got off to a bad start. I'd phoned the club beforehand to make sure it would be all right for me to see the show what with my not being a member and everything, and they had assured me that it would be fine, and I could 'bring a young lady with me' if I wanted. In spite of this, when I arrived at the club, I was taken into a little room whilst the committee of grim-faced middle-aged men looked me up and down and to decide whether they should let me in or not.

The show was supposed to be celebrating the re-opening of the newly decorated concert room. It looked, well, as nice as flock wallpaper can possibly look. I wouldn't have fancied playing the gig myself. It was a big, cavernous room, with bad acoustics and poor sightlines. The audience huddled round tables and flocked to the extensive bar. There was an alarming age-range among them, from little kiddies to old-aged pensioners, but two things unified them: they were almost exclusively white and working-class.

The show itself didn't do much to cheer me up. The compere was a committee man who didn't even attempt to be entertaining or charismatic, he just shouted the acts' names and dragged them on. The first two acts were, loosely speaking, musical. There was a middle-aged boy/girl duo who sang the hits of the '60s with stiff but well-rehearsed dance routines. The man, bald-headed, wore tight trousers and a little bolero jacket, the woman a low-cut silver dress slit to the top of her thigh. Both costumes seemed to accentuate their middle-agedness. They rejoiced in the name 'Timeless'. Following them was a bloke with a silver quiff, who was billed as a 'tenor'. He bellowed out sub-operatic songs in a deep, wobbly voice. It seems that the key qualities in club singing are volume and wobbliness. Then total silence descended on the concert room whilst a couple of games of bingo were played. The caller approached his job with grave sincerity. He was obviously a bit of a celebrity in the club.

Eventually, the comic hit the stage. She started her set with an interminable soul ballad, and for a couple of dreadful minutes, I wondered whether maybe I had got it wrong, and that she was not a comedian but a singer. Either way, she looked and sang like a cross between Bonnie Tyler and Bobby Ball. All evening, the musical backing was provided by the club's resident musicians, an organist and a drummer. They were as competent and soulless as the music that accompanies the television test card.

This first interminable soul ballad was followed by a second interminable soul ballad, and then she started the comedy. It was about ten minutes into her act before she got into her favourite comic groove, namely slagging off any racial or regional group that she wasn't a part of. 'Any Welsh people in?' she asked, and followed up the question with a gag about a Welshman doing it with a pig. This was followed by 'Any Irish people in?' and 'Any Scottish people in?' It was fifteen minutes into the act before she used the word 'coon', in a gag about 'a black feller, a white feller and a poof'.

She didn't get really vicious, though, until the routine which began with the question, 'Any Pakis in?' This got a laugh in itself. The very idea that there should be Pakistanis in their club was a right hoot. This was a bastion of white supremacy in a multi-ethnic area. The comedian assured us, 'I'm not a bloody racialist. I don't mind 'em at all. They can stop 'ere as long as they bloody like,' before launching into some genuinely savage stuff. There was the one about the Pakistani who gets his testicles kicked in after a dispute with his neighbour, and the one about the twenty Pakistanis who are tricked into plummeting to their death from the top of a burning block of flats, and the one about the chemist who gives the Pakistani cyanide by mistake then runs after him, not to save him, but because he realises he has undercharged him by forty pence. How they roared at that one.

What really made me wince was that in spite of the fact that the punters had laughed at the very idea that there should be any 'Pakis' in their club, there actually was one young Asian chap in the concert room. He was there with his white girlfriend, standing by the side of the stage where the comedian couldn't see him. While the audience guffawed at gags about people like him being killed or having their testicles mangled, he grinned and bore it, laughing along with them as best he could.

The comic's political analysis never got more sophisticated than calling Margaret Thatcher ugly, and her idea of witty repartee was telling a member of the audience that he had 'a face like a twisted pisspot'. The most impressive thing about the act was its sheer brutality. One line in particular stuck out. The one about people in Liverpool not catching AIDS 'because they're never off their arses long enough'. The genius of this line is that it manages to cram anti-Scouse prejudice, homophobia and insensitivity about a fatal disease into a single one-liner. Eventually, after a couple more dreadful songs, the act came to a close. It had lasted no more than three-quarters of an hour. I left the club, and walked back to the bus stop. The bus I had taken to the club was the same route I had taken a couple of months earlier, when I had gone to the Northern General hospital to visit a friend who had tried to commit suicide. I honestly don't know which was the more depressing experience. Coming out of that working men's club, I felt like I had just witnessed the Nuremberg rally. The worst thing was not the jokes in themselves, but the reaction they got. Previously, I had fondly imagined that this kind of naked prejudice was a thing of the past, but the three hundred or so people crammed into the club that night proved me sadly deluded. The fact is that thousands of people all over the country go and sit in their local club to laugh at comedy like that every night.

Forgotten history

It would be wrong to suggest that working men's clubs are simply evil dens of fascism, and it shouldn't be forgotten that stand-up comedy is only a tiny part of what they exist for. They play an important part in many working-class communities, and have a rich and surprising history. The working men's club movement was started by a Unitarian minister called Henry Solly, who founded the Working Men's Club and Institute Union (CIU) in 1862. He was backed by aristocrats, capitalists and clergymen, and their aim was to improve the character of the British working man by weaning him off beer. Alcohol was banned in the early working men's clubs, and the main form of entertainment they provided was sitting on hard wooden benches and listening to informative readings.

It was not long before the British working man got thoroughly fed up with this, and the members began to seize control of the CIU from its philanthropic founders. Beer was introduced to the clubs, and women were allowed to join them, but only as 'associate members', a situation which persists to this day. For a time, working men's clubs were hotbeds of political radicalism, playing host to socialist speakers like George Bernard Shaw and William Morris, and organising the 'Bloody Sunday' march on Trafalgar Square in 1887.

Gradually politics was elbowed out by entertainment, and the club movement continued to expand, often with help from the breweries. There was a big boom in the number of clubs after the first world war, and another in the 1960s with the growth of new housing estates. As the Victorian slums were bulldozed into oblivion and their former tenants moved into brave new concrete estates, working men's clubs were set up within them as a way of generating a new sense of community. In the 1950s, when the variety circuit was in its final downward spiral, the club scene was boosted by a newcomer on the entertainment scene: the big, privately owned, social club.

This was the big brother of the working men's club, run for profit by a proprietor, rather than for the members by an elected committee. Social clubs had bigger capacities than the working men's, and with as many as fifteen hundred people turning up to booze, eat chicken-in-a-basket and watch the show, they allowed obscure northern towns to attract big stars. Frankie Howerd, who moved onto the club circuit in the 1960s after the variety circuit had breathed its last, reckoned that it was possible to tour for three years without playing the same club twice. It was a peculiar time in history, when one of the most important venues in the country was a club in Greasbrough, near Rotherham, and stars of the magnitude of Louis Armstrong appeared in the small West Yorkshire town of Batley.

Sadly, the big social clubs started dying off in the 1970s.

The introduction of the breathalyser meant that nights of watching celebrities, smoking, eating fried food and getting tanked up on Double Diamond before driving home in the early hours were no longer such an attractive prospect. Getting stopped by the police after hurtling dangerously through the darkened streets with alarming amounts of alcohol pumping through the bloodstream must have put a damper on even the finest evening's entertainment. By the mid-'70s, comics were even starting to make jokes about the decline of the big social clubs. Bespectacled Irishman Frank Carson, for example, cracked this one at a show at Cesar's Palace in Luton, in 1976: 'I was up in Aberdeen three weeks ago, and I went out the back, and when I came back half an hour later the place was a supermarket.'

The working men's clubs continue to survive, although they have been hit hard by the economic recessions of the '80s and '90s. As traditional working-class communities fell apart under the strain of increasing poverty and mass unemployment during the Thatcher years, more and more clubs found their memberships dwindling, and their cash disappearing. Clubs which had thrived for decades found themselves slipping into receivership. The number of venues advertising in the Sheffield clubs listings magazine, *Our Clubs*, has shrunk from fifty-three in 1988 to around thirty in 1996.

The surviving working men's, together with an ad hoc assortment of privately owned clubs, nightspots and large pubs, form a circuit populated by an army of mainly obscure professional and semi-professional entertainers. It's a hidden world, largely ignored by mainstream culture. A town like Sheffield still boasts at least thirty clubs, but you could live here for years and remain totally unaware of the big brick or concrete buildings, flanked by gravel carparks, tucked away in little back streets in outlying areas. The shows they put on are advertised on hand-drawn posters displayed in the bar, or in the inky listings guides distributed among the clubs themselves, so they can go completely unnoticed by the outsider. Being hidden doesn't mean club entertainment isn't popular, though. In 1982, the CIU still boasted three million members nationwide.

The lost generation

Just as the history of working men's clubs has been largely forgotten, there is also a forgotten generation of club comics. When I became interested in club comedy, I went to talk to Eric Thomas, who wrote a weekly column in *Our Clubs*. The first thing he said to me was that the traditional stand-up comic was dead, killed off by a newer, bluer style of club comedy. He went on to describe the club comics of the 1950s, with their slow, laid-back delivery, and their proletarian stage costume, consisting of a flat cap, a scarf, and 'probably an old football jersey to add a bit of colour'. He mentioned names like Harry Bendon, Bobby Thompson, Harry Buxton and Ron Delta.

Intrigued, I tracked down Ron Delta at a concert at Upper Heeley Working Men's Club in Sheffield, in 1988. His style was indeed different from that of his modern counterparts. Instead of an evening suit or a colourful approximation of high-street fashions, he wore an old cardigan and a flat cap. He took time over his jokes, using accents and funny voices to flesh out the characters that appeared in them. There were wife jokes and Irish jokes, but they lacked the hard, cruel edge of modern club comedy. He even managed to swat aside taboos by making jokes about his blindness.

It was when I stumbled across the work of Bobby Thompson that I discovered just how different this lost generation of club comics was from the modern breed. Thompson hailed from Penshaw, County Durham, and had worked as a miner before starting his career in comedy. He started performing at smoking concerts and Friday-night suppers in local working men's clubs, and after losing his job at the local colliery because his constant joking was deemed to be distracting his fellow workers, he turned professional, building up his career in a tight circle of North-East Federation clubs. In the 1950s, he gained wider exposure through a regular spot on a show called *Wot'cheor, Geordie*, broadcast on the BBC regional Home Service. Two decades later, he released a pair of bestselling LPs of his stage routines, which led to lengthy tussles with the Inland Revenue. Partly as a result of the debts he incurred, he continued working into old age, right up to his death in 1988.

Bobby Thompson was working-class through and through. You could see it as soon as he shuffled onto the stage, licks of Brylcreemed hair escaping from under the peak of his flat cap, his hands appearing from the ragged sleeves of a tatty pullover, his legs encased in big, baggy trousers. He had an industrial-strength North-East accent, almost unintelligible to an outsider. Then there was the material itself, delivered slowly and confidentially. He used a crumpled little cigarette to helps his timing, taking a drag to punctuate a sentence, or perhaps blowing out a plume of smoke to separate the build-up from the punchline. He didn't just bang out the gags, he meandered through long routines, creating a cast of imaginary characters along the way.

Like his contemporaries in the variety theatres, he had a hideous wife figure, and a tyrannical mother-in-law. His dearly beloved had breasts like the Cheviot Hills, and when she lay sunbathing on the beach, she looked like 'a bag of coal on a bike.' Her cooking skills were typically nightmarish. She made 'claggy' tinned tomato sandwiches, and had a truly disgusting method of boiling eggs: 'Then she starts, "What d'ya want fa ya brikfast?" I says, "I'll have a boiled egg." "You can have a boiled egg, but there's nay tea na nay coffee, 'cos there's nay watter." I *still* don't know how she boiled that egg. *(Loud laughter and applause)* Good job I didn't want it poached, and er . . .' *(Loud laughter)*

Elsewhere, his comedy was more peculiarly working-class. His jokes were about living with hardship, coping with poverty, dodges to lessen the strain of hard industrial labour.

Some of the gags drew on his previous occupation in the mines. One of his finest comic techniques was discussing the rich and powerful as if they were working-class. In a routine set in the second world war, he talked about meeting the Duke of Gloucester in a working men's club, about the Queen having to go round to her mother's to take her the catalogue money, and about Neville Chamberlain's wife putting a pan of chips on while her husband is out collecting sea coal.

He had a healthy disrespect for patriotism and the Protestant Work Ethic. His Second World War routine began with him shuffling onto the stage in a scruffy army uniform several sizes too big for his tiny frame, before coming out with his opening line: 'You're lookin' at a little lad noo that fought, fought and fought. And still I had to gan.' *(Laughter)* In his civilian act, he was as reluctant to go to work as he was to go to war: 'No, but I think if you're . . . if you're off work, ya shouldn't be skitted. I don't mean on the dole, I mean you've got a job, but you're not keen.' *(Laughter)*

Perhaps his most daring idea was to openly tackle the subject of poverty. The people who smoked and drank round the tables in the North-Eastern clubs where Thompson was king of comedy might have had trouble finding the money to pay the gas or electric bill, or meeting the weekly instalments for the things they bought from catalogues, but he had the nerve to tease them about their problems, and the empathy to get away with it without causing offence. He'd start his act by asking 'How's ya debt?' and the audience would laugh with him as he cackled away. He'd turn to a woman on one of the front tables and say: 'I'll tell ya what I'll do with ya, pet, I'll gi' ya a glass o' brandy . . . and Bob says 'e'll give ya a bottle o' brandy . . . if you can tell me ya pay the 'lectric bill before ya get the red letter. *(Laughter)* I've 'ad that brandy for ten year, wa ha ha!' *(Laughter)*

Then he'd declare: 'Why, this would be a nudist camp if aall the women took their catalogue stuff off.' *(Laughter)* He wasn't lording it over them as an outsider might, he was talking as one of them, somebody who shared their problems and knew there was no point in keeping quiet about them. He'd talk at length about his own money problems:

'Ee though, I'm not laughin', I cannat sleep for debt. I'm up to there *(puts hand up to forehead)*. I wished I was a bit taaller. *(Laughter)* You believe Bobby Thompson – if you pay what you owe, you'll nivver ha' nowt. *(Laughter)* Let them worry that wants if off ya. The dole is my shepherd, I shall not work. *(Laughter)* Mind, I thought I was out o' debt last Monda' mornin'. There's a knock at the door, I wasn't at woork. I wasn't clever. *(Giggle)* "Mr Thompson in?" I says, "I'm Mr Thompson." He says, "I'm from Littlewoods," I says, "God bless ya! *(Laughter)* I've won the Treble Chance." He says, "No, your wife's up for shopliftin'" *(Laughter)* Lad, she's a lazy-lookin' b— woman, that one! *(Laughter)* Lad- d'ya knaa what? There's some of these knockers, d'ya knaa what I mean? Credit callers. All that snaa wa had – nivver kept one away from our door. *(Laughter)* Come on a sledge. *(Laughter)* And ya knaa, let's be, we're only human, aren't wa? There's some of them that comes to ya door, they're not, they're not right man, they've got no sense. Come to ya door with the book *open*!! *(Laughter) I'm not laughin'. (Laughter)* And they'll stand there: *(mimes knocking at door and looking at book)*. And they knaa ya not in. *(Laughter)* Let them knock, the paint lasts longer than the skin.' *(Laughter)*

To Thompson, debt wasn't something to be ashamed of, it was something to bring out into the open and laugh at. Instead of being guilty about owing money he was defiant, prodding his bony finger and shaking his wrinkled fist as he talked about his battles with his creditors. He laughed particularly loudly at those who hid their debt, social climbers who pretended to be above it all: 'But we call it "debt". Others calls it "credit". Committee men's wives "on account", yaaah! *(Laughter and applause)* Well I'm in debt on account o' not bein' able to pay me credit!' *(Laughter)* Even the way he finished his act shouted his allegiance to a disappearing working-class culture. Instead of murdering the latest Andrew Lloyd Webber smash, he'd get out his mouth organ and play a traditional tune, wiggling his hand to create a thin, reedy vibrato.

There was this feller . . .

As the working men's circuit got hooked up to the big new privately owned social clubs in the 1960s, the entertainment scene changed. Out went the traditional flat-cap-and-football-scarf working-class comics, and in came the brighter, glitzier breed of entertainer. By the end of the '60s, television was starting to look to the clubs as a source of new talent, with acts like Les Dawson breaking into the mainstream, and at the beginning of the '70s, Granada Television unveiled its massively successful club comedy showcase, *The Comedians*.

Looking back at footage of the first episodes of *The Comedians* nearly a quarter of a century after they were first broadcast, the first thing that stands out is the laughably dated fashions. It's a synthetic-fibre parade of mauve kipper ties with big knots, enormous collars, dinner suits and dickie bows, turquoise frilly-fronted nylon shirts, and gleaming Harmony hair-sprayed hairdos with huge sideburns, against a psychedelic backdrop of coloured blobs.

The next thing you notice is the number of comics it featured who went on to become big names in the world of light entertainment: Lennie Bennett, who would star in the now-forgotten TV hit *The Lennie and Jerry Show*; Stu Francis, who later became a presenter on the long-running children's programme *Crackerjack*; Jim Bowen, now famous as the host of the cult darts-based game show *Bullseye*; Russ Abbott, star of numerous series of his own sketch show; and Les Dennis, who teamed up with the late Dustin Gee before being given his own comedy show and presenting *Family Fortunes*.

What *The Comedians* made obvious was that the common currency of club comedy is the pre-packaged gag. The gag that comes ready-wrapped, complete with build-up and punchline. The gag that starts 'This feller . . .' or 'This Irishman goes for a job on a building site . . .' The gag that anybody can re-tell after a single hearing. The comics on *The Comedians* did little more than tell the kind of jokes that people tell each other every day in pubs, works canteens or school playgrounds all over the country. It's only the superficial details that distinguish one comedian from the next. There are no comedy costumes, no larger-than-life stage personas, no song-and-dance numbers. There is none of the all-round-entertainer frills that brightened up the act of, say, Max Miller. Most of the comics don't even have a catchphrase. Stand-up comedy has been whittled down to the basics of a person standing behind a microphone, telling packaged gags one after the other. The only thing that gives each act a modicum of individuality is accent and appearance. Bernard Manning is a fat Mancunian, Mike Read a burly Cockney, George Roper a tubby Liverpudlian, Charlie Williams a black Yorkshireman and Frank Carson a cackling Ulsterman (who does have a catchphrase: 'It's the way I tell 'em!'), but beyond that there isn't much to tell them apart. Some tell their gags quickly, some slowly, some are friendly, others aggressive, some are jolly, others morose, but the actual jokes are interchangeable.

In this sense, *The Comedians* was an accurate portrayal of what stand-up comedy was and still is like in working men's clubs. The main difference is that the television programme cut the acts up into bite-sized two-minute chunks, whereas in an actual club a comic is on stage for about forty-five minutes, starting and finishing with a straight song. One of the drawbacks of such a gag-encrusted style of comedy is that it encourages a grinding, yawning, deadening lack of originality. Packaged gags come complete with a beginning, a middle and an end, and you only have to hear them once before you can repeat them and pass them off as your own. Before I'd ever seen a comedian in a working men's club, *Our Clubs* columnist Eric Thomas told me: 'You will find that if you go and watch one one night, you will probably hear a lot of the same material from one that you do from the other, and everybody's pinching one another's material, you see, borrowing it, taking it, whatever.'

I soon found out he was right. I didn't have to see much club comedy before I started hearing the same jokes again and again and again, each time coming from a different mouth. For example, Jos White told a joke about his Chinese neighbour on a 1971 edition of *The Comedians*. In it, the neighbour, whose house is identical to White's, asks him how much wallpaper he bought for his front room. He tells the neighbour he bought sixteen rolls. The neighbour goes off to paper his room, and comes back a week later to complain that he has six rolls left over. 'So have I!' replies White, laughing. A 1977 recording of Bernard Manning performing at his own Embassy Club in Manchester includes the same gag, with hardly a detail changed. The victim of the gag could be a member of any minority group, it's not essential that he's Chinese, but he's still Chinese in Manning's version. There's also an incidental joke in the build-up, a complaint that the Chinese neighbour leaves a trail of rice all over the path, which appears in both White's and Manning's version.

The fact is that club comics get material from wherever they can find it. They steal from the past and future of comedy. A 1993 commercial video showcasing club comedy sees some acts retelling old Max Miller gags, and the Billy Bennett one about the man with a hair on his nose that cracks like a whip, while others pilfer material from alternative comics like Alexei Sayle, Sean Hughes and Bruce Morton. Stealing material is a way of life for club comics. Johnny Wager is a Mancunian who bore a passing resemblance to a young Leonard Rossiter when he appeared on *The Comedians* as a young comic in the early 1970s. Today, he still plays the northern clubs, sporting a gingery blow-waved hairstyle. He is quite candid about the attitude he and his fellow club comics take to finding material: 'Sometimes I make up a joke myself, without any assistance from outside. I think if anybody's speaking frankly, this doesn't really happen so much, I think that people glean humour from different avenues, and probably put 'em together themselves, and say they've written it themselves, but in actual fact, they haven't, they got it in a sly way from someone else.'

In 1992, there was an incident which threw the joke-stealing habits of the club comedian into sharp focus. A comic called Mike McCabe appeared on Granada Television's revival of *The Comedians*, and did a five-minute routine about the documentary series *Crimewatch UK*. It was a direct copy of a routine Jack Dee had performed on his own series on Channel 4. When Dee complained, McCabe replied: 'You can't have a monopoly on jokes. Once they have been told, they spread. If a comedian wants to keep a gag to himself, then he shouldn't tell it.'

Apart from direct stealing, there is another reason why club comedians tend to duplicate material: some use the standard joke-sheets which are sold through small ads at the back of *The Stage*. These are cheaply printed booklets or stapled wads of photocopies which cost about ten pounds each. Some come with advice on how to deliver the jokes. One warns: 'Don't use the "heckle stoppers" or the more "offensive gags" before you have some experience of possible reactions from your audience. You could get a punch on the nose!' It also offers advice on how the budding comic can improve his offstage activities: 'The easiest way to pull the best-looking bird every night is to throw a few well chosen one-liners at her, half an hour later find the girl, apologise profusely and offer to make amends by buying her a drink – it works every time.'

The actual gags are usually weak, often unoriginal. They

are typed out one after the other, sometimes with key words underlined to make sure the user actually understands them. Anybody who buys these joke-sheets is free to use the jokes they contain, so they inevitably lead to more joke-duplication on the stages of the working men's clubs.

Working the clubs

There are good reasons why club comics have taken such a light-fingered joking-by-numbers approach to stand-up, particularly given how hard it can be to play the clubs. Their lifestyle is very different from that of their predecessors in variety. To start with, weekly engagements are a thing of the past. In the 1960s and 1970s, the big privately owned clubs would book acts for a week, but the comedians who work the working men's clubs today have to make do with one-night stands, or noon and night bookings on Sundays.

Rather than being sent all over the country by the booking agent of a big theatre chain, club comics tend to build up their work in the area around their home town. Acts can go on like this for thirty or forty years, making themselves local legends while remaining complete unknowns to the outside world. Talk to people in the club scene, and they'll say things like, 'Of course you'll've heard of Ronnie Delta – he were the daddy of them all, he were the best comic that ever lived,' completely unaware that you don't know him from Adam.

The clubs are more difficult to play than the variety theatres were. However unruly variety audiences might have been, a comic could at least be sure that they had come specifically to be entertained. This is not true in the clubs. People go there for a night out, possibly to enjoy a drink with the family or a game of bingo, and to them, the idiot telling jokes on the stage may be little more than a minor irritation. There is rarely an extra charge for sitting in the concert room, so there is no financial commitment on the people sitting in it to pay attention to the acts. This tends to create less of an audience, more of a random assortment

106

of individuals. People wander about, streaming to the bar or the toilets, and the background chit-chat is constant. It seems that club audiences have always been like this: when William Morris lectured in working men's clubs in the late nineteenth century, he complained that 'the coming and going all the time, the pie-boy and the pot-boy, was rather trying to my nerves.'

In many ways, stand-up comedy is the least suitable form of entertainment for this environment. Comedians are vastly outnumbered by singers and groups. Singers work to an organ-and-drums backing in clubs which employ musicians, and backing tapes in those that don't, and groups provide an entire musical package. In either case, they do a selection of chart hits past and present, or numbers from West End shows. Singers and groups stand a much better chance than comics in a noisy, often hostile club atmosphere, because they can outblast background chatter with sheer volume, and in many ways they require less attention than comedians. At worst, they can act as background music, but background comedy would be a hard concept to sell.

Strippers also stand a better chance than comics in the harsh club environment. Big-haired, false-smiling women slowly shedding cheap imitations of leather and lace sophistication to reveal forbidden portions of fake-tanned flesh are far more likely to capture the attention of a concert room full of men than some poor comedian. Strippers are engaged to offer the working men a bit of Sunday lunchtime titillation, and I can only imagine what drooling and whooping male bonding rituals they inspire, but it must be a far cry from the indifference the club comic has to try and overcome. As a nod to sexual equality, some clubs also put on ladies-only nights with sub-Chippendales male strippers, sometimes supported by a female impersonator.

Another type of act with more attention-grabbing qualities than the average stand-up is the occasional speciality act which does the rounds on the club circuit. There are mime acts, like Sheffield's The Discoes, who do mimed sketches to backing tapes, perhaps taken from adverts or TV programmes. Then there are the more outlandish acts. There's Ratman and Robin, for example, who put rats down their trousers and eat live cockroaches. There's a magician called Orchante, who swallows a ball of string, then apparently cuts a hole in his stomach and pulls the string back out of it. A lone person with a mike trying to tell gags couldn't possibly compete with such talents.

The form of entertainment which is perhaps best suited to the club concert room, and certainly the most popular, is gambling. Bingo is by far the favourite form, but there are others. Films of long-forgotten football matches or horse races are hired out from local firms, and members bet on the outcome. It'd be easy to sneer at the hallowed silence which descends over a previously rowdy club audience as soon as the bingo starts, but the fact is that there's money at stake here. Club members have a vested financial interest in shutting up and listening to the bingo, especially given that clubs tend to be filled by poorer sections of the community.

Stand-up comedy is far more vulnerable, because, at the very least, it needs to be heard. Nobody will laugh at a joke if the punchline has been drowned out by a loud conversation on the next table. Crucially, comedy also requires attention and thought. Songs can often be enjoyed without the aid of a brain, but even the most basic joke needs to be understood to be laughed at. Given the chatting, half-listening audience which most club comics face, it is hardly surprising that they tend to be so unadventurous. The string-of-unrelated-packaged-gags style makes perfect sense in this context. Packaged jokes are like buses: if people in the audience miss the beginning of the current joke, they can be sure that there will be another one along in a minute. Long, involved routines would not make sense in the clubs, given that a fair proportion of the audience would probably miss crucial bits of it while they were going to the bar or talking to a friend.

Stolen jokes also make sense in this context, for both

comedian and punter. Given the uphill struggle the club comic faces, he or she can't be blamed for wanting to use material with a proven track record. Getting heard is enough of a task in itself, without worrying about originality or writing your own jokes. Recycled gags are better for the audience, because if you've already heard a joke, you don't have to think too hard or pay too much attention to be able to get it. It's not surprising that innovation is rare. Trying to pioneer new comic techniques in venues where many of the punters think of you as little more than a minor irritation over there on the stage would be asking a lot.

Working conditions have affected not only the style, but also the content of the comedy. The fiercely working-class identity which was so visible in the Bobby Thompson generation has all but disappeared. When the emergence of the privately owned social clubs brought the club circuit onto the fringes of international celebrity glamour, the scruffy pullover look became inappropriate, and there was a vogue for comics to wear evening dress, swapping worker's clothes for the clothes of the aristocracy. Most of the gags about pawnbrokers and poverty disappeared with the flat caps.

In the 1990s there might also be the odd yuppie joke, like the one that a young comic called Lee J. Simple told on Granada's revival of *The Comedians* about two yuppies playing 'Shove Access Card'. On the other hand, the few jokes about class which club comics do tell are as likely to ridicule working-class people as those higher up the social structure. In the 1970s, there was a fashion for gags about lazy British workers, and dockers were a particular target. George Roper, a corpulent Liverpudlian comic, used to tell the one about the docker who kicked a tortoise to death, because it had been following him round all day.

My wife, my wife . . . (2)

The preoccupation with working-class lifestyles and problems has been replaced with a more aggressive approach to comedy. Modern club comedy is about finding as many targets as possible, and giving them a good kicking in joke form. Something the modern club comic has inherited from his predecessors in variety is the wife joke, which has evolved in opposite directions. On the one hand, there are comics like Johnny Casson, a Yorkshire comic with a friendly, eye-twinkling manner. He wears a patterned mauve jacket and the lacquered, slightly bouffant hairstyle of an ageing rocker; indeed, he started out as a drummer. His delivery is confidential almost to the point of being camp, and he puts his hand to his face with his little finger disappearing into the corner of his mouth, unconsciously echoing the great variety sketch comic Robb Wilton. Casson's angle on the wife joke is to make himself the butt. This one dates from 1992: 'But I've said to 'er, I said, "Listen love," I said, "you just stop at 'ome," I said, "you just do the cooking and the cleaning and the washing and the ironing and the gardening and the shopping and the painting and the decorating." 'Cos I don't want my wife to work.' *(Laughter)*

He's deliberately developed this angle, having noticed that 'most comics tend to, you know, be sexist towards women' and that as a result, women 'don't actually go for comics as much as men do'. His reasoning is, that by telling jokes at his own expense, he can go down better with the women in the audience and increase his popularity.

On the other hand, there are comedians who have gone in the opposite direction, making the wife joke darker and uglier than it was in the variety theatres. There are gags about wives who risk getting harpooned when they get in the bath and mothers-in-law who are too ugly to be raped by a gang of burglars. Tony Gerrard is a tubby, bespectacled, wheelchair-bound comic from the South-East, white-haired and balding. His warm, almost avuncular delivery masks the implicit violence that lies behind some of his wife jokes: 'I got married again last year, 'cos my first wife died in a wishing well, and . . . *(Laughter)* I didn't think they work, but they do. *(Laughter)* If you push 'em hard enough, any well'll work.' *(Laughter)*

Something blue

Sex is a big subject for club comedians, and the 'blue' jokes they tell are a far cry from the nudge-nudge, wink-wink sex gags the variety comics used to tell. Most club comedians are quite prepared to call a cock a cock. Although they bring sex out into the open, this is not so much about sexual liberation or breaking taboos, it's more about making sure those taboos stay firmly in place. The basic assumption underlying blue gags is that normal sex is something a man does to a woman. He lies on top, pushes it in, grunts a bit, then lies back, sated. Any deviation from this is enough to make the average club concert room resound with dirty laughter.

In variety, wife jokes reinforced an ideal of what the perfect wife should be by ridiculing deviation from that ideal. The blue jokes which club comics tell work in exactly the same way. Men with small penises are hysterically funny. There's a Johnny Wager gag about a man whose doctor can't help laughing at his half-inch penis. Then it turns out he's seeing the doctor because it's swollen. The all male crowd laughs it up. The implication is that a man's penis ought to be respectably large, so he can assert his sexual dominance. By the same token, a woman's vagina should be small, to match her sexual subservience. That's why club sex jokes are filled with enormously-endowed women, boasting huge, cavernous genitals. There's the one about the bus conductress who has room for five standing inside, the one about the woman who can fit five pints of Guinness in hers, the one about the woman who thinks she's tight because even though you can fit two hands up it, you can't clap.

In the same way, club audiences find gay sex funny because it deviates from their narrow model of normal sex. Lesbians can't match up to this phallic, penetrative ideal, so in blue jokes, they are constantly trying to find unlikely penis-substitutes. Bernard Manning, for example, gets a laugh with a joke about two lesbians in Belfast, fighting over a rubber bullet. A gay man is more of a threat, because he might see any other man as a passive sexual partner, thus threatening his dominance. In blue jokes, gays desire all other men. A straight man need only bend down to provoke a gay man to hop on top and bugger him. Johnny Wager, for example, has a gag about staying in a rough hotel: 'Went in, there's a big sign on the wall, it said, "Beware of homosexuals," walk along, there's another sign, said, "Beware of homosexuals." Walk along, there's another sign nearly on the floor. I bent down, it said, "You have been warned – twice."' *(Laughter)*

It's male sexual paranoia that gives these jokes their appeal, the fear of being robbed of sexual power. They're part of the same kind of anxiety that leads rugby players to shout, 'Oo, backs against the wall, lads,' if they suspect somebody of being homosexual. Since the 1980s, the advent of AIDS has taken the gay joke to new depths of insensitivity. You might hear, for example, the one about the gay man who goes to the doctor to get the results of his AIDS test. The doctor tells him he's got AIDS, but not to worry, he's also got Alzheimer's Disease, so he'll have forgotten about it by the next morning.

Curiously, it is the very tastelessness of club comedy that has allowed it to be turned into a cult commodity. Comics like Bernard Manning, Jim Davidson, Roy 'Chubby' Brown and Jimmy Jones have built up a huge following, allowing them to move out of the clubs and into big thousand-seater theatres. Their success has been boosted by the increased popularity of the live comedy video, and their video sales have been phenomenal. Roy 'Chubby' Brown's *Jingle Bollocks* sold 350,000 copies, and his sales net £5 million per year.

These comics have been marketed on their outrageous-ness. Their videos are splashed with sensational warnings in bold lettering:

'THIS VIDEO CONTAINS MATERIAL WHICH SOME WILL FIND OFFENSIVE!'
'IF EASILY OFFENDED, PLEASE DO NOT BUY!'
'THIS VIDEO IS ABSOLUTELY BLOODY DISGUSTING!'

Several use the title 'Live and Uncensored'. The cover of *Bernard Manning Ungagged* shows a sneering Manning, handkerchief in mouth, giving the finger to the camera. Manning's underground appeal has been assured by the placing of adverts for his videos in the cult *Viz Comic*. An essential part of the superstar blue comedians' rebel stance is the idea that they're too rude to appear on television. PolyGram's Pete Smith has been quoted as saying: 'You can almost say that the product sells better if the artist is not a current TV star.' An 18-rated certificate is also vital, to the extent that Bob Monkhouse included a stripper in his show specifically to bump the video certificate up from 15 to 18.

This kind of marketing has succeeded in bringing club comedy to a wider public, but the actual material is largely unchanged. The comics tell the same unoriginal packaged gags about the same targets. The main difference is that there's more sex. Sometimes there's a brutal edge to it. Jimmy Jones is a genial, grey-haired Cockney who comes across as more of a raconteur than a stand-up comic. Perched on a bar-stool, and without a microphone stand to divide him from his audience, he has the manner of the father-of-the-bride giving a particularly salty after-dinner speech at a big family wedding. Behind the jovial manner, some of the jokes are surprisingly violent: 'I'm not as evil as one bloke I know. Took a bird out who was deaf and dumb and 'e raped 'er. Then 'e broke all 'er fingers so she couldn't tell 'er mum and dad what 'e done.' *(Laughter)*

Even when there's no violence, the superstar blue comedians turn sex into a filthy cartoon in which penises are twelve inches long and four inches thick, sex aids are the most popular form of consumer goods, and men regularly do it

113

with camels, kangaroos or even moles. The ultimate blue comedian is Roy 'Chubby' Brown, because he discards most of the racist trimmings and sticks almost exclusively to sex. There is the occasional comment about the Chinese being 'fuckin' slinty-eyed bastards', but most of his gags are about genitals, fornication or defecation. Brown's audience is surprisingly broad. There are smartly dressed middle-aged couples and parties of old ladies as well as the inevitable drunken lads.

'Chubby' Brown is the mutant bastard offspring of Max Miller. Like Miller, Brown wears a brightly coloured costume, a patchwork suit worn with a red bow tie and a flying helmet. Like Miller, he overflows with cheek and charm, although his Geordie banter is much earthier than Miller's smooth-talking patter. Crucially, they both talk a lot about sex and portray themselves as libertines, although Brown's approach is far more graphic and explicit, poetically describing what Miller could only hint at.

Essentially, their technique is similar: pushing against the boundaries of acceptability to get laughs. The audience goes to see them specifically to see something shocking and dangerous. There's an extraordinary explosion of laughter, applause and whistles when Brown gleefully licks his lips around an explicit reference to cunnilingus. The audience is delighted to hear something so unashamedly outrageous. It's exactly like the nineteen-second laugh that Miller got for his fan dancer gag. Interestingly, Brown is capable of getting a bigger laugh for saying 'fuck me!' in the build-up to a joke than he does for the punchline. The lads laugh with joy at hearing their own kind of slang being used on stage. The middle-aged couples and old ladies laugh at the thrill of hearing somebody using such appalling language.

This colour problem

The racial gag has just as important a place in the club comic's armoury as the blue joke. When *The Comedians* was first broadcast at the beginning of the 1970s, one of the things that stood out was the sheer number of jokes about Irishmen, Pakistanis, West Indians and immigrants of any description. More recently though, the racial joke has gone into hiding. In 1987, Granada Television produced a video of clips from the early series of *The Comedians*, and all the immigrant jokes had mysteriously disappeared, discarded on the floor of the editing suite. Then in the early 1990s, when they relaunched the series with a new set of comics, they made sure nobody told any racial gags. Johnny Casson, who appeared on the revamped series, told me: 'They didn't want any, you couldn't do any ethnic jokes really. I mean they didn't actually, they told us not to, they said. "You can do what you want, but they won't go out on the programme." It's like I did a Christmas *Comedians* and Bernard [Manning] was on it. Ha ha ha, he come on like a, he was like an Exocet missile, I mean his language was abominable. And of course, he only had a fifteen-minute spot and they couldn't show above two or three minutes of it.'

This kind of whitewashing creates a false impression, because jokes about race are still popular on the club circuit of the 1990s. The basic unit of the race gag is the stereotype, the idea that a racial group can be reduced to a given set of characteristics. Perhaps the club comic's favourite stereotype is the thick Irishman, as in this joke, told by *Crackerjack*-presenter-to-be Stu Francis, when he appeared on the first series of *The Comedians* in 1971, as a fresh-faced, long-haired twenty-two-year-old: 'You know what it's like when you arrive at the airport, and y'ear all the announcements: "The flight bound for Majorca, Spain, will leave at twelve hundred hours. The flight bound for New York will leave at thirteen hundred hours. The flight bound for Dublin in Ireland will leave – when the big finger's on the twelve . . . and the little finger's on the six."' *(Laughter)*

In the 1970s, the thick Irishman stereotype was applied to the political situation in Northern Ireland. There was a

115

joke about an IRA bomber telling his driver to slow down, so the 400lb-bomb in his lap didn't go off. The driver told him not to worry, they had another one in the boot.

A slightly less well-used part of the stereotype is that Irish people are welly-wearing labourers, and everything they do is coloured by their pickaxe-shovel-donkey-jacket approach to life. In 1993, for example, Frank Carson was telling the one about the Irishman who had a leg transplant which went wrong because the welly rejected the new leg, and in the late 1980s, Johnny Wager was telling the one about the Irish teddy boy who carried a 'flickhammer'.

Afro-Caribbeans are another group with a popular stereotype attached, the myth of the black man with the unfeasibly large penis. Jim Davidson was born in 1953, and started playing the pubs and clubs in the early 1970s, before shooting to fame by winning the television talent show *New Faces* in 1976. He has built a career on playing the charming London bad lad, with twinkling blue eyes, longish, dirty blond hair, gold jewellery and the odd tattoo. One of his gimmicks is his imaginary black friend 'Chalkie', who he imitates in a voice somewhere between a Black and White Minstrel and Fozzie Bear. Inevitably, Chalkie offers an excuse for Davidson to relentlessly pump out the big penis jokes, one after the other. There's a 1990 television routine, for example, about going to Barbados on holiday with Chalkie. His penis scrapes the bottom of the swimming pool, gets caught up in weed while swimming in the sea, when he swims on his back he can't get under the pier, and somebody mistakes him for a windsurfboard.

The psychology of the big-black-penis joke is puzzling. Given that big genitals are supposed to be desirable in a man, it's a perverse kind of racial insult. All kinds of sexual paranoia could lie behind it. Perhaps the black man has a bigger penis because he is thought to be wilder, and nearer to the animals? Perhaps having a large progenitive organ relates to fears that the black man will produce enough offspring to take over the world? Perhaps white comics have a suppressed homosexual desire for black men? Whatever the explanation, given the way black men are treated in other gags, you can be sure that big penis jokes aren't meant as a compliment.

The Irishman and the West Indian are just two of a vast range of stereotypes which the comic can draw on. Club comedy is a kind of self-service buffet of bigotry, with all prejudices catered for:

1. *Liverpudlians: workshy scroungers or criminals*
   Example: A prostitute asks a Liverpudlian if he wants a 'blow job', and he asks if it'll affect his dole money.
2. *Welsh: prone to bestiality*
   Example: Comedian tells any Welsh people in the audience that he'll make them homesick, then plays a tape of a sheep bleating.
3. *Italians: greasy*
   Example: Italians haven't got freckles because they slide off their faces.
4. *Gypsies: filthy*
   Example: The reason seagulls have wings is so they can beat the gypsies to the rubbish tip.
5. *Jews: mean with money*
   Example: The Jewish Father Christmas comes down the chimney, and offers to sell children their presents.
6. *Germans: sunbed stealers*
   Example: German reunification means twice as many Germans will steal your sunbed on holiday.
7. *Ethiopians: famine victims*
   Example: There's a new nightclub in Ethiopia called 'Stringyfellows'.
8. *Koreans: eat anything that moves*
   Example: A Korean mistakes the Greyhound bus for a fast-food delivery service.
9. *Iraqis: ugly (in the context of the Gulf War)*
   Example: Iraqi women are so ugly they have to get their vibrator drunk before they can use it.

117

Racial stereotypes make predictable jokes, and that's why they're perfect for the club concert room. An ale-sipping, drink-buying, toilet-going, chit-chatting, kiddie-minding, smoke-wreathed audience has a short attention span, and the stereotype, like the packaged gag, is a helping hand, allowing them to get the joke without thinking too hard about it. As soon as they hear the phrase, 'There was this Irishman . . .', they can be pretty sure the joke will be about somebody doing something stupid. As soon as a black man is mentioned, they'll have a good idea that a big penis joke will be along shortly.

Stereotypes also fuel prejudices. Racial prejudice is the vodka in club comedy's Bloody Mary. It's what gives it its kick, its bite. It's what intoxicates its audience. The 1970s were good times for the racist. Enoch Powell had set the tone in 1968, with his 'Rivers of Blood' speech, which predicted apocalyptic violence if the government didn't put a stop to immigration. The tabloids ran scare stories about Britain being swamped with illegal immigrants. By 1973, member-ship of the National Front had grown to seventeen and a half thousand, and Far Right parties were starting to enjoy half-respectable votes in local elections. Meanwhile, on *The Comedians*, you could enjoy polyester-suited comics trotting out gags about explorers tracking down the lost Matazuki tribe living over a chip shop in Bradford, or switching on the radio on Christmas Day to hear the new Queen Mother talking in an imitation cotton-picking black accent. You could laugh and have your immigration paranoia stoked at the same time.

At its most dangerous, there's a sinister atmosphere of violence lurking beneath the laughter. Bernard Manning is the comic who's most closely associated with this trend. Born into a poor working-class family in Manchester in 1930, Manning started in showbiz as the singer for the Oscar Rabin Big Band after the war, and moved into comedy when he landed the job of resident compere at the Northern Sporting Club in 1955. In 1959, he opened the Embassy Club, run by his family and compered by himself. Throughout the Swinging Sixties it played host to international stars like The Beatles, Matt Monro and Jimmy Tarbuck, and it's still going strong today, with Manning as very much the main attraction.

Predictably, Manning's big break was appearing on *The Comedians*, but unlike most of his contemporaries, he has stayed in the public consciousness, largely due to his extraordinary gift for self-publicity. He has built his reputation on notoriety, his willingness to lay into anybody and everybody with his jokes. In practice, that means just about every creed and colour feels the sharp end of his comedy hobnail boots. There are hundreds of club comics who use similar tactics, but they lack Manning's high-profile media image.

A huge hulk of a man, his bushy eyebrows are the only things that stop his tiny, twinkling eyes from getting lost on his fat dumpling face. He radiates not so much confidence as defiant smugness as he spews out his jibes. Sometimes these are plain racial insults, not even encased in a joke format. Black footballer Paul Ince walked out of one show after Manning called him a 'coon'. In a video filmed at the Circus Tavern, Purfleet, you can see him picking out a young Asian man, and telling the audience they'll be having a lynching later on. The hapless victim's white friends laugh with guilty delight at this sinister teasing, and he does his best to join in the merriment. Perhaps more sinister still is Manning's angle on the Rodney King beating that sparked off the Los Angeles riots. His reaction to seeing the video footage of it is that it wasn't right, because there should have been more police there. He included this in a performance at a private police function, which was secretly filmed by *World in Action* in 1995. It caused a media storm, and it's not hard to see why: it wasn't just Manning's violent angle on one of the most serious racial confrontations in recent history, it was also the sight of an audience of British police officers shouting with laughter at it.

The most common target of violent racist jokes is

'Pakistanis', a term which seems to be used for anybody who comes from the Indian subcontinent, and not necessarily just for people from Pakistan. Although they no longer appear on television, in the smoky concert rooms of clubs all over the country, Pakistani gags still get them rolling in the aisles. There are jokes which dehumanise Pakistanis by implying that they are objects, not people. There's the one about how they smuggle them into the country in separate parts, then assemble them in Wolverhampton, for example. Then there are ones which simply imagine extreme acts of violence. I heard this one told by Johnny Wager in a Sheffield working men's club in 1988: 'Big queue of cars on the M6, feller comes, said. "What's wrong 'ere?" Feller said, "Pakistani – middle of the motorway. Poured petrol on 'imself, burnt 'imself. We're havin' a collection for 'is relatives." He said, "How much have you got?" He said, "Ten gallon."' *(Laughter)*

Occasionally, there's a kind of warped ingenuity about this sort of thing. There's a joke which has become common currency among club comics, which goes something like this: 'Have you noticed there are fewer Pakistanis around since the Chinese found out they taste like chicken?' What's clever about this is that it manages to squeeze three different flavours of racism into a single one-liner:

Stereotyping! It taps into the idea that the Chinese will eat anything that moves, serving up dog in their take-aways, etc.

Dehumanising! It suggests Pakistanis are a non-human species, with bizarre, chicken-like qualities.

Violence! It implies Pakistanis are being chopped up, cooked and eaten.

It's difficult to find any redeeming features in this strand of humour. Indeed, on the *World in Action* programme on Manning, a race relations lawyer called Geoffrey Bindman argued that his jokes could constitute an incitement to racial violence, making him liable to prosecution under Section 18 of the Public Order Act. The simplest explanation of why club comics tend to adopt this wife-beating, gay-bashing, black-battering brand of comedy is that it reflects their own right-wing views. Jim Davidson, for example, has links with the right wing of the Conservative Party, and Bernard Manning expressed some reserved respect for Adolf Hitler in a 1980 *Sunday People* interview, admiring him for 'cleaning out the workshy parasites and spreading the message that it is a fine, rewarding way of life when you work hard for your family and country.'

Hostility

On the other hand, there is something in the atmosphere of a working men's club that might encourage comedians to wheel out the racist gags, regardless of their own opinions. Club audiences aren't just inattentive, sometimes they can also be positively hostile. This can be more than just rowdy high spirits, sometimes fights actually break out. There's a historical rivalry between the comics and the clubs that employ them. Comedians resent the clubs for being so difficult to play, and routines sending up the whole club scene are quite common. There's also a tendency for the clubs to resent the comics they employ. This dates back to the 1960s, when the club scene boomed. What had been a ramshackle, semi-amateur circuit suddenly became big business. The new privately owned social clubs set higher rates of pay, and the smaller working men's clubs struggled to meet the new costs. The situation reached crisis point, and in 1968, the CIU backed a three-month entertainments ban in South Yorkshire clubs to try and force fees back down.

The resentment of club committees can easily filter down to the ordinary members. In his autobiography *A Clown Too Many*, Les Dawson recalls an incident in a club in Wales, in which the compere announced they would have to play an extra game of bingo before the comic came on, to make enough money to pay him. He told them exactly how much Dawson was getting, which was more than most of the audience got for an entire shift. They started heckling furiously, and fights began to break out. When Dawson eventually hit the stage, he lasted no more than a few seconds before he was dragged off and given a fraction of the original fee.

This is not just an isolated incident. Club committee men relish the power they have over the acts. The ultimate sanction is to pay somebody off, in other words paying them half the fee and cancelling their second show. An ex-concert secretary of Dial House, one of Sheffield's biggest clubs, proudly told me about the time he paid off Cannon and Ball early in their career: 'They did a spot at dinner time, and I said, "Right, don't bother coming tonight, here's your money, and on your bike," and I got somebody else for t'night. And in fact, they did mention it. They were at City Hall the other month, couple of months since, and t'little un said, "Where's that concert secretary from Dial House, is he in? What paid us up, like." Wish I'd been there, actually. I don't rate 'em now, Cannon and Ball.'

One possible response to this hostile atmosphere is to try and be as friendly and attention-grabbing as possible. Bernie Clifton started out as a stand-up on the club circuit before going on to a successful career in children's television, doing comedy sketches on programmes like *Crackerjack*. His props-based, family-entertainment approach to comedy was his response to the fear he felt on stage: 'As far as I was concerned, one of the reasons I started doing visual comedy twenty years ago, rather than just doing patter like a lot of other people were, was that I was afraid of being caught out. That's when I was doing working men's clubs. I wanted to go in and do something different that would make sure I could survive an evening in what was really a cauldron.'

Scapegoating

The more common approach is to fight fire with fire. Vicious gags about Pakistanis and homosexuals are a useful tool in the comic's struggle with a potentially hostile audience. They allow the aggression which could be directed at the comic to be deflected onto unfortunate scapegoats. This scapegoating process is at its most visible in a standard club technique: the comic asks. 'Any Irish in?', and when nobody replies, he or she follows it up by saying, 'Oh, question too difficult, was it?' This is the cue for a whole string of Irish jokes. Suddenly, it's no longer comic versus audience, it's comic and audience versus the Irish. The same ploy can be used for any minority group, and a comic can get a good ten minutes' worth of material out of it, following, 'Any Irish in?' with 'Any Scottish in?', 'Any Pakis in?', 'Any poofs in?' and so on.

In its purest form, scapegoating doesn't even have to involve a minority group. In the show I described at the beginning of this chapter, the comedian finished her set by dragging the concert secretary on stage and turning him into the scapegoat. Telling the audience how he'd referred to them as 'miserable buggers' in a conversation before the show, she whipped up whoops of laughter by laying into him, calling him a 'creeping arsehole', and forcing him to apologise to the punters.

If club comics do pick minority groups to deflect hostility, it's because they're playing to prejudices which are ingrained in the culture of the working men's clubs. Women are still second-class citizens. Although about a third of all club members are female, they are still only allowed to become associate members, ineligible to be elected to the committee. Some clubs have autonomously decided to change this rule, but attempts to officially allow women full membership have been consistently defeated. As recently as 1995, the CIU voted to keep things the way they are. The clubs are one of the last bastions of male supremacy in an increasingly equal world. It's hardly surprising that wife jokes go down well with audiences that still enjoy watching Sunday lunchtime strippers. In such an atmosphere, a good way of currying favour with an aggressive crowd would be to tell the one about the mother-in-law who's too ugly to get raped, or the woman with the enormous genitals.

Racial prejudice is also ingrained in the ethos of many working men's clubs, and it's not surprising that comics play up to it. Frankie Allen, a young comedian currently working the circuit, has admitted to putting racist gags in his act just to please the crowds, saying that if he doesn't do any Pakistani jokes when he's on in Yorkshire, the audience won't take any notice of him. It's not just a question of individual members being racist, sometimes the clubs themselves actually ban black people from joining. As recently as 1990, a Birmingham working men's club, the Handsworth Horticultural and Allotments Association, was reported to the Commission for Racial Equality after it was found to be operating a formal colour bar.

Black Yorkshire comedian Charlie Williams used to find himself playing to clubs which wouldn't have allowed him in as an ordinary punter. Winning over the audience in a place like that must have been a thankless task. Williams was born in Royston, near Barnsley, in 1929, and started playing the clubs in the early 1960s after working as a miner and a footballer with Doncaster Rovers. As with so many others, it was *The Comedians* that made him a TV star, and it led on to a stint hosting the game show *The Golden Shot*. Comics like Williams, and black Liverpudlian comic Jos White, had the cards stacked against them. Audiences could resent them not just because they were comedians, but also for their skin colour. Both rose to the challenge in the same way. They were warm and friendly on stage, winning the punters over by smiling and laughing along with their own jokes. Williams in particular had a real homely charm, flavouring his gags with his old-fashioned Yorkshire vowel sounds. Both also took a leaf out of the white comic's book, telling the same kind of anti-immigrant jokes. Here's a chunk of Charlie Williams' act in the early 1970s: 'I were talkin' to our saviour, Enoch Powell, you know. *(Laughter)* Eh, no, I wa', because see, I'm a Yorkshire lad, you know, and I told 'im about job, I said, I told 'im straight, I says, "Nocker – come 'ere, cock." *(Laughter)* I did, I said, "There's too many," you know, I knew, I knew. *(Laughter)* 'Cos I were 'ere fust, they're spoilin' it for me, you know. *(Laughter)* But it's these Pakistanis, you know, they freeten me. *(Laughter)* Eh, in't there a lot, in't there? They're comin' ovver 'ere, aren't they, on barrers, camels . . . oil slicks, owt they can gerron, aren't they? *(Laughter)* Eh, you shouldn't laugh, I'm feightin' like 'ell, me, to keep 'em out, I'm feightin'!' *(Laughter)*

If a naive liberal had wandered into a club and heard this sort of thing, he might have imagined that it was some sort of ironic satire on racist attitudes, but for the audience of the day, the meaning of the gag was quite different. The joke was actually that it was incongruous for these comics to moan about immigration, when as black men they were seen to be part of that very problem themselves. They were taking a position which, from the audience's point of view, they had no right to take.

In the same kind of way. Williams could get laughs by saying, 'I'm a Yorkshire lad, you know. There's not many of us left.' The audience laughed because he was black, and to them, that meant it was ridiculous for him to claim to be a Yorkshireman. What I find sad about this is that he was turning himself into a joke for the pleasure of a white audience. The fact is that although they laughed when he claimed to be an anti-immigration Yorkshireman, that's exactly what he was. He was born and bred in the Yorkshire area, played for a Yorkshire football team, and according to his autobiography, *Ee, I've Had Some Laughs*, he really did think that immigrants were 'spoilin' it' for him: 'It sounds daft coming from me, but in some ways you've got to go along with Enoch Powell. I reckon that immigration should be on a measured scale and under proper control . . . While ever the coloured immigrants keep coming over here in big numbers, you're breeding fear and unrest.'

Exceptions

It might seem that I've painted a deliberately bleak picture of club comedy, implying it's little more than comics trotting out second-hand bigoted gags to try and win over near-impossible audiences. What I haven't mentioned is that there are some comics who have managed to triumph over adversity, creating their own highly individual styles of comedy rather than just ripping off other comics, and yet still managing to get the laughs.

Tom O'Connor is better known as a TV quizmaster than a comic, but he started his career doing a stand-up act in the working men's and social clubs. This silver-haired, silver-tongued Liverpudlian appeared in the early series of *The Comedians*, and he stood out because he preferred observational routines to straight packaged gags, with the cosy, confidential delivery of a tour leader taking a party of pensioners to the seaside for the day:

'I mean let's face it, today the world's goin' mad, isn't it, and I, I think one of the worst experiences anyone can undergo for the first time or, you know, first sort of sensible time in their life is the dentist's, you know the place, don't you? You go in, you sit in the waiting room, the coathanger's full o' coats, and there's nobody else there. *(Laughter)* And from the back room comes, "Ahhahahh!!!" *(Laughter)* And a feller with blood all over 'is wellies runs out and says, "Next." *(Laughter)* And 'e's laughin', 'e's got a full set, you know. And 'e takes yer in, and 'e puts yer in the chair, and 'e fills yer mouth up with cotton wool and iron. And you're like that. *(Giggle)* And as soon as your mouth is chock-a-block . . . 'e starts askin' yer questions. *(Laughter)* "Has it always

126

hurt yer?" "Ughh gkhuh urr gurr gur uhh!" *(Laughter)*
Then 'e puts the mask over yer face, and you're off.
"Nineky nine, *(giggle)* nineky eighk, *(giggle)* nineky
hheven . . .' *(giggle)* and you're away – you and Brigitte
Bardot, *(giggle)* running through the cornfield, *(giggle)*
like an action replay. *(Laughter)* And she's got a shift on.
(Giggle) So 'ave you. *(Laughter)* And yer catch up to
'er. "Hallo!" And throw 'er into the waving corn, lobbo!
(Laughter) And fall beside 'er. And she looks up and
says *(woman's voice, bored:)* "Spit in the bowl, love."'
(Laughter)

Not everything in this is entirely original. The line about
there being nobody else in the waiting room in spite of the
coathanger being full, for example, originates in a 1961
routine by hip American comic Shelley Berman; O'Connor
was a big fan of imported American comedy LPs. However,
drawing out the absurdity from everyday incidents, using the
catchphrase 'The world's going mad' to get from one subject
to the next, was a far more subtle and skilful approach than
simply reeling out aggressive second-hand jokes.

Another who stood out from the crowd in *The Comedians*
was Ken Goodwin. His material was far from special. He
told just as many packaged gags as the next comic, and
they were often weaker than average. What was remarkable
was that the jokes he told were just a vehicle for his comic
persona, a Lancashire simpleton with echoes of George
Formby. Goodwin was a living embodiment of fun, like a
child so excited he could wet himself at any moment. It was
all he could do to contain his crazy gurgle of a laugh, which
exploded uncontrollably as soon as he had blurted out his
infantile punchlines.

In fact, the majority of the laughs came not from the
actual punchlines, but from the goofy asides that he slipped
in between the jokes themselves. His most important tool
was not the gags, but his crazy laugh. The sheer magic of
his technique was that he could get laughs by doing nothing

more than laughing himself. There'd be a burst of laughter at his apparently uncontrolled mirth. Then they'd laugh again at the fact that he could go on laughing so long. Then he'd say, 'What yer laughin' at?', and they'd laugh yet again.

Goodwin's simpleton approach was an interesting way round the problem of audience hostility. Instead of trying to fight back with aggression or by picking on minorities, he made himself as daft and lovable as possible. Anybody who shouted abuse at somebody like that would come across as being unreasonably cruel. It'd be a bit like kicking a beggar.

The king of club comedians was Les Dawson. Born in Collyhurst, Manchester, in 1931, Dawson slogged his way to the top of the club circuit before breaking into television with an appearance on *Opportunity Knocks* in 1963. After guest appearances on programmes like *Billy Cotton's Bandshow* and *Cilla* throughout the '60s, by the end of that decade he'd got his own show on Yorkshire Television, entitled *Sez Les*. Dawson is unusual in that he's one of the few club comics to have enjoyed sustained success on television. *Sez Les* was followed by *The Dawson Watch* and *The Les Dawson Show* as well as stints hosting game shows like *Blankety Blank*, and he continued to make regular TV appearances right up to his death in 1993.

Television allowed him to develop his comedy beyond the straight stand-up format, and his shows were packed with sketches, music and a wild array of comic characters. There was his Cissie and Ada double act, performed in drag with actor Roy Barraclough as his sidekick. A conscious tribute to the variety comic Norman Evans' 'Over the Garden Wall' sketch, this involved them dressing in an impressive collection of floral nylon and Crimplene dresses and gossiping about medical matters, mouthing silently any words too rude to be uttered aloud in public. Then there was Cosmo Smallpiece, the lust-crazed pervert. With unkempt hair, pebble glasses, a shabby suit and a spotty bow tie, he'd start off reading something perfectly innocent, perhaps train announcements or a nursery rhyme. Then he'd start to read sexual meanings into it. Giggling with desire, he'd grossly gesticulate, purse his lips into a disgusting heart shape and shout obscene phrases before being hooked round the neck with a shepherd's crook and hauled off camera. Dawson's favourite party piece was to play the piano, playing a few bars before coming in with a perfectly timed bum note.

On the surface, he was the archetypal club stand-up: fat, northern, dinner jacket-wrapped and constantly harping on about his wife and mother-in-law. On closer inspection, though, he must have stuck out like a sore thumb when he played the clubs. Like Ken Goodwin, he had an obvious stage persona, but it was the very opposite of Goodwin's cheery halfwit. Grumpy and gloomy, he looked as if he was far more concerned with his own troubles than with making the audience laugh. His eyebrows were knotted in a permanent frown. He spoke in a deep Mancunian growl, the sort of voice you might expect of a thousand-a-day smoker. His face was a big rubbery sponge, and he could get extra laughs just by twisting it into unlikely shapes, sometimes hoisting his lower lip right up to his blobby nose. Occasionally, he'd crack a big, eye-gleaming smile, as if to let the audience know that the gloomy demeanour was just a gag.

The wife jokes he did tell were far from run-of-the-mill. Instead of handing out simple comic abuse, he'd conjure up a surreal kind of domestic disharmony, perhaps saying that his wife had thrown a fried egg at him, in revenge for his having spilt cocoa down her nightdress whilst wearing it himself. He'd insult his wife more imaginatively than most, painting grisly word pictures. He might catch the sunlight dappling the warts on her lips, for example, or describe her as a 'bilious Gunga Din'. His mother-in-law got the same treatment. He'd talk of her picking the cabbage out of her teeth with her Iron Cross.

His choice of language was just like his piano playing:

perfectly wrong. His routines were jarringly poetic, liberally strewn with ornate and ostentatious words. Even the most functional punchline was an excuse to wax oddly lyrical. He'd describe the stars in the night sky, 'like pieces of quicksilver thrown carelessly onto black velvet,' before coming out with a punchline about needing to put a new roof on the outside lavatory.

This was the contradiction at the heart of Dawson's stand-up: here was a gruff, northern comic with a voice like heavy machinery being dragged over a concrete floor, who incongruously filled his routines with highfalutin cracked poetry. This was very much a reflection of his own life. He'd started out aiming for artistic greatness and ended up in light entertainment. His original ambition had been to become an essayist, and he had moved to Paris in his early twenties with this in mind, living the Bohemian lifestyle and playing piano in a Left Bank brothel to pay the rent. He ended up having to go back to Manchester and sell insurance. He started playing the pubs and clubs and eventually made it big, but even then he had greater artistic ambitions. Not content with being a mere stand-up, he wrote novels and took the odd straight acting role. In a *Guardian* interview in 1975, he said: 'I'm not going to stand on stage, or in front of a camera for the next thirty years telling caustic gags about a mythical mother-in-law.' Sadly, he died less than thirty years after making that comment, and in that time he never fully escaped those caustic mother-in-law gags.

When the big social clubs sprouted up in the 1950s and '60s, dragging the working men's club scene into the big, glamorous, glittery world of showbiz, stand-up comedians faced a real challenge: how to survive in such a beery atmosphere. The way they rose to that challenge reflects the best and worst of human behaviour. While most took the easier road, becoming living gag-machines running on recycled jokes and pandering to the audience's worst prejudices, a few comics like Les Dawson, Ken Goodwin and Tom O'Connor proved that even in the direst circumstances it is still possible to do your own thing. Each had their own very unique style, their own individual way of getting the laughs, and each still managed to taste success. They were very much the exception to the rule, but even without them there is still room for optimism. Club comedy may be dominated by bigoted, imagination-free hacks, but it was precisely reaction against these qualities which sparked off one of the most important developments in the history of British stand-up: the alternative comedy revolution.

Chapter Five

The Confidence Trick

Being a stand-up comedian is about saying witty things and telling clever jokes, but, more importantly, it's about making the audience believe that you're funny, creating faith in your own funniness. Famous comedians go onto the stage with a huge advantage. The audience has come along knowing their reputation, having already experienced their humour, and fully believing that they are going to have a good time.

Unknown comics have no such luck. They have to start from scratch every time they face an audience, getting the punters to make that leap of faith by their sheer performing skill. This is why confidence is so important. If a comic shuffles onto the stage cringing under the glare of audience attention, fiddles with the microphone, and reels out the first joke in a terrified, wavering voice, the chances are it will be greeted with an embarrassed silence. If on the other hand, the same comic swaggers onto the stage, grabs the microphone as if it is his or her own private property, and tells the same joke without apparently caring what the audience thinks of it, it will probably get a healthy laugh.

Stand-up comedy is a confidence trick. It's about making the audience believe that you know what you're doing. It's about creating the impression that you are in control of the situation. Your jokes may be old, stale and predictable as hell, but if you can go out there with enough confidence to persuade the audience that you are the funniest thing since the custard pie, the laughs will come thick and fast.

I'll never forget the first time I managed to pull off the confidence trick. It was at a student show at the Exeter Arts Centre, and I'd decided to do a kind of performance poetry act, with a rap and a song on the mandolin. I had utter contempt for the other acts on that night, because they seemed to me to be typical student revue-style rubbish. The fact that they were going down well with the audience pumped me up with swollen-headed arrogance. I walked onto the stage wearing nothing more than a huge pair of boxer shorts, a cub scout scarf, army boots, and a pair of sunglasses, and my costume alone was enough to get an enormous, seemingly endless roar of laughter. This seemed too good an opportunity to waste, so I launched into a ten-minute improvised routine about dogs, based on a private joke I'd enjoyed with a friend. Every time I got a laugh I was encouraged to try another line, and every line I tried got a laugh. It felt unreal. I finished off with what I had prepared, and went off to heart-stopping applause.

I spent about a year trying to recapture that experience, but the fact was that it was a fluke. The confidence trick is an acquired skill, and it can take years of experience to be able to pull it off consistently. You need to learn how to do it in different situations, the tricks that can help you to achieve it, and the pitfalls to avoid. One of the most obvious mistakes is to apologise when a joke flops. It is possible to rescue a joke that has flopped with a bit of cheeky self-deprecation, but this only tends to work if the audience is already with you, and even then you can't try it more than a couple of times. The chances are that pointing out comic failure will just make the audience uneasy, and destroy their faith in your funniness.

Audiences are razor-sharp in spotting signs of confidence-deficiency. Like a dog, they can smell your fear, and they will not believe that a frightened comic has the power to make them laugh. Stand-up comedians must learn to control their nerves, to make themselves confident even when they are quaking inside. My own approach to nerve-management is to focus as little attention as possible on the fact that I'm about to walk out in front of a group of strangers and try to make them laugh. I used to think that having a beer or two before going on was a useful way of grabbing a little instant inner calm, but since I have started driving to gigs I have found that going on stone-cold sober is actually a better idea.

Nerve-management becomes a particular problem after a bad show. When I've gone down like a plate of veal at the Animal Liberation Front annual dinner-dance, I often find that I get a bit nervous about the next gig. The danger is that dying on stage can damage my own faith in my funniness. I find that I can't wait to perform again, so I can restore my belief in myself. The problem with this is that I expect too much of the next show. Nothing short of uproarious, explosive laughter is enough to dispel the nerves and restore the faith, but it's difficult to get this while I'm still edgier than usual. As a result, my confidence remains shaky and the laughs remain limp and half-hearted. It's a vicious circle. My confidence crisis will last until I can put it out of my mind, tell myself that it doesn't matter, and believe I'm funny again without having to have an audience prove it for me.

Beating off hecklers is another part of the confidence trick. Non-comedians might imagine that heckling is the most terrifying occupational hazard facing the stand-up, but in fact I rarely worry about being heckled before I go on. Again, having the correct state of mind is essential. Answering a heckler is all a matter of not showing fear, of showing that you are still in control of the situation. A clever pre-prepared put-down that you've sweated for hours over in the comfort of your own home will fall flat if it is delivered in shaky-voiced terror, but a wit-free comment delivered with confidence will work every time.

There are some stock put-downs which are considered

common properly among comics, like 'I'd shake you by the hand, but I can see that you're using it,' or, for the particularly drunken heckler, 'Yeah, I can remember *my* first pint as well, mate.' One standard heckle put-down that was frighteningly common in the early 1990s was slightly more involved:

HECKLER: You're crap! *(or whatever)*
COMEDIAN: I'm sorry?
HECKLER: You're crap.
COMEDIAN: No, I heard what you said, I'm just sorry.

This might look innocuous on the page, but in practice it was almost foolproof. What makes it effective is that in saying, 'I'm sorry,' the comic appears to have been stumped. Sensing victory, the heckler smugly repeats the heckle, and the comic goes in for the kill with the punchline, making it clear that the whole thing was a set-up. It used to work every time until audiences finally caught on to it, but even now you still hear it being wheeled out occasionally.

Of course, comedians also invent their own personal anti-heckle lines, but often the most effective put-downs are the spontaneous ones, that are only funny in that particular situation, and couldn't survive out of that context. These are the products of pure confidence. When I'm totally relaxed, and my comedy is in full flow, I can swat away a heckler without even thinking about it. The right thing to say pops into my head unbidden, and without a second thought it trips straight off my tongue.

For the comedian, some of the least inspiring heckles are the most obvious ones. The most immediate answer for, 'You're not funny!' is 'Yes I am, actually,' which is far too pathetic to say onstage. I've often been tempted to respond to, 'Get off!' by casually saying, 'Right, see you then,' and walking off, but sadly, there is the small matter of fulfilling the contract. As with any other kind of heckle, these can only be dealt with by being completely unafraid of them. A useful technique is to ask the rest of the audience if they feel the same as the heckler. They will usually pitch their weight behind you, and you can get them to shout insults at the heckler in unison. However, this only works if the audience *is* already behind you, and I have seen inexperienced comics try this with a hostile audience, with the effect of provoking everybody in the entire room to shout, 'You're not funny!' or 'Get off!' or whatever.

Compering a comedy show is a particular skill, because the compere carries the confidence-can for the whole show. It's the compere's job to take the chill of a cold audience at the beginning of the evening, and to create faith in the whole show, to establish the idea that this is going to be a funny evening. It's an especially tall order for the resident compere, who has to do all this with hastily scrabbled together scraps of new material. The trouble with new material is not only that you can never be sure whether it is funny or not yourself, but also that until you have tried it a few times, you don't know how to make the most of it. After a few airings, you begin to learn which bits to draw out and milk, and which bits to skim over.

On the other hand, being a resident compere has its advantages. You get to know what to expect of an audience, you learn the kind of gags that will hit home and the kind that will fall flat. In some cases, you also build up a continuing rapport, and the audience comes along expecting you to be funny. I was lucky enough to witness Eddie Izzard and Frank Skinner in action before they attained household name status, when I played their respective clubs, Screaming Blue Murder and the 4X Cabaret. Their comic styles are very different. Izzard is surreal and whimsical where Skinner is matey and obscene, but they did have two things in common. Both had the ability to pour out seemingly endless amounts of new gags, and both had built up such a following that the acts became little more than an interlude between their routines.

Personally, I have never experienced such hero worship,

and I still have the misfortune to get nothing but bemused stares from the audience at my own club in Sheffield on occasion. The one redeeming feature about committing comedy suicide at the beginning of the show is that it doesn't necessarily destroy the whole evening. Following somebody who has died can go two ways. If you manage to get a big laugh within the first couple of minutes, you're likely to whip up a storm of enthusiasm. The audience has been longing for the opportunity to laugh, but hasn't been given the chance. Your first laugh shows that you're up to the job – now they believe that you're funny, and their relief is instantly translated into big laughs. On the other hand, if you fail to get that big early laugh, a terrible thought flashes across the audience's collective mind: 'Oh God, here's another unfunny one.' Then it's a constant struggle to make them believe you are actually funny.

The compere's job doesn't end with setting things up at the beginning of the evening; he or she must also repair the damage if an act goes down badly. It is vital to acknowledge what has just happened, which normally involves a bit of hefty ridicule. This is harder than it sounds, particularly if the unfortunate act is a friend. I once had the skin-crawling experience of introducing one of my comic heroes only to watch him suffer the worst death I have ever witnessed. His apologies for his joke-failure were dredged from the depths of his soul, making it seem that we were witnessing more than just the failure of a stand-up comedy act: he actually seemed to be going through a major nervous breakdown. The audience squirmed in their seats. I paced about in the toilets, racking my brains for a way of defusing the situation when he came off, and in the end I managed to think of a joke which acknowledged the awfulness of what had just happened without insulting him. It is vital to admit when an act has gone down badly, because otherwise you destroy the audience's trust in you, and their faith in the funniness of the evening as a whole.

The fact that I run my club as well as compering it creates

an interesting ego dilemma when an act goes down badly. Of course, the insane egomaniac part of my personality always enjoys seeing another comic failing, but when it's in my club, it's different. The showbiz impresario within me is screaming and fretting, worrying that the audience is going to go away unsatisfied and never come back, leaving me penniless and destitute. Cash worries always triumph over ego boosts, so I sweat a bit when an act dies at the Last Laugh.

Perhaps the finest confidence trick available to the resident compere is the joke competition. The audience is given the skeleton of a joke like. 'What's the difference between [*a well-known public figure*] and [*a household object*]?' for which they must provide a punchline; or you show them a picture for which they must provide a caption. The jokes are written down and collected, and later in the show the compere reads them out. The one that gets the best reaction wins a prize. Milking the laughs out of a joke competition is childishly simple. There are many easy ploys, like pretending to disapprove of a particularly outrageous gag, mercilessly ridiculing pathetic attempts, pointing out spelling mistakes, or simply cheating. Saying, 'Well that didn't go down very well, but I'm putting it through to the final because my mate wrote it,' always seems to get a big response. All these things create the illusion of spontaneous wit. You are responding to things that people have written, apparently off the top of your head, and there is nothing like the apparent ability to be spontaneously witty for making an audience believe in your funniness. Joke competitions almost always go down well, and, while comedians tend to find them useful but tedious, audiences never seem to tire of them.

Chapter Six
Misfits

Tied down by the problems presented by the variety theatres and the club circuit – censorship, management troubles, tough audiences – there were limits to what comedians who worked these venues could do with their comedy. Eventually, alternative comedy would tear through these restrictions and revolutionise the whole process of stand-up comedy in Britain. But even before that, there were some comics who worked outside the conventional circuits, finding their own audiences and their own unique approaches to the job of making people laugh for a living.

Dave Allen

Dave Allen became one of the biggest stars on British television in the early 1970s, just as shows like *The Comedians* were leading stand-up into a blind alley. Allen (real name: David Tynan O'Mahoney) was born into a literary Irish family in 1936. His father was the managing director of the *Irish Times*, and his aunt was the poet and novelist Katharine Tynan, a leading figure in the Celtic literary revival. Allen hoped to follow his father into journalism and moved to England in 1955 with this in mind, but impending poverty forced him to become a Butlin's Redcoat. This led to the bottom rungs of the showbiz ladder, touring pubs, clubs, summer seasons and the dog-end of the dying variety circuit. In 1959, he made his first television appearance on *New*

Faces, but his big break was a nightclub tour of Australia in 1963, which led to an Australian TV series, *Tonight with Dave Allen*. This opened doors in British television, and a regular spot on *The Val Doonican Show* and an ATV version of *Tonight with . . .* were followed by his seminal '70s series *Dave Allen at Large*.

Throughout his career, Allen has never stopped evolving. In the '60s, he was fast and manic, his routines fizzling and crackling with life, propelled by cartoon characterisation and insane energy. By the beginning of the 1970s, a remarkable transformation had taken place. Now Allen was quiet and urbane, sitting calmly in a chair, armed with cigarette and whiskey. Suavity oozed from every pore. He was like the club comic's more sophisticated cousin, telling packaged gags, but with theatrical precision, every stroke of the hair, every sip of the whiskey, every puff of the cigarette adding to his delivery. What distinguished him from the joke-a-like acts on shows like *The Comedians* was that he would mix packaged gags with the looser, more observational material that would eventually become his stock-in-trade. This was quite an innovation, because up to this point there had been no tradition of observational comedy in British stand-up.

Something else that marked Allen out from the crowd was his sheer inventiveness. In one classic 1970s routine, he suggested ways of staving off boredom when you find yourself stuck in traffic. Most of these involved freaking out other motorists: he'd pretend to swim underwater, or take his eyeballs out and polish them on his jacket and sew up his top lip. The missing half of Allen's left index finger has made it one of the most famous digits in British comedy; in this routine he used it for laughs, pretending to pick his nose with it, creating the illusion that he'd rammed a good couple of inches of finger up his nostril.

By the 1980s, Allen had changed again. The packaged gags had been completely phased out, replaced by free-flowing, philosophising routines. Possibly influenced by the rise of alternative comedy, he got faster and harder throughout the decade. His expletive count went through the roof, and he'd stand up to deliver his material instead of sitting, keeping the chair onstage only as a reminder of his calmer past. As the '80s made way for the '90s, he became more overtly political, perhaps comparing Ronald Reagan to a Cabbage Patch Doll, or drawing out the intrinsic comedy of the Poll Tax fiasco.

What makes Dave Allen special is the intelligence and subtlety of his comedy. In the 1970s, when other Irish comics were going for easy laughs by playing on the idiot stereotype, Allen took a much more thoughtful approach to his nationality. In one routine, he talked about the reasons why the Irish leave their home country: not for economic reasons or religious persecution, but to get more sex – that's why the Irish are so good at populating other countries. Another time, he talked about Irish attitudes to death, and the irony of wakes, in which you have the best party of your entire life, but you're the only one who can't join in the fun; as an afterthought, he added that if you did join in, you'd be drinking on your own. In the '80s, Allen further undermined the thick Irishman stereotype by talking about the illogicality of the English. He'd laugh at signs in English theatres that request the patrons to leave by the exits only.

As well as intelligence, Allen brought back a sense of danger to stand-up comedy. He has never shied away from taboo subjects, joking about religion and religious figures, for example, with joyful savagery. *Dave Allen at Large* was peppered with sketches showing priests knocking down pews like dominoes, bishops whose crosiers become erect in the presence of pretty nuns, and monks who get tripped up by their halos when they ogle young women. In his sit-down stand-up routines, he'd impersonate terrifying Paisleyesque preachers, reducing their fire and brimstone rhetoric to pure nonsense.

This approach has meant that he's no stranger to controversy. In the 1970s, a sketch which showed the Pope doing a striptease caused a Fleet Street furore, and the parishioners of St Wilfred's church, Northwich, even got up a petition against him. He topped this in 1990 by saying 'fuck' on his BBC1 show. The tabloids went mad. 'STORM OVER BLUE DAVE', screamed the front page of the *Daily Star*, which went on to berate him in the editorial, saying, 'It seems a shame for Dave to spoil his much awaited return to our screens by resorting to the language of the terraces.' The irony of this was that the word hadn't been used with casual yobbishness, but in the context of an intelligent joke about time and stress. After pointing out that we live our lives by the clock, clocking on and off at work every day, he asked, 'What do they give us when we retire? A fucking clock!' Blinded by the impact of the word, people ignored the context in which it had been used, and the storm raged for days. Incredibly, the incident was even discussed in the House of Commons.

In spite of his willingness to offend, Allen takes an ethical approach to his comedy. Although not above using the odd wife or gay joke in his time, by 1990, perhaps influenced by alternative comedy, he was speaking out against this sort of thing. He explained his position in an interview in the *Guardian*: 'If I were a woman I would be very angry about comedy over the years, because it makes things tacky. The idea that it's all right to talk about big boobs and use humour against homosexuals is very tiny-minded. Instead of broadening your mind it closes it. You end up with stereotypes – all Irish are thick, all Jews are mean, all Frenchmen are lascivious.'

The folk comedians

Dave Allen wasn't the only ground-breaking comic of the 1970s. Throughout that decade, the folk music scene produced a whole group of performers who expanded the possibilities of stand-up. It started with the folk revival of the 1960s, when a singer and musician called Hamish Imlach began spicing up his shows with quips and funny stories, thus paving the way for a hybrid blend of folk and comedy. This style was developed further by a young performer that Imlach had taken under his wing, a Glaswegian called Billy Connolly. Born in 1942, Connolly, after leaving school at fifteen, spent several years as an apprentice at Stephen's shipyard on the Clyde as well as serving in the Territorial Army. His showbiz beginnings were in a folk group called The Humblebums, with Tam Harvey and Gerry Rafferty. After they split up, he went solo and began throwing in gags and routines between the songs. Gradually they became the most important part of the act.

All over the country, others began to adopt the style. Jasper Carrott (real name: Bob Davies; born Birmingham, 1945) set up a folk club in Solihull called The Boggery with a £50 loan from a friend, appointing himself as resident singer and comedian, and from there began to play the folk circuit. Mike Harding (born Crumpsall, Manchester, 1944) worked as both a solo jokes-and-folk act and with his band Hedgehog Pie. There were other northerners like Tony Capstick and Mike Elliott, Welshmen like Max Boyce, Scots like Bill Barclay, and Londoners like Richard Digance and Derek Brimstone. They played in venues like the Brunswick Hotel, Preston; the Brown Cow, Mansfield; and the Wigan Rugby Club.

The gags and monologues were thrown in between numbers or even between verses of songs which covered most of the folk spectrum: they'd sing their own compositions, traditional unaccompanied ballads, ragtime, blues, banjo instrumentals or songs about drunkenness and incontinent poodles. Some songs were serious, others funny. Billy Connolly could even pull off the incredible trick of getting laughs out of an instrumental. There was some ambivalence about the folk scene though, and Connolly would quip about being fed up of seeing civil servants in pullovers singing 'The Wild Rover'.

The musical element was part of what was so different about folk comedy. Stand-up comedy had always contained elements of music, but the music which the folk comics made was young and fashionable. Some of them had hit records. Jasper Carrott's career only really took off when his single 'Funky Moped' got to number five in 1975. Mike Harding also had a hit in 1975 with 'Rochdale Cowboy', Tony Capstick's 'Capstick Comes Home' charted in 1981, and Billy Connolly had three chart hits, 'D.I.V.O.R.C.E.', which reached number one in 1975, 'No Chance (No Charge)' in 1976, and 'In the Brownies' in 1979. In the 1970s, he sold more albums in Scotland than anybody else except the Beatles.

As well as the music, the costumes they wore also linked these comedians with youth culture. Gone were the smart suits of the club comic, replaced by clothes which, whilst oddly revolting now, were fashionable at the time. Mike Harding wore dungarees and a Sergeant Pepperesque moustache-and-spectacles ensemble; Jasper Carrott appeared in denims, with long hair and big side-burns; and Billy Connolly had a whole range of outlandish stage wear including black catsuits, flared polka-dot pyjamas and banana-shaped wellington boots.

In some ways, the actual comedy was not such a big step forward. At worst, it was little more than a few Irish jokes thrown in between traditional songs about sheep stealing, and the actual Irish jokes they did tell could be every bit as harsh as the ones that did the rounds in the working men's clubs. There was the one about the Irishman up on a rape charge, for example: when the victim walked through, he piped up with, 'Dat's her, dat's definitely the one!'

There was also a vein of beer-soaked laddishness. Jasper Carrott would quip about his mother-in-law being 'a test pilot in a broom factory' and describe women drivers as 'just like any other normal psychopath'. One of his classic routines was a gleefully puerile take on the children's TV puppet show, *The Magic Roundabout*. It was included as the B-side of 'Funky Moped', and promptly banned by the BBC. It was this ban, as much as anything else, that took the single into the charts. The jokes are very much pitched at the lads in the audience, with Dougal wondering whether Florence is a virgin, and Dylan replying, 'Drops 'em for certain!' On the recording, the audience sounds exclusively male, lapping up the gags with the guttural cheers and drunken enthusiasm of a rugby club social. Mike Harding took much the same approach, in spite of claiming sympathy with 'women's libbers'. In a late 1970s routine, he talked about chatting up girls at a disco. His friend gets stuck with a 'slag'eap with legs on', and uses the immortal chat-up line, 'You don't sweat much for a fat lass, do yer?'

There were other aspects of the folk comedians that were far more interesting, though. Like Dave Allen, they broke free from the tyranny of the packaged gag. Billy Connolly's routines are a million miles from the standard set-up/punchline formula. They're more like comic trains of thought, starting with a couple of ideas and going wherever they take him. Over the years, his shows have got looser and looser, blending autobiography, observational material, philosophising and fantasy. He'll start off on a theme, then drop it in favour of something else, only to return to the original theme half an hour later, having launched into a dozen subjects in the meanwhile.

Jasper Carrott is just as jokeless. His routines unfold as easily and naturally as everyday conversation; his cosy Brummie accent screams ordinary blokishness. The only thing that differentiates his stage routines from brilliant pub table anecdotes is that they're so well constructed. Sometimes, he even works sitting on a bar-stool. Whether he's talking about going on holiday to America, driving a truck, or being one of a handful of Birmingham City supporters in a stadium full of Manchester United fans, he never appears to be straining to get a laugh. In one of his classic 1970s routines, he spends a full eleven minutes talking about how he got rid of a mole from his garden, and there's hardly a single punchline in the routine that could be taken out and used on its own. His great talent

145

is to get a constant flow of laughs by describing everyday experiences, and one of the best examples is his 'Nutter on the Bus' routine:

'When you're on a bus. When, when the nutter gets on the bus. *(Laughter)* Does the nutter sit next to you? *(Laughter)* The nutter always sits next to me, do you know that? *(Laughter)* Why is that, why do I always get the nutter? *(Laughter)* I'm the same as everyone else, they . . . It happened the other day like, I was on the top deck of the bus. *(Hums)* Bus stopped, you know, couple of people get on, starts off . . . *(hums)* Then you could 'ear the nutter comin' up the stairs. *(Laughter)* "Ereep! *(Laughter)* 'As anyone seen me camel?" *(Laughter)* "It's a nutter! *(Laughter)* Please God, don't let the nutter sit next to me. *(Laughter)* I bought a *Watchtower*, please . . ." *(Laughter and applause)* Everyone starts stretching out on the seats, don't they? *(Laughter)* I'm on the bus, no problem, they'll spot me, "Whoo-oo!" *(Laughter)* I must have this aura above my head, "nutter lover", you know. *(Laughter)* "Is this anyone's seat?" "Er, no." "Oh good, heh!" You can hear the visible sighs of relief from everyone else on the bus, "Ohhh! Ohh thank God 'e's got the nutter! *(Laughter)* Ohh! I thought I was for that one, you know." "Yeah, I know what you mean." *(Laughter)* "It's a camel job, they're the worst, aren't they?" *(Laughter)* Nutters love showing yer things, don't they? *(Laughter)* "Eh eh! I've got an atom bomb here!" *(Laughter)* It's a corned beef tin, you know.' *(Laughter)*

Even the less successful folk comedians would work outside the packaged gag structure, going off on whimsical flights of fancy. Derek Brimstone used the fact that the average height of the population is constantly increasing to reason that the knights in the Court of King Arthur were only two feet seven inches tall, and St George had actually killed a newt, not a dragon. Tony Capstick, a short, moustachioed comic with an accent as traditional as Yorkshire puddings, used an article in the *Lancet* as the start of one of his routines. In the 1970s, the very idea of referring to such an erudite journal in a stand-up comedy routine was pretty unusual in itself: 'I read that when y' 'ang somebody, or when somebody gets hung – which is a subtle difference between the two of course, erm – it's something to do with the carotid nerve or the spinal system or something, but they get an erection on. It only 'appens wi' men. *(Laughter)* And er . . . I read this in the *Lancet* and I was intrigued, you know, because I don't 'ave any trouble now like, but in a few years it might come in 'andy, you know wha' I mean? *(Laughter)* And er . . . I remember, I remember mentioning this to me grandad you know, 'cos 'e an't 'ad an erection since VJ Night, you know. *(Laughter)* 'E went an' 'ung 'isself. *(Giggle)* 'E's been in the kitchen now three months, me granny won't let us near 'im. Anyway . . .' *(Laughter)*

Something else that made the folk comedians stand out from their contemporaries was their politics. Tony Capstick did gags about Watergate, and even before she was Prime Minister, Mike Harding was doing Thatcher jokes, saying, 'She reminds me of every woman who'd never let me 'ave me ball back when I was a kid.' In some cases, the political commitment went beyond just jokes: in 1974, Billy Connolly made a party election broadcast for the Labour Party.

They were also political in a broader sense. The whole folk movement leaned towards the Left, and idealised a kind of flat-capped notion of the common people. The folk comics went along with this, playing up their regional, working-class roots. It's difficult to disassociate Mike Harding from his homely Lancashire tones, Jasper Carrott from his Brummie twang or Billy Connolly from his Glaswegian lilt. Connolly's comedy was steeped in the working-class culture of Glasgow, the accent, the slang, the drinking habits. 'Everybody in Glasgow's called "Jimmy",' he'd observe, 'even the women.'

147

The most nationalistic folk comic of them all was curly mop-topped Welshman, Max Boyce. Boyce's big thing was the Welsh rugby team. His Wales scarf and outsize rosette were as important a part of his stage gear as his acoustic guitar, and he shamelessly played up to the almost religious devotion his fans had for their national team: 'Outside Twickenham, there was this lad, I'll never forget. He didn't have a ticket an' 'e was shoutin' up to these English lads on the terraces, "Whoss 'appenin'?! Whoss 'appenin'?!" This English lad shouts down, "All the Welsh team have been injured," 'e said, "and the only Welsh man left on the field is Gareth Edwards." *(Laughter)* Twenty minutes later, there's a big roar from the crowd. *(Makes crowd roar sound)* And this Welsh lad shouts out, "What 'appened? Gareth scored, has he?"' *(Laughter and applause)*

This routine dates from the days when Gareth Edwards was still the Welsh team's star player, and at that time, Boyce also did a poem anticipating the day Edwards would be dropped from the team – at the age of seventy-eight. What's interesting is that when he announced the poem, before he'd got to the punchline the crowd hissed with disapproval at the very idea that their hero would ever fall from grace.

There was also a kind of working-class earthiness to the comedy, and a cheeky scorn for middle-class values. Jasper Carrott made fun of the 'surface wealth' of the ladies who walked around the Solihull supermarket he used to deliver for, lording it in their fur coats, then buying nothing more luxurious than 'a rasher of bacon and two eggs'. Mike Harding had a routine about being invited to a middle-class party, chock full of cartoon impersonations of toffee-nosed posh people with names like Roggers and Ju-Ju. The beginning of the routine, with its reference to dodging the rent man, harks back to the poverty comedy of Bobby Thompson: 'You know you should never've gone. You know, 'cos there's more trees than people. *(Giggle)* You know, and it's really posh, the garden gnomes are better dressed than you are, you know? *(Laughter)* An' all

148

the dog muck's in real neat piles. *(Laughter)* You know? And there's no rent-men's eyelashes 'angin' out the letterboxes.' *(Laughter)*

Another side to this earthiness was a love of toilet humour. This was a far cry from the variety comic's hidden references to laxatives or flatulence. It was a gleeful and explicit fascination with bodily functions. Harding had a seminal routine about vomit, for example: 'And you look down – and there's always carrots. *(Laughter, applause and cheers)* You may never've eaten 'em in yer life. *(Laughter)* You may've lived a totally carrot-free existence. *(Laughter)* You may've lived on a desert island where there were no carrots. *(Laughter)* But there they bloody well are! *(Laughter)* I think they come up the plug 'ole, me. *(Laughter)* "Someone being sick up 'ere, Ron." "OK, give us a hand up 'ere!"' *(Laughter)* The association of sick with carrots has become so popular that 'diced carrots' is now an established euphemism for vomit.

The master of the toilet joke was Billy Connolly. Connolly would dominate the stage, stomping about and illustrating his ideas with big, big gestures, his voice sometimes surprisingly gentle and lilting, sometimes gratingly loud in a mock-furious rant. With his long, flowing hair and his goatee beard, he came over like a foul-mouthed Jesus. Excrement was a never-ending source of inspiration, and in one particularly inventive routine, he described the life cycle of the excrement produced by airline passengers, imagining it dropping into the sea, being eaten by fish, the fish getting caught, eaten and eventually excreted again by an airline passenger. Every stage of his crazed reasoning got a big laugh, climaxing with tumultuous applause.

Like Dave Allen, Connolly could whip up real controversy, particularly with his religious material. His most famous early routine was a reworking of the Crucifixion story, set in Glasgow, which showed Jesus as a hard-drinking Glaswegian, who constantly comes out with unbiblical phrases like. 'Oot all mornin' doing they miracles, I'm knackered!' or 'See you, Judas, you're gettin' on mah tits.' Nowadays, this might seem like little more than a bit of irreligious fun, but in the early 1970s, in a devout and sectarian country like Scotland, it was dangerous stuff, leading to protests from the Church and even street demonstrations by religious groups.

The folk clubs hadn't always immediately welcomed the idea of having comedians in their midst but, once it was established, the relatively laid-back atmosphere allowed comics to find new ways of being funny, beyond the gag-gag-gag approach of working men's club comedy. The scene couldn't last forever, though. Folk music became less popular, and the clubs became smaller and fewer. The big names, like Connolly, Carrott and Harding, moved on to bigger things with hit television shows and national tours in thousand-seater theatres. The lesser-known comedians moved into other areas, like acting or local radio.

Victoria Wood

Another comic who has made a career outside the main circuits is Victoria Wood. Like Dave Allen and the folk comedians, this has allowed her to take a highly individual approach to comedy, but, unlike them, her stand-up career doesn't predate the alternative comedy revolution. Wood was born in Prestwich in 1953, and after studying drama at Birmingham University she began to dabble in showbusiness, winning the TV talent show *New Faces*, which eventually led on to a regular spot on *That's Life* in the mid-1970s, singing topical songs. Her big break came in 1982, when she was given a television series, *Wood and Walters*, which she wrote and starred in alongside Julie Walters. It was not until after this that she did her first solo stand-up show, *Lucky Bag*, at the King's Head in Islington in 1983. Throughout the '80s, she built up a huge following, boosted by two highly successful series of *Victoria Wood As Seen On TV*. By 1993, she had enough pulling power to fill the Royal Albert Hall for a fifteen-night run.

The material itself has an impressive gags-per-minute rate, but the packaged joke is completely alien to her. Much of her comedy is about putting an absurd twist on everyday things. She'll complain, for example, about sitting next to a woman on the train 'who's eating the individual fruit pie by sucking out the filling through the hole in the middle.' It's not simply the ability to pluck a grotesque image out of something as mundane as a fruit pie that gets the laughs, it's also the attention to detail: it's not just a 'fruit pie', it's an *individual* fruit pie'. Another big source of laughs is her skill in character comedy. She draws on her Lancashire roots, often slipping into a female version of the George Formby-style northern dimwit character. Slurring whole syllables into oblivion, she twists her mouth into a gormless sneer, and sticks her tongue right out to achieve the vowel movements, in routines like this one, which recalls her schooldays: 'Everybody was on a diet the whole time, and we thought that yoghurt made you thin so we used to eat yoghurt all the time, and we used to say *(slurred Lancashire tones:)* "Sandra. If you're going up town get us a raspb'rry yoghurt? *(Laughter)* If they 'aven't got raspb'rry get us summat else." *(Laughter)* She used to come back and say *(identical voice:)* "I couldn't get yer raspb'rry yoghurt . . . so I got yer meat 'n' p'tater pie."' *(Laughter)*

In a longer character piece, she impersonates a hapless cosmetics demonstrator in a department store, desperate to interest customers. The comedy grows out of her inability to make meaningless advert-speak sound convincing, getting her phrasing slightly and deliciously wrong:

'Welcome to the world of Sasharelle. *(Laughter and applause)* This is Madelaine speakin'. *(Laughter)* I'm over by the escalators, between the health bar and the toupees. *(Laughter)* Wendy and myself are just about to give a demonstration of Sasharelle's new Autumn range of cosmetics and skincare preparations. *(Laughter)* So if any lady would care to step up *to* the Sasharelle counter, that's right by the escalator between the health bar and the toupees, Wendy will be very happy to give that lady a free make-up. And I must stress that it is free, totally free of charge, whichsoever. *(Laughter)* 'Course, any lady or gentleman wishing to purchase *from* the new Sasharelle range we have a special offer on special offer. *(Laughter)* A free gift coming to you free with any purchase worth thirty-six pound or more. *(Laughter)* Free gift comprising of suede-effect pochette *(Laughter)* . . . packed to the drawstring with handy-size oddments. *(Laughter)* Total in-mouth blot, eye-wipe and shimmering cleavage enhancer.' *(Laughter)*

Throughout the routine she strains to sound bright and cheerful, but as she gets more flustered, the nasal attempt to sound sophisticated collapses, and she reverts to the comedy Lancashire accent: 'So this is Madelaine asking for the last time for *one frigging volunteer*! *(Laughter)* Will you drag your bums up please! *(Laughter)* To the magical piggin' world of Sasharelle!' *(Laughter)*

Unlike Dave Allen, or the Billy Connollys and Jasper Carrotts of the folk comedy scene, Wood is neither controversial nor political. Feminism is a basic assumption in her work, but polemical gags about gender politics are not her thing. When she does talk about, say, sexual harassment, she's more cheerful than aggressive: 'I think the only good thing to be said about leotards is that they're a very effective deterrent. *(Giggle)* Against any sort of unwanted sexual attention. *(Laughter)* 'Cos if you think, if you're wearing stretch knickers, and stretch tights, and a stretch lycra leotard – well, you might as well try and sexually harass a trampoline. *(Laughter)* 'S almost worth letting them have a stab, I think. *(Laughter)* Just to watch them boing off and bang into the hatstand.' *(Laughter)*

What could be a bit of furious comedy ranting is transformed by the fact that Wood delivers it not with a sneer, but with a beaming smile that suggests she's more interested in enjoying the idea of bouncing off a leotard than political point-scoring.

Perhaps Wood's greatest achievement is that, together with sketch duo French and Saunders, she has re-established the idea that female comics can be successful. In spite of the fact that variety comedy boasted many female stars, by the 1970s there was a serious comedienne shortage. For many, this tended to confirm the sexist assumption that women are just not funny. By propelling themselves to stardom, Victoria Wood and French and Saunders have thoroughly scotched that myth, and it is possibly because of this that they inspire such devotion in their fans. It is not unusual to come across people, young women in particular, who can reel off whole Victoria Wood or French and Saunders sketches verbatim.

Comedians like Dave Allen. Billy Connolly and Victoria Wood have an impressive record. They held out the possibility of stand-up comedy being a highly individualised art, whilst all around them was a sea of conformity. They made stand-up original, exciting and often controversial, more about flights of absurdist fantasy than stale old gags. But however successful and brilliant they are in their own right, the fact is that they are blips, one-offs, exceptions which prove the rule. It wasn't until alternative comedy came along that somebody thought about tearing up the rulebook.

Chapter Seven
The Right Circumstances

If stand-up comedy is about creating the right frame of mind in the audience so that they have faith in what they see and hear as funny, I should point out that this state of mind is not created just by the compere or the comedians. What goes on onstage is only part of the story. The whole way the gig has been set up is also vital in creating the right atmosphere. Perhaps the most crucial factor is whether people have paid to get in or not. An audience that has paid to come and see a comedy show is infinitely easier to convince than a haphazard collection of punters who have just happened to wander into the venue. Non-paying audiences have no investment in having a laugh, so they may not even bother to listen.

I have found myself performing in the corner of the main bar of a pub. To the ordinary customers, I have been an invader, an idiot in the corner with a microphone, disturbing their quiet drink. On one recent occasion, this was compounded by the fact that there was a constant stream of customers walking directly in front me. It was their only route to the toilets. Trying to persuade an audience like that of my innate comic genius was a thankless task. The same is true of comedy shows in discos, where the punters have come along quite reasonably expecting to dance, not listening to somebody desperately churning out the funnies.

Other factors which affect the audience's state of mind

are the time the show starts and the seating arrangements. A gig with an early starting time, say 7.30pm, will probably have a more formal atmosphere than a gig which starts at the more usual time of 9pm. The audience will be less excited, less willing to go mad, less likely to give you big laughs. On the other hand, a late gig starting at, say 11pm, might be all too lively, with drunken punters who have only come for the late bar licence shouting incoherent abuse. Seating has the same kind of effect. Ranked theatre seating makes for a colder, more polite audience than chairs around tables with drinks on.

I always take the circumstances of the gig into account when judging how well I have gone down. There are comedians on the circuit who think that if you go down badly you should only ever blame yourself, but it is no exaggeration to say that some gigs are almost entirely impossible. Sometimes I feel angry with myself after a show, because even though the circumstances have been appalling, I feel that I haven't done everything I could to overcome them; but blaming yourself for getting no laughs in a beer-stained bearpit seems counterproductive to me. It can bring about an unnecessary confidence crisis, and it might lead you to tinker with things in your act that don't actually need tinkering with. On the other hand, being too quick to blame the circumstances of the gig can also be dangerous, because if you are actually doing something wrong, you need to be aware of it so you can change it. When I give myself a post-mortem after dying on stage, I always try to work out how much of it was my fault, and how much was the gig itself.

An example of a near-impossible gig that immediately springs to mind is a Red Grape Cabaret show at Nene College in Northampton in 1992. We arrived to find a room which literally stank. The floor was sticky with spilt beer, the chairs strewn around the edge of the room were a foam-rubber graveyard and the contents of an egg salad sandwich were scattered across the stage. The student who had booked us gave us a cheery grin and naively tried to reassure us: 'Don't worry lads, we've got the rugby squad *and* the football team getting pissed in the other bar, and they'll be coming through to watch you.'

University sports teams are not known for their high position on the evolutionary scale, and sure enough, they were out for blood that night. As soon as the compere went on the chanting started, and the guttural wall of noise they produced lasted the whole night. Just five minutes into the show, the neanderthal comedy king of the rugby squad leapt onto the stage, grabbed the microphone, and launched into the least Rolf Harris-like Rolf Harris impression I have ever seen. His friends roared with laughter. That was an achievement we could not match, not least because of the simple physical fact of not being able to be heard above the din. Afterwards, somebody told us that Jack Dee had been there the previous year and suffered a similar fate.

Another impossible gig that sticks in the memory was a Red Grape show at Huddersfield University in 1994. We arrived at about 8pm, only to discover that we were performing at a beer festival, and our audience had been drinking solidly since ten o'clock that morning. The first thing that happened was that the fire alarm went off, and the entire building was evacuated whilst the fire engines arrived. Somebody told us this was the fourth hoax call-out that day. When we went back in, we were told that our stage was a corner of the balcony. We were expected to stand there with the microphone and deliver our routines to a chaotic mass of alcohol-sodden debauchery fifteen feet below. Again, the rugby squad was involved. They marched up the stairs and grabbed the microphone from one of the other comics, telling him to get off in no uncertain terms. When it was my turn, I decided to cut my losses and deliver my material to a single bearded mature student who happened to be up there on the balcony with us. His face never once cracked into a smile, but after each punchline his solemn Irish voice said things like, 'Oh, that was quite a good one,' or, 'No, I didn't like that one much. A bit corny.'

In circumstances like these, the wisest course of action is probably to simply give up any hope of going down well. Oddly, this sometimes brings about the right state of mind to achieve the impossible. I remember a spine-chilling gig in Birmingham, based on the misguided belief that putting a few comedy acts on before the disco started might be a good idea. The ritual of heckling off the comedians before the music came on was quickly established, and the night I played there was no different. I was due to go on last, and, one by one, the acts before me had their jokes and their egos gleefully torn to shreds. I walked on, certain that the same thing was going to happen to me, and not really caring. As it turned out, my fatalistic attitude was perfect for the circumstances because it made me completely confident. The first thing I did was to take the microphone out of the stand. It fell apart in my hands. There was a huge laugh. It was at my expense, but it was a start. I laid into one of the hecklers, and got approving cheers. I oozed confidence, so they believed in my comic abilities, and all the vehement negativity that had been used against the other acts was converted into positive energy. The laughs and applause I fluked out of them that night were every bit as loud as the heckles had been.

The same thing happened at a show in Derby. There was a bar promotion offering cheap bottled beer, which sold out in the first ten minutes. There were tables of lads, each with twenty bottles of German lager in front of them. The organiser said we were too late for a sound-check, and put us in a room with no light whilst the sound system blared out painfully loud indie music. The first act was shouted down in minutes, destroyed by feedback from the PA system as well as the solid wall of bellowed abuse. I went on fully expecting the worst, and in spite of the PA wailing like a banshee every time I moved, my total apathy came across as confidence and they lapped

157

up my gags as if I were topping the bill at the London Palladium.

Perhaps the hardest gigs are the ones without many punters. A non-comedian might imagine that an audience of eight is less daunting than an audience of two hundred, but in fact it's hard to fill empty rooms with laughter. Small audiences start off cold and defensive. Because there are only a few punters, each one feels exposed. Comedy-goers tend to be scared of being ridiculed from the stage, and if there are only a few of them in the room, the chances of being a victim are statistically higher. Small audiences also tend to be plagued by the collective fear that this will be a limp, slightly depressing evening, and that they might have had much more fun if they had gone somewhere else. They find it hard to have faith in your funniness. Then there's the simple matter of numbers. Laughter is infectious, but when there's only a handful of people in the room, the chances of cross-infection are that much smaller. Nobody notices if three or four people aren't laughing in an audience of two hundred, but if there's only eight people in the room, that means half the audience isn't laughing.

The secret of turning a handful of embarrassed people into a viable comedy audience is part of the confidence trick mentioned in chapter 5. The key is not to let the gloomy atmosphere overwhelm you. It's essential to be able to break free of your set routines and improvise freely. I like to storm on and cheerfully draw attention to the sorry state of affairs, perhaps starting by getting everybody in the room to introduce themselves. I will pick out individual responses, make people part of the act, comment on the poor quality of my own material, but all the time I make sure that I am beaming with enjoyment at what I am doing. This usually creates a kind of party atmosphere, allowing people to enjoy the fact that the evening has been a bit óf a flop. Turning on the instant cheerfulness in the face of adversity isn't always easy, but I try to remember that at least there is nothing to lose with a small audience. If things go horribly wrong in normal circumstances, I am faced with the thought, 'Those hundred people will go away from the gig thinking I am the worst comedian in the world.' If I die in front of eleven people, only eleven people end up thinking that.

The near-impossibility of some gigs is immediately obvious. In rowdy gigs, there's a bearpit atmosphere even before the show starts. The whiff of testosterone fills the air, individual tables spontaneously erupt into football chants and the beer consumption is alarming. Similarly, a vast hall with three people huddled together at the back presents an obvious challenge. Occasionally though, the danger for the comic is less visible. It is difficult to tell in advance, but some audiences have strong allegiances, and treading on their prejudices is a good way of making them instantly withdraw their belief in your funniness.

Sometimes these prejudices and allegiances are political. I remember working at a club in a West London pub which was packed with rich, mouthy Jewish teenagers who regularly went there because it was a soft touch for under-age drinking. I wouldn't have realised they were Jewish, but luckily I had gone to the gig with a friend who is Jewish himself, and he pointed the situation out to me. If he hadn't, what followed would have been a mystery to me. By coincidence, the first act was also Jewish, and when he referred to this onstage, he got a hearty cheer. Later, he did some thoughtful material about Jewish politics which was implicitly critical of the Israeli government, and suddenly the cheers turned to disapproving jeers. He weathered the storm, but it was a peculiar crowd to work to and I was relieved that I didn't have any jokes like that in my own act.

Audience prejudices can be much more trivial than this, though. Just recently I did a show at Derby University, and I used a line which I always use in student gigs. I say, 'It's funny playing at [*name of academic institution*], because I was actually going to come here at one point to study. But then I passed my A-levels.' It's a deliberately cheeky line, which normally gets a delightfully outraged response. On this occasion, it was different. After a solid start, with laughs in most of the right places and the odd bit of spontaneous applause, I launched into the line, and there was instant uproar. It was only when it died down that I realised that it was the wrong kind of uproar. What had been a comedy audience had turned into a sullen, hard-eyed crowd, challenging me with their stares. Somebody shouted. 'You're shit!' and got a cheer. I put him down and got a groan. I kept hitting tried and tested punchlines to no response. I had insulted their honour, and they refused to laugh any more. I felt like saying, 'Hey, it's me, I'm funny, remember? You were laughing a minute ago, we were having a good time, remember the dog-in-the-overcoat gag, you loved that didn't you?' Whatever I did, I couldn't win them back. Afterwards, I was a little shell-shocked. I was amazed that a joke that was so obviously just meant to be a cheeky tease, a harmless bit of fun, should have left such a bad aftertaste, particularly because I'd got away with it twice before at the very same university. I found the idea of people being so sensitive about their exam results extraordinary.

Just a few weeks later I had another experience with over-sensitivity. I was compering my own club in Sheffield, and I had got onto the stage to start the show when an ostentatiously drunk punter started shouting indistinct, confused comments. His athletic intake of alcohol had filled him with love for everything and everyone. I mentioned Cliff Richard, and he shouted, 'I FUCKIN' LOVE CLIFF RICHARD!!!' I mentioned the Conservative Party, and he shouted. 'I FUCKIN' LOVE THE CONSERVATIVE PARTY!!!' All this was very good for getting instant laughs, but it made it difficult to get back into my rather tepid topical gags. After a couple of minutes. I decided to cut my losses. Every time I raised a subject, I asked him what he thought of it, each time getting the inevitable response, 'I FUCKIN' LOVE IT!!!' Then I got onto the subject of contraception, and when I asked him. 'What do you think of contraception?' he replied, rather perversely, 'I FUCKIN' HATE IT!!' It was a set-up. I snapped straight back with the line, 'Well, I expect you don't have much use for it.'

The audience response completely threw me. First there was the beginning of a huge burst of laughter, but before it could reach a climax it was drowned by a tidal wave of booing. My mind whirred, frantically trying to work out what I had said wrong. As I soldiered on, my alcohol-soaked friend continued to shout, and each time I put him down, there was another boo. Somebody shouted, 'Leave him alone!' I found it hard to believe that somebody so dedicated to making an exhibition of himself could have attracted so much sympathy. Eventually it clicked. I said, 'Do you know this bloke or something?' and a chorus of voices shouted back 'yes' without any hint of embarrassment.

It turned out that Mr Drunkard was celebrating his birthday, and had brought twenty-seven friends with him. Their thin-skinned presence dominated the front half of the room. I was careful what I said about him after that. What I found astonishing about the whole episode was their loyalty. Most people seem to accept that a heckler is fair game for a few insults from the stage, but these people were completely unashamed of being associated with somebody who was making a drunken idiot of himself in public.

Because the circumstances of the gig makes all the difference as to how hard I have to work, part of my job is to start weighing up the venue as soon as I get there. It's important to know as much as possible in advance. I try to get the feel of the room, its size, its shape and the sightlines. If the stage is in the middle of a long, thin room, or in the corner of an L-shaped room, I need to be prepared to work to both sides. If the sightlines are poor, I need to work out the best way of making my visual gags visible to everybody. If it's a large, cavernous hall, I need to be aware that the audience's responses will get lost in the high ceiling, and that a distant, ghostly rattle of a laugh is all I am likely to hear.

I often ask the person in charge of the gig what the audience is like. Generally, he or she will try to put the best possible gloss on things, but a comment like. 'It's sometimes a bit thin in here,' means I'll probably be facing no more than a couple of timid punters who have wandered in by mistake, and, 'They get a bit rowdy sometimes,' probably means an angry, wailing mob, fired up for a good lynching. By the time the show starts I'll know exactly how big the audience is, but I will also have checked for any peculiarities, for example if it is dominated by older people or teenagers. When the show starts, I will watch to see how the other acts are going down. This gives me an idea of whether I am likely to get great strength-giving bellows of laughter, timid little titters or abusive shouting.

All this advance knowledge is useful because what I find most dangerous is the unexpected. Facing a blood-out-of-a-stone non-laughing audience will only tend to throw me if I am expecting a big, excitable crowd. Dealing with poor sightlines is more difficult if they take me by surprise. A drunken heckler can wreak more havoc on my act if he (and it usually is a he) comes out of the blue. On the other hand, it is important not to prejudge an audience too much. I remember a feeling of dread coming over me as I sized up the audience in York Arts Centre before a Red Grape Cabaret show. It was a distinctly middle-aged audience, with a sizable minority of pensioners. I was convinced that my act was doomed. The jokes that they didn't find offensive would be too youth culture-orientated for them to under-stand. As it turned out, they lapped up the menstrual blood routine, guffawed at the ejaculation gag and applauded the impression of the 1970s cartoon character Scooby Doo.

More recently, I had a similar experience in Sunderland. After a gruelling drive, I turned up at the venue, which turned out to be a smart pub on a deserted riverside development miles from anywhere. My first thought was that I'd be playing to the other acts and the bar staff. I was pleasantly surprised when enough people dribbled in to make a respectable comedy audience. My next worry was that most of the punters were working-class Sunderland folk, and I thought they'd be expecting me to be a kind of cut-price Bernard Manning. My prejudices about their prejudices turned out to be quite wrong. It was certainly different from playing to the more usual type of middle-class alternative comedy audience, but it was no less pleasant. One thing that worried me, though, was the fact that there was a huge, round man sitting on the table to the right of the stage who wasn't even cracking a smile. He looked like the sort of person who'd be handy in a post-pub Friday night punch-up, and the hard, funereal stare which he'd fixed on me was strangely unsettling. After the show, he came up to me, and I flinched as he held out his hand to be shaken. His face still bore no hint of a smile as I heard his North- East accent say, without sarcasm, 'That was really funny, I thoroughly enjoyed it.'

Chapter Eight
Alternative Comedy

Revolution

May 1979. A Soho strip club. A room accessible only via a tiny lift which can carry no more than a couple of people at a time. The place reeks of glitzy cheapness, the stage backed by the long, glittery strands of its silver slash curtains. The audience sits around tables drinking wine straight from the bottle, eager to shout abuse at the acts on stage. Rik Mayall and Ade Edmondson are hanging around in the background as mere punters. Alexei Sayle is compering the show in a leather jacket with a full head of hair. He introduces a series of amusingly bad acts. There are cheery Cockney Max Mill-er-likes in red waistcoats and bowler hats. There are fat lunatics in false beards putting floral-patterned boxes on their heads and making silly noises. There are bottom-rung working men's club comics being heckled for telling tired old lesbian gags. When the audience's baying reaches a certain level, Sayle steps back onto the stage and bangs a gong and the offending act's ordeal is over.

This was the opening night of the Comedy Store. It was an unlikely setting for a comic revolution but it was here that a whole new breed of comics stalked out onto the stage. They shouted and swore, they delivered weird routines with quiet menace, they turned seditious politics into jokes. They threw aside the stolen Pakistani jokes of their predecessors and instead lashed out at the mood of the times, attacking wine bars and Sony Walkmans ('deaf aids for trendies' – Alexei Sayle) with as much venom as they did the newly elected Thatcher government.

Now, more than a decade and a half after alternative comedy emerged kicking and screaming into the world, it is difficult to imagine the impact all this had on the unsuspecting late-'70s punter. Ian Stone, a comic on the present-day altcom circuit, used to go to the Comedy Store in the early days as an under-age drinker: 'Most of the people of my sort of age were brought up on a diet of *Terry and June* and crap '70s sitcoms . . . and suddenly I'm sitting on the front row of the Comedy Store and I've got Alexei Sayle spitting and swearing in this tight suit and just looking like nothing I'd ever seen. I thought it was incredibly exciting. And there was an energy about it that I really liked. I went every week for a year 'cos I thought it was fantastic.'

The Comedy Store wasn't purpose-built for a comedy revolution. Peter Rosengard, the novice impresario behind the venture, had visited a comedy club (also called the Comedy Store) whilst on holiday in Los Angeles, and had come back determined to set up something similar in London. He had no real idea what to expect. As it happened, the new venue brought together a set of individuals who were determined to turn comedy upside down, but the rag tag parade of amateurs, the Max Mill-er-likes and the low-grade working men's club comics, were as much a part of the Comedy Store as the new comedy pioneers. There were even appearances by famous television comedians like Les Dawson and Lennie Bennett. For a year or so, the old guard shared the stage with the new wave of comedians, with a kind of rivalry that the eccentric hippy anarchist Tony Allen has described as a 'civil war', before they were eventually swept away and the Store became a *bona fide* alternative comedy venue.

Even before the civil war was won, the Comedy Store was important, not only because it brought a handful of comic revolutionaries together, but also because it gave them a

165

stage on which they could learn to be funny. The first to stand-up and deliver were refugees from the alternative theatre scene. There was Alexei Sayle, a portly Liverpudlian of working-class Marxist parentage, who had toured with an anarchic cabaret troupe impersonating Bertolt Brecht. There was Tony Allen, who had written and acted with radical theatre companies like Rough Theatre and had a history of ranting at audiences as a regular at Speaker's Corner in Hyde Park. There were also ex-members of some of the bigger touring companies: Andy de la Tour had been in Belt and Braces, and both Pauline Melville and Jim Barclay had worked for John McGrath's 7:84. Then there was former Borstal boy Keith Allen, who had worked with a surrealist theatre group called Crystal Theatre of the Saint as well as having been involved in various bits of Situationist mischief.

Hot on their heels came a second group of comics, mainly ambitious graduates of the student drama scene. There was the double act 20th Century Coyote, made up of Rik Mayall and Ade Edmondson, which had grown out of an improvised theatre group at Manchester University. Later they were joined by fellow Manchester graduate Ben Elton. Another double act, Nigel Planer and Peter Richardson's The Outer Limits, was the continuation of a partnership formed at LAMDA.

The Comedy Store brought these people together and, in doing so, created the momentum for a whole new comedy movement which quickly became too big to be contained by its four walls. Shortly after the Store opened for business, the new-style comics it attracted banded together in a loose collective called Alternative Cabaret. They toured around pubs, colleges and arts centres, averaging four gigs a week by December 1979. They also set up altcom's second regular venue, the Elgin in London's Ladbroke Grove, which in an earlier era had been the local pub of the murderer John Christie. In many ways, the foundation of Alternative Cabaret was every bit as important as the opening of the

Comedy Store, because it established the idea of running comedy shows in small venues around London, and thus sowed the seeds of the network of pub-based gigs that grew up in the capital throughout the 1980s.

The third regular venue was the Comic Strip, which opened in October 1980. Like the Comedy Store, it was based in a strip club. It was run by a group of performers, the student-theatre wing of the new movement, and soon began to acquire even more kudos and media attention than the Store. It was here that French and Saunders were introduced to the world of comedy. Later, the Comic Strip would evolve into a touring group and eventually a production company producing a successful series of television films.

Rock'n'roll

Alternative comedy completely redefined what it meant to be a stand-up comic. For the first time, stand-up comedy became a young person's thing, as close to rock'n'roll as it was to family entertainment. In an interview with *The Face* in 1981, bug-eyed manic genius Rik Mayall was quoted as saying: 'I wanted to do rock'n'roll because it seemed the best way of getting through. But I can't play an instrument and I can't sing. So I did comedy instead.' He and his fellow Comic Strippers played in joke bands like Nice Weather and Bad News as a sideline to their comedy. Keith Allen had been involved in punk festivals, and played drums in a band called the Tesco Bombers. Later he released a trouble-making reggae record about homosexuality under the pseudonym Sex Boots Dread, and wrote the 1990 England World Cup song with New Order. Andy de la Tour's first forays into the world of stand-up were when compering a rock theatre show, and Tony Allen regularly appeared onstage alongside the cult anarchist punk band Poison Girls. The links with punk bands were more than mere coincidence: the first alternative comedians shared punk's aggressively anarchic approach to performance, together with its insistence that passion was more important than technical ability.

Rock'n'roll may have been nothing more than a sideline for most of the new comics, but for Alexei Sayle it was a highly successful one. In 1984, he had a Top Thirty hit single with 'Ullo John! Gotta New Motor?' This was nothing new in itself. Comedians had been hitting the hit parade for decades, but usually with novelty comedy songs. Altcom produced its fair share of these, but what was unusual about 'Ullo John! Gotta New Motor?' was that it sounded like a proper rock'n'roll record, a rap with the kind of Frankie Goes To Hollywood-style synth-funk production that was all the rage at the time.

Rock'n'roll was also there in the actual stand-up material. Heavy Metal came in for abuse from Alexei Sayle, who gagged scabrously about the Knebworth Rock Festival and bands like Motorhead: 'Somebody shouted out, "Sexist crap!" and they thought it was a request.' *(Laughter)* Peter Richardson and Nigel Planer's sketch double act, The Outer Limits, also got a lot of comedy mileage out of pop. In among their hit-and-miss barrage of song snatches, computer games impressions and movie parodies, they'd slip skits of ageing heavy rockers, medleys of punk songs sung in a Radio 2 easy-listening style and Nigel Planer's solo character piece, a mumbling, atonal hippy folksinger who'd stumble on and announce: 'I'm gonna do er . . . couple of numbers for you, erm. Off my latest, er, demo tape. *(Laughter)* Never mind, they're both pretty short, OK?' *(Laughter)*

Death to the joke!

The comics who had got to the top of the showbiz tree via the variety theatres or the working men's clubs were the first up against the wall in the alternative comedy revolution. Alexei Sayle would sarcastically refer to Bruce Forsyth, Charlie Drake and Bob Monkhouse as 'great, great comedians', and Keith Allen claimed to be driven by 'an intense hatred of Max Bygraves'. Before he became a comic himself, Allen had disrupted one of Bygraves' London shows whilst working as a theatre stage-hand, by walking onto the stage stark naked during one of his routines.

It was not just individual comics who came into the firing line. Alexei Sayle's comic technique often involved little more than brilliantly timed animosity. By choosing his targets well, conjuring up a sudden fury apparently from nowhere, or by the simple fact of standing on stage shouting into a microphone really looking like he meant it, he could turn low and common abuse into something an audience would laugh at. One of the targets on the receiving end of his baseball-bat-round-the-head comedy was the whole variety tradition: 'Actually, people are always going on about erm, about the British music hall, you know, and erm, how and why it died out. I'll tell yer why it died out, 'cos it was *SHITE*!!! *(Laughter)* Have you seen a bigger . . . bigger load of old shite than the Royal Command Variety Performance, you know? All them old fuckin' acts going, "Ey oop, mind thee marrows! Heyyyy! Ah ha ha ha ha!"' *(Laughter)*

Specific comic devices of the old school of stand-up were sent up. Another target of Sayle's venom was the catchphrase, the verbal trademark which cemented the cheery, matey relationship between variety comic and audience. In one gag he fingered the right-wing bigotry that underlies a lot of traditional comedy by following up two genuine catchphrases, from Jim Davidson and Larry Grayson respectively, with a very different kind of phrase: 'You've gotta have a catchphrase as well, you know like "Nick nick" or "Shut that door" or "*Sieg Heil!*"' *(Laughter)*

The comic device which came in for the most stick was the packaged gag, which was assaulted, battered and turned inside out by the new comedians. Ben Elton, whose combative comic style owed something to Sayle, would belt out carefully written routines at a pace designed to

169

be too fast for hecklers to get a word in edgeways. His angle on the packaged gag was full-on attack: 'We're like politicians, stand-up comedians tell lies, it's our job. I mean imagine what it'd be like if stand-up comics started telling the truth. What a true joke would be like. "A bloke goes into a pub. Orders a pint. Drinks it. Fucks off again," brilliant eh? *(Laughter)* I mean it wouldn't work would it, 'e's gotta 'ave a crocodile up 'is arse or something!' *(Laughter)*

Others took a different approach, reinventing tired old joke formats by subverting their structure. Rik Mayall and Ade Edmondson's double act, 20th Century Coyote, was almost exclusively dedicated to taking jokes apart to get laughs in new and unexpected ways. Often, this meant taking it in turns to run forward and shout things at the audience, or a violent new form of slapstick involving frequent punch-ups and crushed testicles. They'd take a popular joke formula, like the three-line riddle, and give it a sharp twist:

RIK MAYALL: What lies at the bottom . . . what's *yellow* and lies at the bottom of the Atlantic Ocean?
ADE EDMONDSON: I don't know, what?
RIK MAYALL: Sand! *(Laughter)*

The idea of finishing the riddle with a plain, factual answer to the question rather than something whimsical and jokey is a brilliant invention. 20th Century Coyote took a similar approach to the knock-knock joke ('Knock knock', 'Who's there?', 'Open the door!!'), and in one of their most famous routines they spent several manic minutes tearing apart the joke 'What's green and hairy and goes up and down? A gooseberry in a lift.'

Another standard comic style that got a good kicking was the observational routine. Alexei Sayle gave it a strange new twist by starting off with something which might plausibly be a shared experience and slowly making it more and more frantic and surreal:

170

'Didn't you used to stand in front of the mirror when you was a kid? You did, didn't yer, yeah, you'd stand there in just yer junior Y-fronts wouldn't yer eh? *(Laughter)* Lookin' at yerself goin', "Oo, you're a lot nicer than them dirty girls you are aren't yer eh?" *(Laughter)* And you'd get some o' your mum's lipstick wouldn't yer, and you'd put it around yer mouth wouldn't yer, and you'd draw lines right round your body and round your nipples wouldn't yer eh? Ha ha. *(Laughter)* That's right, and round yer belly button, you're smilin', it's all coming back now isn't it eh? *(Laughter)* Then you'd get your underpants, you'd pull 'em tight underneath your arm-pits, get your dad's crash helmet out the wood shed and jam it on yer head really tight, eh? *(Laughter)* It's a wonderful thing innit, eh, childhood, PITY ABOUT THE FUCKIN' 'EADACHES, EH??? *(Laughter)* Get your industrial gauntlets you'd pull them on really tight eh, you're smilin' it's all comin' back to yer now, eh? *(Laughter)* Big pair of fishing wellies, pull 'em up over your thighs and you'd rub Marmite all over your crotch wouldn't yer eh, that's right. *(Laughter)* It's all comin' back now. Then you'd jump up and down, you'd bang you 'ead on the wall, and you'd shout at yerself in Welsh, "Yakky da, yakky da, yakky da, yakky . . . !!!!" *(Laughter) DIDN'T YER??!!' (Laughter)*

This is a classic piece of Sayle mania. What you don't see in a cold reproduction on the page is the increasing desperation in his eyes as the childhood memories get stranger, and he becomes more and more aggressively insistent that these are shared experiences. The final falsetto-shrieked 'Didn't yer??!!' may seem an unlikely punchline on paper, but in performance it somehow feels like a logical climax to an insane routine.

Old joke structures weren't just taken apart and examined in front of the audience, they were also given new uses. Jim Barclay was a politically motivated agit-prop comic whose basic approach to stand-up was to make himself ridiculous. He wore a silly stage costume which made him look like a throwback to the variety era, when comedians often made themselves look like human cartoons. Barclay wore yellow tights, a gaudy jacket, a T-shirt with the slogan 'Loot British' printed on it, and a hat with a couple of wacky attachments: a false nine-inch-nail-through-the-head, and a set of deely boppers. A short-lived late-'70s craze, Deely boppers had a headband with two rigid springs attached, each of which had a glittery plastic ball on the end. The effect was to make it look as if you had some kind of alien antennae coming out of your head. They quickly became the uncoolest fashion accessories around.

Barclay would harangue his audience in a gravelly Cockney accent, whilst somehow generating a real sense of fun at the same time, smearing a grin across his face and punctuating his gags with 'eh?'s and 'ha ha!'s. A typical technique was to squeeze a political point into a standard joke format, for example using a riddle to comment on the nuclear warning system errors which were alarmingly frequent in the early 1980s: 'What is the difference between a flock of Newfoundland geese and five hundred SS20 missiles homing in on Manchester and Birmingham? *(Giggle)* Answer, as far as the Fylingdales early warning system is concerned, there isn't any difference, ha!' *(Laughter)*

One of the main reasons the alternative comedians attacked their predecessors was because the old guard were seen as bigoted reactionaries; often, the attacks were overtly political. Anarchist Speaker's Corner veteran Tony Allen was one of the first to argue that comedy had to shed its old prejudices, and his act included a parody of the club comic's easy-target approach: 'Right, stand-up comedy, I know what you want, stand-up comedy right. Er, there was this drunk homosexual Pakistani squatter trade unionist, and 'e takes my mother-in-law to an Irish restaurant, right?' *(Giggle)*

Similarly, one of Ben Elton's earliest routines attacked the Benny Hill school of breast-based double entendres. In

1981 he appeared on BBC2's *Oxford Road Show*, looking impossibly young, with close-cropped hair and wire-framed glasses, and after reeling out a set of such gags ('I've got some lovely little nibbles back 'ere', 'We can see that, Gloria') in an imaginary sitcom called 'Can You Show Me The Way To Oldham', he laid into the idea that breasts are intrinsically funny: 'Women's tits, that's the best thing in the world, we've got 'undreds in the audience tonight, why aren't you wettin' yourselves? *(Laughter)* I don't know. I mean dear me, girls, 'ow do you get dressed of a morning? You must die. Up comes your nightdress. "Oo look, there they are, laugh, I nearly did." *(Laughter)* Wonderful. Girls, d'you know. I know why you ain't in any of the bloomin' jobs in this country, you must all be sat at home laughing at your tits, aren't you? *(Laughter)* Sexism in comedy, watch out for it, thank you, goodbye.' *(Cheers and applause)*

Political satire!

Before altcom, the idea that stand-up comics could be political animals was unthinkable. In 1979, Eric Midwinter wrote a book about comedy called *Make 'Em Laugh*, in which he asserted: 'It would be difficult to conceive of, for instance, a Marxist comedian treading the boards of one of the private theatre circuits, not just because the management would object, but because the audience would feel uncomfortable.'

That very year the alternative comics sprang from nowhere and proved his assertion embarrassingly incorrect. Obese Scouse shouter Alexei Sayle proudly proclaimed himself a Marxist as he bounced about the stage. Jim Barclay made the more grandiose statement of calling himself a 'wacky, zany Marxist-Leninist comedian' and, with his tongue rammed hard into his cheek, he got laughs by boasting, 'I tell jokes which precipitate the downfall of capitalist society.' Tony Allen was a self-professed anarchist comic, who wore his Bohemian connections on his sleeve.

173

He chose his own version of the fashions of the day as his stage costume, claiming to be 'Ladbroke Grove's best-dressed squatter three years running', before eventually settling on his trademark black suit/black trilby look. When introducing Alternative Cabaret shows he would play up their subcultural connections, announcing them as 'a sort of collective of comedians, musicians, dope-smokers, dole scroungers, tax evaders, sexual deviants, political extremists.' The idea of stand-up comedians being openly political and happily attaching factional labels to themselves was totally new. Bernard Manning's frequent savage jibes about immigrants are nothing if not political, but that's something he probably wouldn't own up to: it's unlikely that he would refer to himself on stage as a 'wacky, zany Enoch Powellite comedian'.

Alternative Cabaret also took one of altcom's most important political steps when it adopted a non-sexist, non-racist line. It was the first time in the history of stand-up that comedians had voluntarily adopted egalitarian moral guidelines in their work, and the repercussions of this are still with us today. Very soon, comics from outside the altcom circuit began to follow the example. Lenny Henry is Britain's biggest black comic, and he started his career in the 1970s in clubs and discos in his native West Midlands. Following the example of Charlie Williams and Jos White, he says he felt forced into 'telling darkie jokes and rolling my eyes'. Appearing as a sixteen-year-old on the TV talent show *New Faces* in 1975, he started his act by telling the audience: 'Ladies and gentlemen, you may've seen some of these impressions before . . . *(puts on comedy black voice and waves his hands minstrel-style)* but not in colour!' *(Laughter and applause)* Some of his earliest television work was doing impressions and telling jokes between the song-and-dance numbers on *The Black and White Minstrel Show*, the last vestige of the Victorian 'nigger minstrel' tradition.

Whilst looking for acts for a show called *OTT*, Henry visited the Comic Strip, and being exposed to comedians like Alexei Sayle turned his own comedy upside-down. The self-deprecating racism was dropped immediately. It was replaced by a fun-packed, family entertainment-style approach to comedy which has made Henry one of Britain's biggest stars. His all-singing, all-dancing style of stand-up includes a gallery of black comic characters like the lust-crazed soul singer Theophilus P. Wildebeeste and the elderly Jamaican Deakus, and between the gags, impressions and silly voices he will occasionally slip in a routine which directly comments on racism. In 1988, he appeared at the Catch a Rising Star club in New York, and talked about being on the streets at night, having been warned to watch out for 'big black guys'. Feeling afraid, he tries to join a group of white people: 'And I thought, "Well, if I walk with these guys, you know, safety in numbers, I'll be safe." So I started to walk toward them . . . and they sped up. *(Laughter)* So I started to walk faster, and they walked faster still. *(Giggle)* Until eventually it was, was like the Olympics, we were both going like this: *(mimes manic running)*. *(Laughter)* They started to throw ten-dollar bills over their shoulder. *(Laughter)* I was picking 'em up saying, "Excuse me, I think you dropped this." *(Laughter)* They were saying, "No no, it's OK, just leave us the fuck alone, thank you!" *(Laughter)* I said, "Please don't run away, I'm as scared as you are!" The guy turned round and said, "A black guy with an English accent, Bob, get over here and listen to this." ' *(Laughter and applause)*

After the conversion of Lenny Henry, the non-sexist, non-racist comedy code gradually moved further into the mainstream. By 1990, the holiday firm Thompsons was banning 'blue' comedians with racist gags from its resorts, and it was not unusual for television comics as anodyne as Les Dennis to declare their respect for Alexei Sayle and Ben Elton and openly reject bigoted comedy, saying, 'I must admit it has worried me, when I've been watching an act with racist humour in it, to see the whole audience laughing.'

The first wave of alternative comedians did more than just give comedy a conscience, they also made politics a legitimate subject for jokes. They splattered out topical quips about the big stories of the early Thatcher years: the Falklands war, the inner-city riots, the Iranian Embassy siege. These were more than just gratuitous witty jokes about the events of the day, they were barbed political comments. Jim Barclay used his eccentric stage costume to send up the gung-ho spirit of the Falklands conflict: 'This gear I am wearing has nothing to do with the act. All I'm doing is modelling the new invasion gear that 'as been issued to the Royal Marines. Eh? *(Laughter)* Nail through the 'ead to show those Argies what hard bastards we can be, eh? *(Laughter)* Red boots to soak up the bloodstains! *(Laughter)* And throughout history, Margaret Thatcher has discovered . . . that all successful invaders 'ad things growing out their 'eads. *(Laughter)* Right? Know what I mean? The Vikings 'ad the wings. Right? The Saxons 'ad the 'orns. So Margaret Thatcher said to the Marines *(pointing at deely boppers)*, "Don't mess about lads, get your bollocks on top of your 'eads.' *(Laughter)*

This is a typical bit of Barclay, because it's driven more by gusto-packed performance than strong jokes. He looks like he's having a whale of a time as he treats very serious events with total irreverence, flying in the face of the rampant nationalism that had been whipped up in the majority of the population.

Andy de la Tour tackled an even more contentious conflict in a routine about Northern Ireland. De la Tour (the brother of actress Frances de la Tour who played Miss Jones in the classic 1970s sitcom *Rising Damp*) had potential altcom credibility problems: his baldness made him look too old for a rock'n'roll image, and his middle-class accent made him sound far too posh to claim working-class roots. He lacked the aggressiveness of an Alexei Sayle or a Ben Elton, but what he did have was a willingness to get gags out of controversial subjects. With a kind of amused charm, he would go into areas which were then largely uncharted by stand-up comics, talking about the elusiveness of erections, for example, or the difficulties of masturbating in a public school dormitory. His Ireland routine achieved the improbable by turning the idea that the situation is of war and not just a series of terrorist acts into a series of serviceable gags: 'You see if they'd only admit there's been a war going on in Northern Ireland for the past thirteen years, twelve years, whatever, think of the war films you could've had. Eh? In the fine old tradition of British war movies? Scene one – a battleship cruising down the Falls Road. *(Giggle)* Sitting on top, Kenneth More in a duffle coat. *(Giggle)* "Paddy's being damned quiet tonight, number one."' *(Laughter and applause)*

Another comic who managed to turn a radical view of Northern Ireland into a laughing matter was Pauline Melville. Melville was one of the gentler comics of the initial wave of altcom, specialising in affectionate ribbing of the left-wing subculture, but she was also capable of more abrasive stuff. One joke, for example, used IRA demands for their prisoners to be given political status to get in a crack at the then Prime Minister: 'Margaret Thatcher hasn't got any political status, so she won't let anybody else have any.' *(Laughter and applause)*

The Left has always tended to dislike the police, and there were anti-police jokes aplenty in the early days of altcom. Jim Barclay impersonated a sinister community policeman, for example, and Andy de la Tour dismissed the report into police methods carried out in the wake of the inner-city riots with a single one-liner: 'All the local bobbies in our area've all got their own copies of the Scarman Report – rolled up with a piece of lead piping stuffed down the middle.' *(Laughter)* Tony Allen managed a radical double whammy, combining cracks at the police with jibes about Third World exploitation by the hands of capitalism, climaxing in a surprisingly savage little gag: 'What I wanna know is where is the cop on the beat when it comes to arresting the REAL criminals? I mean the *REAL* criminals. "Well . . . I was er, walking in a North Easterly direction in the boardroom of Amalgamated Conglomerates . . . er, when I noticed the accused and several other persons unknown making a dubious decision as to the economic future of Latin America, well er . . . *(Laughter)* I cautioned 'im, arrested 'im and bunged 'im in the back of the Transit. *(Laughter)* That's when 'e 'it 'is 'ead." Doesn't 'appen, does it? *(Laughter)* No, I've got a soft spot for the police – Romney Marsh.' *(Laughter)*

The rise of alternative comedy coincided with the resurgence of the Campaign for Nuclear Disarmament in response to the stepping up of the Cold War. It is perhaps not surprising then, that there were plenty of gags about the Bomb. One of Ben Elton's routines ridiculed the reasoning behind the nuclear deterrent by making a link with IRA bombs. In it, he describes being frightened by unattended bags whilst riding on the tube: 'And I say *(whiny voice)*, "Look I know it's embarrassing and it's very silly, it's just an unattended plastic bag, it's probably just an old person's *home* or something, but it *(Laughter)*, you know . . . it could be . . ." 'E says, "Nah. It's a bomb." I said, "What?" "Yeah," 'e says, "it's a bomb. We got 'em on all the tubes. All the trains, everywhere. We got bombs everywhere, weren't you given a bomb when you bought yer ticket? Should've been given a bomb, there's bombs everywhere, couple of tramps over there, they're both wired up with gelignite, I've got a couple of bombs in my pocket, they're bombs." I said, "Whoss that about then?" 'E says, "Well it's part of the new government anti-terrorist IRA offensive, you see. It's based on the same policy as the nuclear deterrent. We put all *our* bombs on the tubes, we're *totally* safe from all of theirs, eh?" *(Laughter)* And at that point the train blew up, yeah! *(Applause)* Bit of satire, OK.'

Margaret Thatcher was elected to office on 3 May 1979, just sixteen days before the Comedy Store opened for business. The new poverty and rocketing unemployment which characterised the early years of her regime provided rich joke-fuel for comedians like Andy de la Tour: 'I'll tell you what it's nice also to be away from, in London, is there's a lot of trendy bastards in London. *(Laughter)* A few up 'ere an' all, aren't there? *(Laughter)* You know what they do? They kind o' look and see what's going on in the real world and they just turn it into a fashion, you know, so you've got kind of like, got all this poverty everywhere right now, so in London they've kind of got this whole poverty 1930s-revival fashion thing, you know. You get a recurrence of rickets in the north of England and in London they turn it into a dance *(dancing)*, err nerrr nerr nerr . . . *(Laughter and applause)* Even got their own clubs, you know, poverty clubs, Monday Night's Diphtheria Night, yeaahhh!' *(Laughter)*

Class and privilege were two of Alexei Sayle's comic obsessions. He joked about his working-class Liverpudlian upbringing ('Our estate was so boring, its twin town was Père Lachaise Cemetery'), and richly abused the trendy middle-class invaders of his local area, laying into the carriage lamps they stuck on their houses ('It's like puttin' up a big sign saying, "Please break in an' steal my video recorder"') and the Suzuki jeeps they drove ('"I think it's so important to have four-wheel drive when you're going down to Sainsburys"'). Never before in the history of stand-up had middle-class values been subjected to such savage ridicule. If Sayle's attitude to class was informed by his Marxism, there was also something deeper and more personal about his anger. In one of his most furious routines, he starts off with a modicum of actual political analysis and ends up with pure class hatred: 'I'll tell yer another fuckin' myth, right. Er . . . It's like education, you know like if, er, you know when you went, when you went to school about twenty years ago they told you if you came out with two CSEs you're gonna be head of British Steel, you know. *(Laughter)* That's a load of bollocks, innit eh? *(Laughter)* You look at the statistics, right, like 82% of top British management've been to a public school and Oxbridge, 83% of the BBC've been to a public school and Oxbridge, 94% of the *KGB*'ve been to a public school and Oxbridge. *(Laughter)* All you get from a public school, right, is, is one, you get a top job. The other thing, the only other thing you get from a public school, right, is an interest in perverse sexual practices! *(Laughter)* That's why British management's so ineffective, as soon as they get in the fuckin' boardroom, they're all shuttin' each other's dicks in the door! *(Laughter)* "Go on, give 'er another slam, Sir Michael!" Whack! *(Laughter and applause)* "Come on, let's play the Panzer commander and the milkmaid, eeuh eeuh eeuh eeuh!!" *(Laughter)* Bastards!' *(Laughter)*

Swearing!

Variety comedians avoided bad language because it was prohibited in the theatres. Club comics have more freedom to talk dirty, and although some of them make a living by plunging deep into the realm of obscenity, most have to exercise a degree of caution. A Mansfield-based club comic outlined his own approach to me: 'You say "piss" once, which mostly you'll get a good laugh . . . If they don't take "piss", then you know they're not going to take "shit" so you've got to try and cut that down a bit.'

There was no such pussyfooting in alternative comedy. The swearing was wall-to-wall, and the poet laureate of the undeleted expletive was Alexei Sayle. His swearing powers were at their height in a routine called 'Say Hello Mr Sweary'. Jamming a pork pie hat over his eyes and shouting in a crazy Cockney accent, he got torrents of laughter with torrents of rude words: 'Shit piss wank fuck cunt all right bollocks knock it on the 'ead do what wanker all right you fucking cunt, eh shit piss wank fuck cunt bollocks knock it on the 'ead all right eh? *(Laughter)* Shit piss fucking cunt wank shit piss wank fuck cunt bollocks wanker fucking cunt all right shit piss wank fuck cunt bollocks do what as it 'appens fucking cunt. *(Laughter)* Eh you fucking wanker, eh shit piss wank fuck cunt bollocks leave it aht do what as it 'appens shit piss wank all right give it a portion be lucky be brief. *(Laughter)* Fuuuucking wanker eh bollocks 'ow you doin' fucking cunt all right shit piss wank all right eh? *(Laughter)* All right eh shit piss wank all right fuck cunt bollocks 'ow's your old fuckin' shit piss wank fuck cunt eh? *(Laughter)* Do what bollocks leave it aht all right shit piss wank fucking cunt all right? *(Laughter)* Fucking wanker shit piss wank fuck cunt bollocks leave it aht all right do what knock it on the 'ead fuck cunt wank all right bollocks shit piss wank fuck cunt bollocks, leave it aht give it a portion be lucky be brief fucking cunt all right you wanker. Shit piss wank fuck cunt bollocks . . . 'ere, I don't 'ave to remember any of this you know 'cos it's all written on the inside of me hat!' *(Laughter and applause)*

To replace any kind of recognisable jokes with little more than pure swearing and still get laughs is quite a feat. It is the sheer unrelenting weight of bad language that gets the laughs. There had been some precedents for this kind of thing, like Peter Cook and Dudley Moore's *Derek and Clive* LPs, the first of which was unleashed in 1976. These recordings presented an improvised torrent of bad taste, complete with cancer jokes and full-on four-letter obscenity. The difference was that Derek and Clive were caged in vinyl, to be enjoyed in the brown paper-wrapped privacy of the listener's own home, whereas Sayle was a flesh-and-blood comedian, delivering his F-word-rich routines to a living audience sitting right in front of him. In the late 1970s, obscene language still had extraordinary explosive potential in a live context. In February 1977, the management of the Rainbow Theatre, London, had stopped a show by punk band The Stranglers after their lead singer revealed the word 'fuck' emblazoned across his T-shirt. Coming just a couple of years after this, Sayle's comedy swearathons must have been quite a shock.

Attack the audience!

The Comedy Store was a tiny, sweaty room, licensed to hold no more than a hundred and twenty people. Its murals, dusty upholstered seats and raised seating tiers reeked of shabby gentility, but there were tacky modern touches as well, like the glittery stage backdrop, and the ridged ceiling tiles that could easily have graced the sets of the *Doctor Who*. It was an extremely tough spawning ground for a new breed of comics. The ritual of gonging the acts off meant that it was comedians versus punters, in a shouty, heckley, gladiatorial contest. Because it was a late-night venue, the chances were that most of the audience would be already drunk. Some might even be asleep.

There were just as many women in those early audiences as there were men, but the place could easily be overwhelmed by a very male yob mentality. If there had been a big sporting fixture in the day, for example, the place might be crammed with alcohol-crazed rugby fans. Occasionally, fights would break out, and once or twice the police had to be called. Ben Elton has described the audience in the early days of the Comedy Store as 'tables of lads competing with each other to see who could be most sort of bored and aggressive during your act.' Martin Coyote, who now plays the circuit himself, was a regular punter in the early days, and remembers one night when the let's-heckle-the-acts-off mentality reached a ridiculous extreme: 'The audience was just in a stupid mood, and they gonged everybody off. And Alexei Sayle came back on after about twenty minutes and said, "You cunts. You've gonged everybody off. You've paid eight quid to get in, and the show's over."'

Given this drunken, battle-zone atmosphere, it's hardly surprising that the early alternative comedians tended to give as good as they got. Alexei Sayle used to hit the audience with a head-on verbal assault. Coming on stage like a hyperactive billiard ball stuffed into a tight suit, he'd jump up and down with his arms flailing wildly around as he belted out his routines in a furious full-throated roar. His aggressive image was stepped up by the fact that he had adopted the hairdo of the most feared youth cult tribe of the day: the skinhead.

One of Sayle's peculiarities was that as well as being terrifying, he was also surprisingly silly. He came over like a psychotic clown, a mime artist with rabies, pulling his face and his entire body into stupid shapes to act out his almost whimsical twists of logic, as well as adopting a whole range of ridiculous voices. Oddly, this did nothing to soften his impact. Even when he was doing something silly, like making strange high-pitched noises or miming Noddy the Social Worker driving along in a Morris Minor, he was still so bile-drenched he seemed to be possessed by Satan. Whilst introducing the acts at the Comic Strip, he had none of the matey audience relationship which the variety comic carefully fostered. His approach was more grab-them-by-the-collar-and-shout-in-their-face: 'Let's have a big, warm Comic Strip welcome . . . Yeah, let's have a big, warm Comic Strip welcome!! *(A few claps)* No, not yet you fuckfaces, know what I mean?? *(Laughter)* This is a people's collective, you do what I fuckin' tell yer, all right???' *(Laughter)*

Keith Allen, whose anarchic audience-baiting antics have made him almost a mythical figure for those who were around at the time, was quieter and more sinister than Sayle. Sometimes, his assaults on the audience went beyond the verbal. There are stories of him throwing darts at the audience, threatening hecklers with broken fruit-juice bottles, or turning a fire extinguisher on a reviewer from the *Evening Standard*. It was not just one-way violence, though. On one occasion, an off-duty soldier in the audience punched him into unconsciousness for making a joke about an IRA bombing.

These are extreme examples, but even when he didn't come to blows, Allen was confrontational and unsettling. An article in a 1981 edition of *The Face* describes how he dealt with a table of hecklers at a show at the Greyhound pub in Fulham: 'The main troublemaker is singled out. "You like me, don't you?" Surprise, but agreement. Allen cajoles a drink. It takes a moment, but you know that he's going to get the mug's beer off him as soon as he asks. Allen grins a bit, turning soft to get round the dupe's unsophisticated defences. The pint is handed over like a détente treaty. Keith tosses it over the stage. By now, the silent majority of the audience is following the leader. The three would-be contenders are plainly so inept at doing what the silent majority would never dream of doing. The majority thinks it's up there with Keith; equals. They approve of the pint blag. Allen turns around. "It's really easy to manipulate people. I'll show you.' He asks for someone to lend him a quid – and he gets it as easily as he got the beer. He hands it over to the nonplussed, drinkless loser. And the heist isn't taken in. The mass of the audience doesn't see that they're all getting the same treatment as the loudmouths.'

Not all the assaults on the audience were so edgy and physical. There were also subtler digs, attacks on the audience's values. The first audiences that were drawn to alternative comedy were a strange mix. As well as the drunken hecklers, many of the punters came from the thriving anti-Thatcher left-wing culture: corduroy-clad, badge-wearing teachers or social workers. As the media homed in on the new comedy phenomenon, the fashionable and the famous started coming along to see what it was all about. One of the regulars at the time was a teenage kid called Phil Gasson, and he remembers noticing the change: 'Everyone seemed to be in smart clothes. We actually thought they'd put a dress code on, and that would stop us getting in. But they hadn't, it was just the audience had obviously changed.'

At the Comic Strip, the glitterati were particularly thick on the ground, with visits from celebrities like Pamela Stephenson, David Bowie, Bianca Jagger, Jack Nicholson and Dustin Hoffman. The presence of the famous at the Comedy Store, with its cramped room and restricted access, made for some interesting encounters. Martin Coyote remembers: '. . . one time getting into the lift having had a few pints and being a bit mouthy, and it was a very small lift, it held four people if you scrunched in, and I was shooting my mouth off, and I turned and the bloke next to me was John McVicar. And I thought, "Right, better shut up here."'

It was the social-worker wing of the audience that came in for the most stick from the stage. There was one gag which several comics used, and many more would recycle over the years, which went something like this: 'You can always tell left-wingers in an audience, they don't laugh, they just take notes, you know. *(Laughter)* "Oh it's very good, I'll laugh at that one when I get home, yeah." You know, breaking up in small groups to discuss it, you know what I mean?' *(Laughter)*

Sometimes the jibes were more specialised, designed to needle a particular faction. Alternative Cabaret succeeded in getting a party from the Communist Party of Britain (Marxist–Leninist) to walk out *en masse* from one of their early shows by telling anti-Albania jokes.

There were also less calculated wind-ups. Although altcom took a moral stance by adopting a non-sexist, non-racist policy, it was not entirely what would now be called 'politically correct'. There were lapses in taste like flippant gags about the International Year of the Disabled, but perhaps the most provocative gesture was the use of the word 'cunt'. This was a hot issue on the Left in the 1980s. The feeling was that using the word for a central part of the female anatomy as a term of abuse was implicitly misogynistic. Several of the early alternative comedians used the word in their acts, and Alexei Sayle said it with particular relish. The more pressure was put on him to drop it from his act, the more he used it: 'We used to do a lot of radical venues, and people would come backstage afterwards and say, "Look, Alexei, we really liked the act, but . . ." I became more and more of a resolute cunt-ist really. I got more hard-line.'

Less provocatively, the values, language and lifestyle of

the Left subculture became the subject of numerous satirical routines. Pauline Melville sometimes performed as herself, but usually adopted the persona of Edie, a well-meaning northerner desperate to be as radical as possible and win the approval of her left-wing friends, but constantly making *faux pas*. She might talk about going to a thrush workshop for women ('I don't see why you laugh, it's about time radical ornithologists got together'), or being expelled from her commune: 'I'd only been there two minutes! Two minutes. They said, "You're on the cooking rota tonight." Well, I panicked. I can't cook. So I went off to the shops, and I saw this book that said, *Mussolini for Beginners*. *(Laughter)* So I thought, "Ooh well I'll get that, that'll be nice for supper. *(Laughter)* Apparently I made a terrible mistake, 'cos somebody in the house got up, furious, and said, "Whose idea was it to get *Mussolini for Beginners*?" I said, "It was mine, I was going to do jam tart for afters."' *(Laughter)*

Rik Mayall ridiculed the then-popular fad for performance poetry with his mad poet character, an ideal vehicle for his manic style, as it allowed him to launch into childish tantrums and shout a lot. After announcing, 'We're a group of feminist poets,' he would launch into nonsensical verse with total, po-faced seriousness:

> 'When we're near-ter
> The theatre
> I ask myself this question.
> I DON'T KNOW. *(Laughter)*
> Perhaps I should ask Vanessa Redgrave.
> But I don't *know* Vanessa Redgrave. *(Laughter)*
> And neither do you *(with venom)*, THEATRE!
> *(snorts)* That's got 'em!' *(Laughter)*

He would then get squeals of laughter by getting furious with the audience: 'It's easy to clap, isn't it? *(Laughter)* I'm sure it's very funny!!' *(Laughter)* It's the kind of laughter you'd hear from an onlooker watching from a safe distance, as a spoilt child screams at its parents. Mayall conjures up a kind of pathetic pride, often seeming to be on the edge of tears as he shouts babyish insults at the audience, perhaps reminding them of a time before they themselves had grown out of such behaviour.

Drugs!

Since the hippy days of the 1960s, recreational drugs have always been a part of the radical alternative culture, and from the beginning, there were drug gags by the bucketload on the altcom circuit. Pauline Melville even likened the whole business of stand-up comedy to drug addiction, in a routine inspired by intense competitiveness among the new comics: 'You go up to one of the others and you say *(spaced-out voice:)*, "Oh . . . er, hey man. Er, can I score a gag off you? *(Laughter)* Erm . . . go on, I'm really feeling bad, you know, I haven't had a gag for three days. *(Giggle)* I'm having to take all the graffiti off the toilet wall, you know. *(Giggle)* . . . I'm really feeling bad." And er . . . and then *maybe* one of the others gives you a gag. And halfway through it, you find it's cut with unfunny stuff.' *(Laughter and applause)*

Sometimes the drug gags were part of the sustained ribbing of the social-worker contingent, other times, comedians used them to bond with the audience. Alexei Sayle took the first of these approaches: ''E said, "I 'ad one toke of this dope, right, just one toke, and I was paralysed from the waist down. *(Giggle)* I lost the use of me fingers *(Giggle)* and I developed every single symptom of typhoid! *(Laughter)* It was fuckin' amaaaazing! *(Laughter)* And they were all going *(jumping up and down)* "Oeuh fuckin' amazing, oeuh fuckin' fantastic *(Laughter)*, oeuh save the shrimp man, yeah!"' *(Laughter, applause and whistles)*

Tony Allen took the second approach, playing to the drug-culture elements in the audience. He could get a laugh just by saying that he was on drugs, and a dig at the drug squad was enough to get cheers and whistles. Instead of making fun of the drug subculture, he'd laugh at the police's pathetic inability to understand it: 'Now you can always recognise the drug squad where I come from on Portobello Road, Saturday afternoon. They're the only people in plain clothes. *(Laughter)* They got like er, khaki anoraks, pressed cords, short but unfashionable hair. *(Laughter)* And sensible boots. *(Laughter)* They look like lapsed Mormons. *(Laughter)* And they're sidling up to Rastafarians saying things like, "Er, hi, man. *(Laughter)* Where can a, er, cat score some er, reefers?"' *(Laughter)*

Anything is possible!

The first alternative comedians had grown up with the standard diet of traditional British comedy, and while they may have been inspired by *Monty Python*, Billy Connolly or even the odd Lenny Bruce album, their actual performing background was in fringe theatre, so they had no experience of the very different dynamics of stand-up comedy. They had to learn as they went along, and looking back on the video and audio recordings of their work in the cold light of the mid-1990s, what strikes me is the lumpiness of their style. Their acts are filled out with long anecdotes or character pieces which don't quite get laughs in all the right places. Sometimes the material feels forced and rehearsed, lacking the spontaneous free-flowing quality which characterises the best stand-up.

On the other hand, the learning-as-you-go-along approach also brought exciting new discoveries. It was a time of hectic creativity, packed with audacious experiments in ways of making people laugh. Comedians felt free to take risks as a matter of course. For a while, it seemed as if almost anything was possible, and stand-up comedy wandered into the realms of performance art. Jenny Lecoat remembers the atmosphere when she first played the Comedy Store in

October 1982: 'There was [the dwarfish] David Rappaport who, of course, went on to do *Time Bandits* and become a big star in America [in films and television], and Andrew Bailey, who worked on the circuit for years, and they were rehearsing this act half an hour before the show opened, they were actually going to do that night, with Dave Rappaport, who was, you know, a little guy, in a bird cage, and Andrew was his master and he was talking to him in the bird cage, and I just walked in and thought, "Fucking hell, this is a mental hospital!"'

The boundaries were pushed back, and people found unlikely ways of getting laughs. Alexei Sayle could do it just by announcing some Albanian poetry and aggressively spouting total gibberish. Keith Allen pushed back the boundaries still further by breaking the most fundamental rule of stand-up comedy: occasionally, he would deliberately refuse to be funny. Sometimes he would get serious just as a way of getting to a punchline. He would tell the audience his father had died and talk about the funeral arrangements, saying that he now felt tired because of the party they had had to celebrate his dad's death. On other occasions there would be no justifying punchline, he would just be deliberately serious, and not even bother trying to get laughs.

Altcom took comedy back to its roots, presenting incongruity in its purest form, unfettered by tired old joke formats, its impact unblunted by years of stereotype-ridden repetition. It was a million miles from the other comedy that was around at the time, and must have come as quite a shock to the uninitiated punter who stumbled across it for the first time. Perhaps because it was so new and confrontational, it sometimes produced less desirable responses than laughter and applause, as Alexei Sayle has recalled: 'A lot of the gigs I did before the Comedy Store would end in kind of fights and stuff, because people didn't actually have a perception of what it was I was attempting to do. There was quite an interesting thing that when me and Tony Allen went to

189

the Edinburgh Festival in 1980, there was a review in a student paper that said, "I don't know what these people are doing."'

Tony Allen's memory of the same Edinburgh Festival stint was of having to change the order of the show. Originally, Sayle had gone on first, but they had to swap their acts around, because his sweary, aggressive shoutiness was scaring people away before Allen had even had a chance to go on. Allen was quite capable of nonplussing an audience himself, though. On an ill-advised foray into a working men's club in Isleworth in 1979, he found himself stunning the audience into an appalled silence with a routine about masturbation.

Andy de la Tour sometimes experienced a similar clamming-up effect as soon as he mentioned Northern Ireland, before he had even had a chance to launch into the gags. In the same way, Jim Barclay has talked about touching a political nerve with his anti-Falklands jokes. He felt a chill reverberate through the audience at a gig at Huddersfield Polytechnic during the war in the South Atlantic, and afterwards, the punters were split as to whether such jokes were appropriate. Spontaneous pockets of debate broke out as locals argued with students, for and against the war.

The schism

If the first wave of alternative comics revolutionised stand-up comedy, they certainly behaved like any other group of revolutionaries. It was a time of factionalism and grand gestures on points of principle. Altcom declared war on all previous comedy, including the Oxbridge review tradition which had produced shows like *Beyond the Fringe* and *Monty Python's Flying Circus*. This was ironic, given that Python was an obvious influence on the likes of Sayle and Mayall. Proletarian roots were exploited and university connections were swept under the carpet. Interviewed for the *Sunday*

Times Magazine before embarking on a national tour in 1981, Peter Richardson described the Comic Strip's style as 'intelligent comedy by people who didn't go to university'. The irony is that most of them *had* been to university.

This kind of posturing was understandable, given that anybody considered not radical enough for the new movement tended to come in for criticism. French and Saunders, for example, were never truly a stand-up act. Most of their material was made up of two-hander sketches and character pieces, and it was only rarely that they delved into controversial areas. They were criticised for their gentle approach, one *Times* reviewer writing them off as being 'too amiably Guardianish'. This made them rather defensive, with Dawn French telling *The Face*: 'We don't tell jokes about the Bomb because we aren't good at it. We are much funnier at making up characters. I'm not ashamed of doing it. We've been labelled as *alternative*, then slagged off for not being. It's very silly.'

In this kind of hot-headed atmosphere, some kind of schism was inevitable. When the split came, it was between politicos and stylists. The politically minded refugees from the radical theatre scene stayed with Alternative Cabaret, and the ex-student drama types who were more interested in the style and the energy founded the Comic Strip. It was not a completely straightforward split though: Alexei Sayle went with the Strip faction in spite of being more of a politico than a stylist. It was the Comic Strip which made the leap into the mass media, propelled by the runaway success of *The Young Ones*, a television sitcom based on some of the characters they had built up in their live work. Rik Mayall's performance poet became Rick the radical student, and Nigel Planer's folksinger became Neil the hippy. It was the success of *The Young Ones* that brought alternative comedy to the attention of the nation at large. Those associated with the Comic Strip went on to enjoy successful television careers, and if French and Saunders had come in for criticism, they were to have the last laugh: by the end of the 1980s, they had become two of the biggest stars in the light entertainment firmament. Meanwhile, the Alternative Cabaret faction continued to work the growing live circuit.

Spreading out

Alternative comedy may have started out in a strip club, but as it spread out across London, the pub became its natural habitat. As the word got out about this vibrant new scene, more and more people became shoestring showbiz impresarios, running comedy nights in the local drinking places. They were driven more by enthusiasm than the profit motive. Jim Barclay remembers: 'It wasn't people on the make, it was people who lived in, say, Crouch End or wherever, you know, and said, "Oh I'd like to have something like that here," you know, and finding a pub and doing it, making it happen, which was great.'

The economics of the blossoming circuit meant it wasn't hard to set up your very own alternative comedy club. All you needed was a friendly pub landlord who was happy to let you use his function room once a week. In many cases, you wouldn't need to pay him for it, because he'd be making money on the increased bar takings. There'd be no need for hefty start-up capital, because most gigs ran on a door-split basis. The money the punters paid to get in would be split fairly evenly between each of the acts and the person who ran the club. This meant there was virtually no financial risk involved: if hardly anybody turned up to see the show you wouldn't make much profit, but at least you wouldn't end up paying the comics out of your own pocket.

Even today, the pub remains by far the most common venue for a comedy club. Usually, the shows are held in function rooms, so that the audience can be charged to get in. This is important not just so the club is economically viable, but also because a paying audience has some commitment to listen. Most London clubs are still run on a door-split basis. Sometimes there is a stage, but it might be tiny. There'll be a microphone and a public address system in all but the smallest gigs. The lighting may be little more than domestic lights hooked up to point at the stage.

If alternative comedy clubs are a little shabby, this doesn't stop them being ideal venues in which to see stand-up, somewhere between a fringe theatre show and a drink with some friends. There's entertainment going on, but between the acts you can talk to the people on your table and have a few pints. You're not tied to your seat, and if you empty your glass or fill your bladder whilst someone is on stage, there's nothing to stop you going to the bar or the toilet, if you're prepared to risk being abused by the comedian.

Pub gigs are also good from the comic's point of view. Facing a drinking, chattering, crisp-munching audience does require a little work. With the tone of your voice, the confidence you exude and the way you react to what is going on in the room, you have to focus the audience's attention on yourself, and lure them away from potential distractions. The reward for this extra effort is a kind of beery intimacy. There is no going straight from the green room onto the stage and disappearing from the venue afterwards, carefully avoiding the autograph hunters. Before the show you are just like another punter, standing at the back of the room and queuing for the bar like anybody else. On stage, you are right on top of them, near enough to the front tables to steal somebody's drink. Your act is a real two-way conversation. They don't just reply to your jokes with laughter and clapping, they groan, whistle, boo and heckle, sometimes supportively, sometimes with genuine malice.

Although the gigs that were springing up in the early '80s were run along much the same lines, they each had their own particular character. One of the earliest clubs was run in a vegetarian restaurant called the Earth Exchange, and it had exactly the kind of *Guardian*-reader ambience that a venue like that might suggest. Even a dying comic was treated with humanity. Quirky Irish comic Ian MacPherson remembers playing his very first gig there: 'There was about a hundred and thirty vegetarians looking very sympathetically at me as I died on stage. I got one laugh. At the end, I said, "I've been in London now for (whatever it was) twelve years now, and it's the first time I've experienced total silence." People laughed, so I said, "Thank you and goodnight."'

At the other end of the spectrum, the Tunnel Club in Greenwich was a very different kettle of piranhas. This notorious comic's graveyard was opened in 1984 by Malcolm Hardee, who had been involved in altcom from the beginning. He and Martin Soan had performed with a group called the Greatest Show On Legs, famous for a naked dance performed with balloons to protect their modesty. They had been Comedy Store regulars and television appearances on *OTT* had sneaked them into the national consciousness.

The hecklers took centre stage at Hardee's Tunnel Club, and their antics have passed into legend. Veteran altcom punter Phil Gasson, who had frequented the Comedy Store in its early days, became a Tunnel regular in the mid-'80s. His approach to the art of heckling is dedicated and discerning: 'Everything they say is true, people heckled the crap acts, things were thrown at them, we used to go in with marrows, you know. And no one would stop us. And you wouldn't try and hit the people, but get it up on the stage . . . this typewriter going on stage was good. That was hilarious, came out of the front row . . . One of our classics we used to do years ago, we were quite famous for it, was to sing, "Show Me The Way To Go Home", right? 'Cos I don't agree with "fuck off" and "wanker", I think they're crap. And we'd sit there, we'd all sing, "Show Me The Way To Go Home", and if you got it going, you'd get the whole audience singing at the act, and the act'd just give up.'

The blossoming pub circuit was boosted when Roland Muldoon's CAST organisation, which had started as a seminal alternative theatre group in the 1960s, was transformed into a variety agency as it set up a chain of gigs in places like Brixton and Wood Green. Meanwhile, the Comedy Store was moving on. In December 1982 the lease on the room in the strip club expired, and Don Ward, who had taken over the running of the Store, moved it to new premises on Leicester Square. It ran for a few months in 1983, before reopening in another Leicester Square venue in July 1985, with a capacity of around two hundred. It continued to run there until December 1993, when it moved to a specially converted four-hundred-capacity basement venue, around the corner in Oxendon Street.

The mushrooming circuit of the early 1980s wasn't exclusively populated by pure stand-ups. Comedians might find themselves sharing a bill with a jazz band, a juggler, a fire eater or a feminist theatre group. The chances are there would also be a performance poet on the bill. Poetry was very much in demand at the time, and poets like Attila the Stockbroker and Benjamin Zepheniah had become cult figures, with music press coverage giving them rock'n'roll credibility. Comics were still in the minority among the various other acts.

By the end of the 1980s, comedy would dominate the circuit, but throughout its history, altcom has always been about more than just stand-up. Its tradition of character comedy which started with Pauline Melville's Edie has been continued by comics like John Sparkes and Harry Enfield. The altcom circuit has produced highly skilled impressionists like Rory Bremner, Phil Cornwell and Steve Coogan, who has gone on to become a hugely successful character comedian. There have been musical comics like Steve Gribbin and Richard Morton. There has also been a string of double acts, following in the wake of Comic Strip favourites like French and Saunders, 20th Century Coyote and the Outer Limits.

The actual stand-ups who worked the emerging circuit of the early '80s came in different shapes and sizes. As well as the new acts that were springing up, people like Tony Allen and Jim Barclay were still around. It was also a time when some of the more obscure acts from the early days of the Comedy Store, like Lee Cornes and Arnold Brown, came into their own. Brown, a middle-aged accountant of Glaswegian-Jewish origin ('two racial stereotypes for the price of one. Perhaps the best value in the West End today . . . perhaps not') had started out as one of the Store's much-gonged amateurs but, helped on by his association with the Comic Strip, he became one of the biggest comics of the 1980s.

Right-on gags for right-on punters

At this time, politics still took centre stage on the altcom circuit. The early '80s was the era of Ken Livingstone's Greater London Council, and the anti-Thatcher left-wing culture was thriving. The social-worker wing dominated the audiences, and the politics of the comedy became less abrasive. While the liberal middle classes still came in for some ribbing, it was far gentler than Alexei Sayle's full-frontal assaults. Arnold Brown, for example, would boast about his local area of London: 'It's all happening in Hampstead. Laura Ashley bin liners. *(Laughter)* The best-selling children's book is the Pop-Up Kafka. *(Laughter)* And people think we're effete because we have organisations like the Campaign for Real Champagne.' *(Laughter)*

Brown's style is a far cry from Sayle's. He replaces aggression with a kind of smoky jazz coolness. He wanders about the stage in a velvet jacket, his eyes narrowed to little crescent moons, microphone held at a jaunty angle as he warmly intones his material in a gentle Scots accent. Instead of breakneck speed, he takes his time with his jokes, punctuating his routines with long pauses. His approach to politics is offbeat and unthreatening, perhaps telling the audience off for applauding ('I don't like too much applause at the start . . . that's how Fascism started') or confessing: 'I cannot achieve an erection . . . under a Conservative administration.' *(Laughter)*

In general, the politics of early-'80s altcom were more

user-friendly to the left-wing audiences than they were at the very beginning of the scene. A classic example of the approach is Jeremy Hardy, who hit the circuit in 1984 with an act about building fallout shelters for teddy bears, but soon settled into a gentle, observational stand-up style, telling tales about his middle-class upbringing in Surrey, with the odd bit of politics thrown in. Gradually, the politics began to take over, but the tweed-clad image remained the same, creating the unsettling image of a Young Conservative possessed by the spirit of Tony Benn. He has the ability to discuss issues intelligently and get laughs at the same time, avoiding preachiness by virtue of his relaxed, civilised stage warmth. Running his fingers through his long fringe, looking down self-effacingly, and never presuming so much as to take the microphone from its stand, he looks harmless enough as he pumps out well-crafted shafts of consistently biting socialist satire: 'People say the Queen has no real power. Well she's got a fucking sight more than us. *(Laughter)* I mean after an election . . . *(Laughter turns to applause)* After an election, the Queen invites somebody to form a government. Now she's got no say in who it is, but you'd think in Thatcher's case she'd've tried to stall her for as long as possible, wouldn't you? *(Laughter)* Steer the conversation onto something else. *(Laughter)* Show her the garden, it's huge. *(Laughter and applause)* Slides, holiday snaps, anything. Show her round the palace *(Queen voice, pointing at imaginary wall:)* "This is where we were thinking of knocking through. *(Laughter and applause)* Into *South* London." *(Laughter)* 'Cos if Arthur Scargill was elected, she'd be shouting through the letterbox of the palace, going, *(Queen voice:)* "They're not here, they've moved! *(Laughter)* I don't know where they are, we're just squatters." *(Laughter)* Which, in a sense, is true, of course.' *(Giggle)*

Unlike earlier alternative comedians, teasing and needling the Left is not what Hardy is about. He's more likely to direct his jokes at the unthinking Right: 'But you can't argue with right-wing people, there's no point. 'Cos right-wing people have no logic. Right-wing people say things like, *(retired colonel voice:)* "So you're a socialist, are you? Well I see you're not too socialist to wear shoes! *(Laughter)* I don't see you sharing them with a family of gypsies!"' *(Laughter)*

Hardy may come across as a decent, polite young chap, but he's more abrasive than his image first suggests. His radio show, *Jeremy Hardy Speaks To The Nation*, which included big chunks of his stand-up act, was the third most complained-about show on television or radio in 1993-94. The left-wing scabrousness and the irreverent treatment of touchy subjects like sex and religion proved too much for some in the genteel, fashioned context of Radio 4.

Mark Steel is a more working-class comic, with a distinct South-East accent and membership of the Socialist Workers Party. His basic comic technique is to draw a political parallel, and then act it out on stage, the laughs coming more from his skill in bringing the characters to life than from deft wordplay or clever jokes. He is a brilliant imitator of regional accents, stretching them just enough to make them funny, but without slipping into cartoonish exaggeration. Whether he is turning Neil Kinnock into a buffoon or bringing to life a nice cop/nasty cop scenario, his character work is not like that of an actor. He slips effortlessly into the voices, in the way somebody might imitate a friend in an everyday conversation, so that the voice work is never presented to the audience as a feat in itself.

Steel's speciality is polemical gags about the class struggle, which don't come across as preachy or tedious thanks to the sheer ease of his performing talent. Sometimes finger-pointingly angry, other times cheerfully cheeky, his strength is that his whole act always comes across more like normal conversation than prepared patter – he sounds like the funniest, cleverest, saloon bar philosopher you're ever likely to laugh with. In one routine, he proves that 'the one thing that determines what goes on in this world . . . is class' by pointing out that everyone in positions of power seems to share the same posh accent. He briefly creates a Colonel Blimp-style general, a high court judge and a member of the House of Lords ('Where the bloody hell am I?') to prove the point, then says that we would find it ridiculous if everybody in power shared a different accent. This is where his voice work comes into its own, as he creates a blue-chip company director delivering his annual report in a thick Brummie twang, and a judge with a manic Geordie accent: 'Aye, ye've gotta allow the prosecution to establish where the defendant was on the naight o'the crime, man, and we can get doon the club for a game o' pool and a Newky Broon, man!!!' *(Laughter, applause and cheers)*

Steel also has the integrity to stick to his political guns. During the Gulf War, he would do ten minutes' worth of gags about it, ignoring the fact that the laughter would get quieter and uneasier until he moved onto a less uncomfortable subject.

Nick Revell hit the altcom circuit at the beginning of the '80s. Starting off as a character comedian, by 1984 he had moved to a more straight stand-up style, mixing political gags about current events with routines about his adolescence in 1970s Pontefract. At this stage, some of the political stuff was more effective as political comment than as jokes, like a gag about leaving a cruise missile outside a burger bar and coming out to find it gone: 'There was just eighteen empty factories there, a couple of empty hospitals and a note saying, "It's a fair swap, Yours, Maggie."' *(Giggle)*

Revell's stand-up style is more theatrical than conversational. Rather than flowing seamlessly, the silly faces and funny voices stick out of the routines, presented as gags in themselves. The gestures are a little larger than life, and certain words are emphasised with an unmissable knowing look. He almost nods as he drives home punchlines or key phrases. A routine about yuppies dating from 1988 is a good example of this. It starts with a gloating reference to the

Stock Market crash of the previous year: 'You remember yuppies? The ones with the smug looks till last October *(screws up face and clenches fist in victory gesture)*, haa!! *(Laughter and applause)* Whilst waiting for a tube train they can only stand in a pose that is in last season's Jaeger catalogue. *(Laughter) (He stretches one leg forward and leans back, pouting.) (Laughter)* And 'e gets the thirty pence out, out of the thirty-pence page of his Filofax. *(Laughter)* Which is the page next to the one that unfolds into a *(yuppie voice:)* windsurfer. *(Laughter)* Next to that the one with the designer condoms, you know. *(Giggle)* They actually do that, buy a page for a, a Filofax with condoms in. You buy it with one condom missing. *(Yuppie voice:)* So it looks like you've *(nonchalantly scratches top of head and adopts smug look)* had a shag recently.' *(Laughter and applause)*

Feminist stand-up

One of alternative comedy's biggest contradictions is that although it adopted a non-sexist, non-racist policy practically from the outset, it hasn't done much to overturn stand-up's traditional dominance by white men. Having said this, it did open things up a little in the 1980s. There were still only a handful of women comics at the beginning of the decade, but it was the first time that outright feminism had ever come into the world of stand-up comedy. Acts like French and Saunders and Pauline Melville had never got many gags out of gender politics, and Melville had even quipped, with a winning smile: 'I am in the Women's Movement. It should give me a lot of strength. The trouble is I'm not in the most militant branch. I'm just in the branch that pulls faces behind men's backs. *(Laughter)* Yes, you may well laugh but there's a lot of us.' *(Laughter)*

Jenny Lecoat started doing stand-up in 1982, and she was very different. Styling herself a 'feminist comedian', she strode onto the stage in a man-scaring uniform of cropped hair and bovver boots complete with a badge bearing the legend: 'Exploited'. She covered her novice's nerves with an aggressive delivery, and spent most of her time getting laughs from the sex war. There were songs about cutting off her boyfriend's penis and boiling it up with kidney beans, and gags about the phallocentric nature of militarism ('When those missiles go launching off Greenham Common, it won't be two-hundred-foot clitorises flying up there.') But the feminism was also there in routines about simpler matters, like urinating in the countryside: 'Actually there, there is *one* thing . . . that men do better than women. Just the one. And that's going for a pee in the open air. *(Laughter)* Well it's true isn't it, 'cos they've got the right equipment. I mean if a bloke is driving through a little country lane in the middle of the night, and 'e wants to go for a wee, all he has to do is find a dark corner, whip it out, do the business and it's all over. Be nice if 'e got out of the car first, but . . . *(Laughter)* Whadda we get? We're out there in the middle of the country somewhere, we're struggling with coats and leotards and thermal underwear and dungarees, you know. *(Giggle)* And we always find the nettle patch. *(Laughter)* Always happens, going for a pee in the country, nettles up the bum, it's always the same.' *(Laughter)*

The feminism is there not just in the begrudging way she admits that this is one thing that men do better than women or the idea that this is unfair, but also in the kind of clothes she refers to: 'coats and leotards and thermal underwear and dungarees' conjures up a perfect image of the typical costume of the 1980s stereotype feminist.

As the decade wore on, Lecoat became less strident, swapping her 'feminist uniform' for frilly dresses, then jeans-and-T-shirt casuals, and dropping the flag-waving gender politics, becoming a highly competent but less unusual circuit comic. Her early '80s contemporaries, like Jenny Eclair and Helen Lederer, had never been as militant, but they still touched on women's issues. Lederer became well known for the gushing yuppie characters she played in TV sketch shows like *Naked Video*, her strange blue eyes glowing with self-satisfied smugness, but her stand-up persona was rather different. On stage, she made herself shy and hesitant, with an almost Howerdesque apologetic stutter and a nervous laugh. One of her routines was her own very distinctive take on what would become an archetypal subject for female comics – menstruation: 'My parents, actually, were very, very good on celebrations, which I think's lovely, and um . . . when I had my first period, sorry to say "period", *period*, sorry *(Giggle)* but period. Anyway . . . when I had my first period . . . um, they put it in the local paper, actually. *(Laughter)* No they did, they did, they said . . . "Lederer, Helen, congrats on your first period." *(Laughter)* Lovely. "Love from Mum, Dad and Uncle Frank." *(Laughter)* Lovely.'

Gay stand-up

As well as bringing the first feminist comedian, the early '80s also brought the first out gay comedian. Gay stand-ups weren't an entirely new phenomenon, but the likes of Frankie Howerd and Larry Grayson were a far cry from the self-professed 'radical gay comedian', Simon Fanshawe. Fanshawe's act was less about sending up camp mannerisms, and more about talking about sexuality and the world in general from a gay perspective. Providing a perfect antidote to the club comic's fear-soaked gags about gay sex, Fanshawe would poke fun at heterosexuals: 'I do know about you boys because I've read *The Hite Report. (Laughter)* And in *The Hite Report* Shere Hite says that forty per cent of all straight guys come within two minutes. Most of you don't know whether to laugh 'cos that's a long time or a short time. *(Laughter and applause)* There's a guy down here going, "My God, my God, some people last two minutes, oh shit!! Oh God!!! What creams do they use??" *(Laughter)* Two minutes! Phew!! "What was that?" *(Laughter)* "Oh that was sex was it, oh I really enjoyed that, let's do it again, you

know." *(Laughter)* It takes four minutes to boil an egg!!'
(Laughter)

Fanshawe could make this kind of thing work for a heterosexual audience by being very charming on stage, the gags spiced up by the fruity poshness of his delivery, his voice a torrent of breathless, high-pitched incredulity. Just as Jenny Lecoat has shoved her feminism onto the back seat, Fanshawe gradually dropped the 'radical gay' tag, and moved onto tackling more general political issues. His stand-up career peaked when he won the Perrier Award in 1989, but he gave up live work shortly afterwards, after an unhappy stint on the TV show *That's Life.*

Julian Clary is not so much a stand-up comic as a one-man showbiz extravaganza. Starting out in the mid-'80s as Gillian Pieface, he became notorious as The Joan Collins Fan Club, appearing onstage in a glittery avalanche of glam costumes, decked with feathers, sequins, diamante earrings and eyeliner applied by the ton, and accompanied by a performing dog called Fanny. Reverting to his real name after threats of legal action from Joan Collins, Clary captured the heart of the nation by appearing on a quiz show called *Trick or Treat* alongside the epitome of bland TV personalities, Mike Smith. The lynchpin of his comedy is a reworking of the variety comic's love of innuendo. The forbidden subject which Clary hints at in his smutty gags is invariably gay sex. Here is a prime example, from a routine about joining the police: 'The other morning they wanted to send me off on a dawn raid. I said, "I'm sorry, but you won't see *me* before half past ten in the morning. *(Laughter)* I don't have my porridge till nine, and I'm not leaving the house without something hot inside me, not for anybody."'
(Laughter and applause)

Very occasionally, Clary will slip a bit of gay politics between the glam and the glitter, for example suggesting he's having a relationship with the ex-Chief Constable of Manchester, James Anderton, famous for claiming to have a hotline to God and for his public pronouncements against homosexuals: 'In private we've got pet names for each other. I call him "Jimbo". And he calls me "the spawn of Beelzebub", so erm . . .' *(Laughter)*

Another of Clary's favourite tricks is to pick on people in the audience ('What's your name? Any idea?'), and by the end of the '80s, his shows had moved away from his own lipstick-encrusted brand of stand-up into a collage of kitsch songs, camp repartee and game-show-style audience participation. Despite his disarmingly glamorous image, he is still able to whip up a media frenzy. An impressive array of shocked tabloid headlines followed his comment at the 1993 British Comedy Awards ceremony that he had been involved in a sexual act backstage with the then Chancellor of the Exchequer, Norman Lamont.

The growing altcom scene of the early '80s also saw the arrival of the first lesbian stand-up in the shape of former performance poet Claire Dowie. Most of Dowie's act is about describing her life as a gay woman to get laughs: 'You've gotta be fit to be gay. 'Cos all you've got is discos and marches you know and I just . . . *(Laughter)* Ridiculous, innit *(mimes disco dancing)* all this just to get laid, you know what I mean?' *(Laughter)*

As a short-haired, denim-clad 'butch dyke', she also has a fabulous routine getting fed up with being mistaken for a man in ladies' toilets, and trying to fend off a staring woman by showing her breasts so as to prove her gender: 'And she came over to me and she said, "Excuse me. Aren't you Claire Dowie?" I thought, "Oh no!" *(Laughter)* I was so embarrassed! I tell you, I was rigid. Just stood there like this *(mimes lifted shirt)* while she was talking about this gig she saw me at at Brixton or somewhere. And I'm really, and I'm going, "Gosh, isn't it hot? *(Laughter)* I'm just taking the air, you know how it is, don't you?" *(Laughter)* Standing like that. And meantime all these other women are walking past saying, "Look at that boy with tits, isn't he odd?"' *(Laughter and applause)*

Trying to get a mainly straight audience to laugh at gay

experiences is no mean feat. I remember seeing Dowie in a small pub room in the West End after doing one of my first London open spots in 1989, and the audience took two or three minutes before they decided to laugh at her jokes. What won them over was a delivery as close as stand-up can get to everyday conversation, complete with nervous laugh and self-effacing smile. By the beginning of the 1990s Dowie was moving away from comedy, using the stand-up format to perform very serious theatre pieces, like *Adult Child, Dead Child*, about an adolescent breakdown.

Strange new comedy

The tearing up of the comedy rule book, the twisting of old jokes, the crazy experiments in laughtermaking that had made the initial explosion of altcom so exciting, continued through the '80s as the circuit spread its wings. There was Kevin McAleer, for example, who presented a surreal mutant mixture of stand-up comedy and slide shows. McAleer would go on to become a huge star in his native Ireland when he returned there in the late 1980s. There was Tony Allen, who continued to push back the boundaries of stand-up, getting laughs from distinctly unpromising comedy subjects like rape, sub-atomic physics, the sex life of orchids and Heisenberg's uncertainty principle. His comedy is informed by his freethinking anarchist philosophy and strung together in an improvisational style and a very distinctive microphone technique: going off at a tangent, he'll step right back from the mic. and use his own unamplified voice, then go back to it to emphasise something, or to return to the original subject. One of my finest memories of his act was seeing him in a small pub room on a stuffy summer night, the door left open to let some air in. While he was on stage the weather broke, and his routines were punctuated by spine-tingling thunder claps. Just as he started talking about chaos theory, the microphone fell apart into several pieces without even being touched. It seemed like he was doing a double act with God.

Then there was Norman Lovett, who came up with a revolutionary approach to stand-up: to deliberately be as dull as possible. Deader than deadpan, he'd punctuate his act with some of the longest pauses in the business, waiting for a full thirty-nine seconds before starting his act in one TV appearance. Bald and middle-aged even when he started out, he looked like Droopy the cartoon canine, with lovable hangdog features and hooded eyes expressing nothing but mundanity. Rather than taking the rush-out-and-grab-'em-by-the-throat approach, he would slowly create his own world on stage, a world that somehow managed to be surreal and humdrum at the same time. 'Cor, I'm bored now,' he would comment, or perhaps he would wince after a particularly weak punchline and apologise, 'Oo I know, I know, but that's why I don't do jokes, see.' Some of the laughs come from playing against type, unconvincingly playing the tough guy ('I take library books back late, sometimes . . . I live on the edge'), others come from pushing the mundanity to the limit. This is from a 1989 routine about buying light bulbs:

'An' I went up to the counter and the man there in brown coat an' . . . collar and tie, an' . . . well groomed, very well groomed man. 'Bout fifty-five, fifty-six . . . fifty-seven could've been at a push *(Laughter)* I dunno, but . . . I said. "Two sixty-watt, two of your *best* sixty-watt bulbs." *(Laughter)* An' 'e said, "I'll just try these for you sir," an' 'e, an' 'e screwed them in the socket to say . . . An' 'e didn't do it quickly to say, "Oo that works, that works," 'e put it in. And stood back with me and watched it glow. *(Laughter)* We stood back and admired it, an' 'e said. "Yeah, that's a good one you got there."' *(Laughter)*

Perhaps the most interesting laugh here is the one he gets by guessing the shopkeeper's age. The pause after 'fifty-five, fifty-six' makes the audience think he is about to move onto something more interesting, but no, he goes on guessing and the audience laughs, amazed he could be so boring.

For a time Lovett moved away from the altcom circuit, moving to Edinburgh in 1989, and getting caught up in television projects like playing the face of the computer in the first series of the comedy sci-fi show *Red Dwarf*. Returning to live work in the '90s, he has speeded up his delivery a touch, upping the surrealism and cutting down the dullness. In a recent visit to my own comedy club in Sheffield, what was fascinating was that whilst the audience was distinctly quieter than it had been in the first half of the show, the mild-mannered Lovett had complete command of the room. There was no background chatter even in bits where there were no big laughs, and hecklers were effortlessly worked into the act.

As altcom slowly colonised every area of London, there were all kinds of comedians working alongside the poets and the jugglers and the feminist theatre groups. As well as the politicos and the innovators, there were gentle observational comics like Roy Hutchins and Mark Miwurdz, finding laughs in everyday experiences and tales of childhood. Even here, the boundaries were pushed back. Mark Miwurdz (who now works under his real surname, Hurst) started off as a performing poet in Sheffield, and after a stint on the cult rock show *The Tube* in the early '80s, he moved onto the altcom circuit. Wearing a Two Tone-style porkpie hat and a boyish grin, his conversational style was flavoured with a warm South Yorkshire accent and pepped up with infectious enthusiasm. There's a clever twist in a routine about his mother's living room: 'And little shitty orniments all ovver. *(Laughter)* Little fuckin' . . . crappy nick-nacks. *(Laughter)* Dvv! Dvv! On every level surface, piled up. *(Laughter)* Dvv! Dvv! Dvv! I said, "Mother, why, why d'yer 'ave all these silly orniments? I'm askin' yer. I've never asked yer this before, but why?" She stopped pourin' me tea. An' looked at me. What's the matter, mother?" "Shut up!" "I'm just a – " "Shut up! You're askin' *me* . . . why I 'ave all these shitty

... little, icky, fuckin' ...", "You don't swear, mother", "SHUT YOUR FUCKIN' MOUTH!! You're askin' me why I 'ave all these little *bastard* nick-nacks all over the fuckin' 'ouse yer little *twat??*" *(Laughter)* "You don't say things like ...", "Shuddup!! What did yer buy me every birthday? *(Loud laughter)* Every 'oliday! *(Laughter)* Every bleeding Christmas! *(Laughter)* A little fuckin' orniment! *(Laughter)* 'Ow did *you* know I didn't want an ... an obscene paperweight??"' *(Laughter)*

This turns the aggression theory of comedy on its head. The audience laughs with him at his mother's tasteless, ornament-strewn living room, but then the joke turns right over and suddenly the audience is laughing at itself: most of us have probably given our mothers a little ornament at one time or another. The aggression theory states that we laugh at the expense of a third party, and that's how this routine starts. The twist is that the end of the routine makes Miwurdz (and the audience themselves) the butt of the joke.

Alongside the observational comics, there were genuine one-offs like the spectacles-obsessed comedy poet John Hegley, and sharp surrealists like Ian MacPherson, Hattie Hayridge, Michael Redmond and Paul Merton. What characterises this brand of comic is a blend of well-scripted gags with logical leaps and often dark themes, almost invariably put across with a deadpan, pause-heavy delivery. The opening of Ian MacPherson's act is typical of the style. Unsmiling, his forehead knotted with puzzlement, he waits a moment before launching into it: 'People often say to me, "Ian ... do you remember where you were when Kennedy died?' I was only eight at the time ... but I do. I was leaning out the sixth-floor window of a hotel in Dallas. *(Loud laughter)* Pphhhw!!! *(Laughter)* Funny how things like that stay with you. *(Loud laughter)* I also remember where I was when the Pope was shot. *(Giggle)* But I don't like to dwell on failure.' *(Laughter)*

By the end of the 1980s the altcom circuit had started to

grow beyond London, with the first clubs springing up in provincial cities, and it had become an important part of the cultural life of the capital. In 1989, it was estimated that over five thousand Londoners were going out to see alternative comedy every weekend. The audience had grown in more ways than one, and by this time it was no longer just a bunch of GLC-type anti-Thatcher left-wingers. People of all different tastes and prejudices were turning up to have a laugh. Another change was that the clubs became less about variety, more about pure stand-up. Steve Gribbin, now a solo act but then half of the agit-pop musical comedy duo Skint Video, believes the bigger audience was responsible for the blues singers and mime artists having to find work elsewhere: 'Slowly, as the circuit grew, the number of venues where, you know, the sort of variety acts, as it were, could ply their trade shrank . . . as it grew, it became more popular as well, and more money became at stake, venue owners and promoters became less willing to experiment, you know, less willing for people to fail . . . and for that reason stopped booking them.'

As pure stand-up became the order of the day, the kind of stand-up on offer changed. The new comedy values that had been built up since day one of the altcom revolution were hacked apart largely by one man, a Glaswegian nihilist called Gerry Sadowitz.

Backlash

Sadowitz is a knot of anger wrapped in a jacket decorated with Dennis the Menace badges, his long, black curly hair spilling out from under his bowler hat. He doesn't so much deliver his jokes as spit them at the audience with the kind of crazy-eyed aggression that harks back to the heady heyday of Alexei Sayle. A magician as well as a comic, he is an expert at close-up card tricks, but the magic in his stage acts is far more anarchic. In some cases it is quite literally 'in-your-face': in one trick he announces 'instead of you pick a card and I find it . . . you pick a card and you bloody well find it!' then hurls the cards right at the audience. Sadowitz was up and running in the Comedy Store by 1985, and the philosophy which fuels his comedy is: 'I fuckin' hate everythin'!!'

In practice, what this means is gagging about any subject as long as it's tasteless, whether it be cancer, senility, the King's Cross tube disaster, Tommy Cooper's onstage death or starving Ethiopians. There's something there to offend everybody, particularly the left-wing social worker types who still dominated the scene when Sadowitz first started shouting at audiences. Political correctness was a particularly annoying bee in his bonnet, and he got a lot of mileage out of deliberately winding up the liberals. Perhaps his most famous gag was the one in which he called Nelson Mandela a 'cunt' and Terry Waite a 'fuckin' bastard'. The punchline implied that these unassailable public heroes had only disappeared from public life because they owed him five pounds. The purpose behind this is obvious: to say the unsayable, to wind the audience up by assaulting their values.

Between the spastic impressions and masturbating with Sooty puppets there was plenty more to upset the Left, whether it be laying into the miners, or having a go at old people. Feminists were a particular sore point. He'd screw his face up while pretending to ram himself into an inflatable sex doll, then rant about how much he bloody hated feminists, asking why they dress like men if they hate them so much. He'd turn to a woman in the audience and ask her, 'Any chance of a fuck?' He'd throw in a beery blue limerick about a girl from Sri Lanka 'whose cunt was as big as a tanker'.

Perhaps most controversially, he'd also do Pakistani jokes. The savagery of the Pakistani jokes in club comedy was one of the things that had sparked off the altcom revolution in the first place, so by introducing them to the circuit, he was breaking a real comedy taboo. Sadowitz's Pakistani jokes

210

weren't as savage as the kind of thing you hear in working men's clubs, but they certainly involved stereotypes. He'd do his own answer to Harry Enfield's Greek-Cypriot character Stavros, for example: a short-changing shopkeeper called Raj, which he'd perform by wrapping a towel around his head and shouting in a Peter Sellers-style cod Indian accent.

Interestingly, most of Sadowitz's comic contemporaries are fans, and it would be wrong to write him off as some kind of right-wing Bernard Manning figure trying to overturn the altcom revolution. Some of his most vicious jibes were reserved for the Right, tearing into the likes of Norman Tebbit, the Queen Mother, the Poll Tax and breast-encrusted soft porn tabloid the *Sunday Sport*. Sadowitz was not so much a second Manning, more a misanthropic anarchist firmly refusing to obey any rules. Whatever his motivations were, though, the net result of the Sadowitz phenomenon was to move altcom away from the principle of refusing to pick on minority groups for laughs. For a time he was one of the most talked-about comedians on the circuit, but after the controversy died down his stand-up career went into hibernation as he seemed to disappear from the circuit.

Others followed in his path, in some cases causing quite a stir. At the Edinburgh Festival in 1987, Sadowitz accused fellow Glaswegian Craig Fergusson (then billed as Bing Hitler) of stealing his act, which in turn led Fergusson to sue him for libel. In fact, the similarities between the two are mainly superficial: both are shouty Scotsmen who do gags about things they hate. The difference is that where Sadowitz picks the most controversial targets, Fergusson's Bing Hitler character was a much cuddlier misanthropist, appearing on stage in a shrunken blazer, a fluffy pullover, a kipper tie and NHS specs, and ranting on about harmless stuff like dentists, *Star Trek* and the DJs on local radio.

Sadowitz's real heirs were the comics who found different ways of following his basic principle. Skulking in the wings

211

behind him, waiting to take the stage in the late '80s, was Jack Dee. He was a calmer hater, standing casually behind the mike stand without ever taking the mike out, and talking lazily, with a begrudging sneer that covered his whole face. The casual slurriness of his delivery masked the cleverness of the material, the careful choice of words. His onstage attitude was that of a child who has had its favourite toy taken away – a permanent sulk. Occasionally enjoying a cruel laugh or adopting a pathetic crybaby voice to imitate his enemies, his approach was totally cynical. A tanker spillage in Alaska provoked him to comment that it was 'a terrible, awful, *awful* waste of oil', and his reaction to anti-smokers wearing badges that say 'You Smoke – I Choke' was that he knew a good deal when he saw one.

Dee's targets were less inflammatory than Sadowitz's. Instead of taking on feminists or Pakistanis, he'd sneer at, say, fat people. One of his most famous early routines was about the film *The Elephant Man*, a sophisticated tearjerker about the hideously deformed John Merrick. He gleefully subverted it by reacting to Merrick's ugliness not with pity, but with callous laughter. This was a real audience pleaser. When it was filmed at the Comedy Store in 1989, the audience laughed along with him so loudly that the soundtrack distorts. The routine goes on to imagine Merrick getting a job in advertising, picturing him appearing in then-current adverts. Dee may have been poking fun at a mere movie character, but part of it was also about laughing at deformity. It's not a million miles from this to the playground 'spastic' joke.

More recently, Dee's comedy has lost its cruel edge. Propelled to fame by his TV shows and a series of adverts for John Smith's bitter, he's changed from a classroom bully to a suave entertainer, replacing his casual stagewear with sharp-cut suits. His television series was filmed in an imaginary nightclub overbrimming with well-dressed sophistication. Though still cynical, he's now more likely to crack jokes about craft fairs or DIY than *The Elephant Man*.

A very different kind of taboo-breaker was the generously proportioned Jo Brand. When she started out, her comedy flew in the face of *Fat is a Feminist Issue*-style arguments about not judging women on their physical appearance. Working under the name The Sea Monster, her technique was to crack brilliant but scathing gags about her own obesity: 'I was the child who always got picked to play Bethlehem in the school nativity play. *(Laughter)* And even then Mary and Joseph used to keep mistaking me for Greater Manchester.' *(Laughter)*

This was more than just simple self-deprecation. The jokes might have suggested she hated herself for being fat, but the delivery said otherwise. She put over the material in one of the most distinctive stage voices in showbiz: bored and toneless, with the characteristic up/down intonation of the man who reads the football scores. This distanced her from the jokes and loaded them with irony. She seemed to be saying, 'This is the kind of thing people say about me, I've heard it all before, instead of simply, 'I'm fat, laugh at me.' The fact that she came onstage in the tribal costume of the '80s feminist with cropped hair, big earrings, Doc Marten boots, and baggy, black clothes added to the impression that the gags were a comment about fattist attitudes rather than just an expression of them.

However, Brand's early material did ruffle a few feminist feathers, perhaps because however ironic she intended the gags to be, it was still possible for laddish elements in the audience to take them at face value and just laugh at the fat woman on stage making fun of herself. There were also gags which, however clever, broke certain feminist taboos, getting laughs out of eating disorders, for example: 'People still say to me – "Jo . . . you're not exactly anorexic, are you?" *(Laughter)* Well I'm not so sure, because anorexic people look in the mirror . . . and think they look fat. *(Laughter)* And so do I.' *(Laughter and applause)*

Like Dee, Brand has changed on the way to the big time. The football announcer voice has been replaced by a cheery,

213

matey rapport with the audience, and a cherubic smile. The fat jokes aren't the main thing any more, and they're not self-deprecating. Instead, they celebrate the idea of stuffing down cake and chocolate in industrial quantities. Onstage, she's as punk as the big, spiky haircut she now sports. She plays the beer-swilling, cigarette-guzzling yob, always looking for a good punch-up. She's more likely to gross the audience out than sneer at herself, perhaps discussing euphemisms for menstruation: 'And among my favourites are, "I've got the painters and decorators in." *(Extended laughter)* "Arsenal are playing at home." *(Laughter)* Erm . . . but er, I have to say actually that my own particular favourite is er, "There's a vast amount of blood squirting out of my cunt, vicar."' *(Laughter and applause)*

Nowadays, her feminist sympathies are much more evident in jokes which reveal her own violent approach to gender politics: 'I've actually got rather a good idea about how women could deal with violence on the streets. I think the government should pass a law for all women to be armed *(Giggle)* with shotguns. Because I think, you know, it'd be great because we could go round, we could shoot rapists. We could shoot muggers, and we could shoot anyone that got on our nerves really, couldn't we?' *(Laughter)*

If one side of the backlash was comedians like Gerry Sadowitz coming onto the circuit, the other side was Ben Elton's fall from comedy favour. Elton first appeared at the Comedy Store in February 1981. By the mid-'80s he had outgrown the circuit, having co-written *The Young Ones* and supported Rik Mayall on big-venue national tours. Appearing on *Saturday Live* (first as resident comic and later as compere) made him a star, but by the end of the decade it was hard to find a single comic on the circuit who had a good word to say about him. He was seen as having sold out, having ruined alternative comedy. He had stopped going to altcom venues because, he said, 'They all take the piss out of me.' A mural decorating the wall of a well-known London comedy club shows the last supper, with Elton in the position normally reserved for Judas Iscariot. Gerry Sadowitz's TV series featured a sketch in which he played a gangster whose henchman delivers Elton's severed head to him.

Elton has been criticised for his delivery, and it's not hard to see why. Once he gets behind a microphone he becomes a hectoring motormouth reaching speeds of up to four words per second. He revs up his Cockney accent and his voice acquires a growliness, like a damaged exhaust pipe. His delivery has several distinct gears: there's the low sinister rasp, the high-pitched tearful voice, the ironic smiley voice, the slow, soft staccato voice. He prowls the stage staring at the audience, as if daring them not to laugh. He preempts his critics by taking on their voices, parodying their viewpoints. His bodywork is deliberately brash: he spent the second half of the 1980s in a glittery suit, his long wavy hair framing a big pair of yuppie-style specs, like a deliberate anti-fashion statement. All of this makes him a gift for impressionists, and Steve Coogan and Rob Newman are just two who have included him in their repertoires.

But a much bigger gripe is that he's seen as a politically correct bore, a painfully right-on prig who sacrifices comedy for socialist preachiness. Certainly, he is prone to sloganising, perhaps using 'sexism in comedy, watch out for it' as a final punchline, or making polemical comments on the marketing strategies of Macdonald's: 'Mums, rot your children's teeth and teach 'em about the friendly face of international conglomerates that fuck up the Third World, MacOrange.' *(Laughter)* He takes the concept of non-sexist language to extremes, turning a Sony Walkman into a 'Sony Walkperson'. He takes his hatred of the Left's folk devils to similar extremes, rewriting Dante's *Inferno* to place the editor of the right-wing tabloid the *Sun* beneath Judas at the bottom of the pit of hell, and portraying Thatcher as the devil incarnate: 'The tendons . . . in 'er 'and . . . were constricting . . . and drawing in the fingers . . . TO FORM A CLAWWW!! And the doctors tried to reverse

215

this! You cannot undo what God is doing. First the claw, then the horns, then the forked tail!!!' *(Applause, cheers and whistles)*

Elton has the wit to play about with his spotless right-on image. In a routine about nude sunbathing on a Club 18–30 holiday ('course, you know they're referring to the IQ there, don't yer?'), he suddenly overturns the audience's expectations: 'Your average dick . . . and believe me, they're *all* average. *(Laughter)* Well mine's not, mine's fuckin' enormous, but yours is . . . *(Loud laughter)* Ooh! And suddenly the alternative pose drops for a moment and the little bit of Benny Hill in us all jumps out onto the stage! *(Laughter)* Ha ha! Recognise the devil within you and conquer it.'

What the gripes about his preachiness and limited onstage style ignore is Elton's huge range. In the late '80s, he did three national tours of thousand-seater theatres. Each show was a marathon lasting two or three hours, with an almost entirely new set of material. All aspects of life were converted into laughing matter, from the hidden horrors of fridges and swing-top bins to the Stock Exchange, from menstruation to fast food, from alcohol abuse to Antarctica. What he lacks as a performer he makes up for as a writer, boasting densely packed routines bursting at the seams with gags and ideas. He has his own comedy language – 'sophisticated' becomes 'sophist.', 'Mrs Thatcher' becomes 'Mrs Thatch', and 'Norman Tebbit' becomes 'Normo Tebbs'. The comic images he conjures up with a handful of words are sheer poetry. A crashed hang-glider becomes 'a cagoule full of purée; overhearing somebody else's Sony Walkman sounds like 'a swarm of bees playing comb and paper'; and a lump of rotten food in the fridge is a 'carrot swamp': 'It's kinda steaming now, and bubbling . . . life cycles and little mini pterodactyls flying about inside.' *(Laughter)*

For somebody written off as a left-wing puritan, he also has an unparalleled penchant for scatology, with a seemingly endless supply of gags about sex, masturbation and toilets, waxing lyrical about pubic hair and unwanted erections. His 1988 routine about public lavatories is a masterpiece, a nine-minute non-stop rollercoaster ride of graphic poetry about the human bowel function and the paranoia surrounding it. In the spine-chilling public convenience he conjures up, there's a ferryman 'to paddle you across the puddle of piss' on the floor, there's an unflushed toilet with a stool in it 'like a chocolate swiss roll', and when he finally moves his bowels it is so loud 'it's like bangin' a dead fish on the surface of a stagnant pond'. Comparing this with the nudge-nudge, wink-wink toilet jokes of the variety comedian shows just how far taboos have slackened and barriers have come down. Forty or so years before, Suzette Tarri got gales of laughter by just hinting at the idea of using her husband's tin helmet as a bedpan, but if she'd taken Elton's full-frontal approach, the chances are she'd have faced a shocked silence and legal action.

Another criticism of Elton is that he does too much material about easy targets like television advertising. It's true that he always includes a big chunk of advert gags in his live shows, but what lies behind these is an idiosyncratic political analysis not based on race, sex or class, but on a different kind of them and us. 'Them' is 'the marvellous world o' the product', 'us' is 'the shitty world o' the consumer'. 'Them' is the unseen controllers of consumerism, the people who decide what to sell in motorway service stations, who replaced towels with hot-air hand dryers, who don't use enough formica in public toilet cubicles. 'Us' is the general public. This analysis is at its clearest in a joke about a late-'80s advert for the Hanson Trust, a blatant bit of corporate flag-waving typical of the Thatcher era: 'Have you noticed . . . how in the last three years, for some inexplicable reason . . . they have started advertising multinational companies? What are they advertising for, there is no reason, they're just sittin' there on the telly sayin', "Fuck off, we're really rich, we've got all yer money *(Laughter)* fuck off, we're really rich, we've got all yer

217

money." Whadda they tryin' to tell us, that's all they can possibly be trying to tell! *(Smug voice:)* "The Hanson Trust – a company from over here doing rather well over there." We DON'T . . . FUCKING . . . CARE!! *(Laughter applause and whistles)* I mean they're not gonna give *us* any of the money, are they?'

The underlying theme is the 'reality gap' between idealised media images and the inability of ordinary people to live up to them in the real world. Even a smut-packed routine about sex has this serious point behind it: 'The media sex conspiracy makes *us* believe that superhuman sexual powers are the norm, and we personally are the only little farties who can't do it that well.' The laughs come from exploiting the gulf between Hollywood and real life, between air-brushed perfection and squelchy reality: 'Kim Basinger was doin' it for *Nine and a Half Weeks*, blimey doesn't she 'ave to go to work in the morning, I mean . . . ? *(Laughter)* For most of us, nine and a half minutes is a major erotic excursion, let's face it. *(Laughter)* This woman . . . did it on the kitchen table, she did it in the attic, she took it there, she took it there. *(Giggle)* Most women don't know whether the G-spot actually exists. She's got 'em all over 'er body. You've only got to tap 'er on the shoulder, she 'as fifteen multiple orgasms. *(Laughter)* Nine and a half weeks, her sheets must've been so soggy Mrs Thatcher could've privatised 'em. *(Laughter and applause)* But never . . . never once did any embarrassing squelches shatter the stillness. Not once did her toot-toot toot. *(Laughter)* What's wrong with 'er? Not once did she salute the fifteenth multiple orgasm with a great, joyous, life-enhancing, gusset-shattering raspberry *(Giggle)* that sent her lover's willy twanging like a jew's harp, boing! *(Laughter)* You never saw Kim's sheets flapping like a sail in a transatlantic race, did you?' *(Laughter)*

The plummeting of Elton's comedy credibility is probably less to do with his own inadequacies, and more to do with what he represents. Coming out of left-wing alternative culture, he has become phenomenally successful not only as a stand-up, but also as a writer of hit novels, West End plays and TV shows. The Left has always tended to see success as the result of a pact with the devil. More importantly, he symbolises the purist left-wing comedy style of the '80s, and by sneering at him, the altcom circuit is turning its back on that kind of political idealism. It's no coincidence that Elton became the epitome of uncoolness in the comedy world just as the mass media were portraying political correctness as the biggest threat yet to civilisation as we know it.

The legacy of the backlash is that whereas run-of-the-mill comics on the altcom circuit might once have picked on Thatcher if they were in need of an easy laugh, today they are more likely to pick on minority groups. Without going as far as Gerry Sadowitz, they crack jokes about old people, fat people or the Welsh, rather than risking gags about Pakistanis or feminists. A bafflingly common target for this sort of thing is people with ginger hair. Gingerism is popular with comedians and audiences, and just as addicts take methadone instead of heroin, ginger gags are a safe, controlled substitute for outright racism.

Post-radical comedy

Because alternative comedy started off as a self-consciously radical movement, it was just about inevitable that sooner or later, it would face accusations of selling out. Just as purists had claimed punk was dead little more than a year after it started, the accusations that altcom had gone soft started pretty much straight away. Probably the first to cry 'sell out' was Keith Allen. As early as 1981, he was laying into his contemporaries: 'All this "alternative" rubbish is just bollocks to me. Their content, virtually all the time is not "alternative" to me. The performance is exactly the same, the structure of the jokes is exactly the same. It's a very traditional approach to stand-up comedy.'

By the mid-1980s, indie pop magazine *Jamming* was criticising altcom for 'confirming the prejudices of "their" audience rather than challenging them', and an article in *New Socialist* magazine was quoting an unnamed alternative comedian as saying: 'It's the first time I can remember when you can make money and a career out of being a right-on rebel. When I read that Sarah Ferguson [the Duchess of York] listed "alternative cabaret" among her pursuits at college, I knew it wasn't something I wanted to be associated with any more.'

When altcom celebrated its tenth birthday in 1989, the cries of 'Sell-out!' had become deafening. The word the press most commonly used to describe the scene was 'bland'. The feeling was that the wild experiments and political bite of the early years had just drained away. There were complaints that comedians were all too ready to stick to certain stock subjects, just as their predecessors in the variety and club circuits had. Instead of mothers-in-law or Irishmen, the altcom circuit was overpopulated with jokes about TV adverts, or cult TV shows like *Star Trek* or *Skippy*. In the mid-'90s, gags about Linford Christie's genitals became very popular. It seems a very small leap from the club comic's gags about big-penised black men to the alternative comedian's jokes about a particular black man with big genitals.

The typical 1990s alternative comedian tells gags which reflect the concerns of the young professional. Alexei Sayle spewed comic bile on people who boasted about going to Sainsbury's supermarket in a Suzuki jeep, but those are the very people that present-day altcom is aimed at. It is lifestyle comedy, exploiting the comic potential of vacuum cleaners and washing machines, of buying clothes or making toast. A more pensive routine might look at the symptoms of oncoming middle age, and for a little rebelliousness, there might be the odd gag about shoplifting. In amongst the groovy, young middle-class lifestyle comedy, there are nostalgic routines looking back to growing up and going to school in the 1970s, jam-packed with references to kitsch '70s culture: Chopper bikes, Spangles and Space Hoppers.

If the material has become less challenging since 1979,

that doesn't mean that performance standards have fallen. If anything, the alternative comedians of the 1990s are far slicker and more consistent performers than their early '80s counterparts. The current circuit is bursting at the seams with seasoned acts who can make the audience eat out of their hands. The likes of Mark Lamarr and Alan Davies are so good at working a room that they can get laughs from improvised freewheeling as easily as they can from prepared material. The best of the current crop can make the smallest, slightest joke get a huge, full-bodied laugh. The problem with this is that it leads to the temptation to stick to the smallest, slightest jokes.

There are obvious reasons why the altcom circuit should have been transformed from a shambolic parade of green-horn comics, attacking the punters with barbed gags about the class system and old joke structures turned inside-out, to a professional class of performers cleverly charming the audience with funny stories about toasters or swimming lessons. First of all, there is pure economics. It's not misty-eyed romanticism to say that the first generation of alternative comedians weren't in it for the money. The fact was that there was very little money involved at all. When the Comedy Store first opened, none of the acts got paid except Alexei Sayle, who got the princely sum of five pounds a night for compering. When Ben Elton played the Store, he was paid fifteen pounds per show.

As the scene spread through London in the 1980s, there was a little more money to be made, but the economic basis of the circuit was still fairly primitive. A *Sunday Times* article in 1984 quoted one comic as saying: 'The advantage for us is that there are no agents, and the money comes in folding blue ones. You don't have to hang around for cheques, or brown envelopes from the taxman.' Most comics lived a hand-to-mouth existence, building up their careers by gradually increasing the number of venues which would offer them gigs for a split of the takings on the door. They worked without agents, getting work by phoning the gigs themselves. The whole scene ran on a very ad-hoc basis, without the interest of big business.

With little money to be made, the alternative comedy pioneers had other aims and objectives. Alexei Sayle talked proudly about making his material 'more agit prop, more against the government [and] the police', and claimed his vicious attacks on middle-class trendies and social working generated 'real solidarity' with working-class audiences. Keith Allen talked of attacking the audience's laziness, making them see they had the power to challenge the authorities and to 'go forward'. He specifically rejected the idea of becoming a career comedian, arguing: 'It immediately suffocates anything you can say, because you're always worried about the laughs.' Even the immediate interest of television failed to compete with more radical motives, because it was viewed with some suspicion. Tony Allen specifically refused to work on television after he'd been censored on the early altcom showcase *Boom Boom, Out Go The Lights*: 'I was onstage at the BBC with two or three hundred people listening, and I got to, "Get your ego out of my . . ." and he cut the microphone so the audience couldn't hear. So I thought, "If you're gonna cut what the audience can hear," I thought, "I'm not playing this game." I stopped doing television.'

In the 1990s, the scene has become much more business-like, and the cash stakes are a lot higher. While the small pub-based gig run by a shoestring entrepreneur is still the bread and butter of the circuit, it is the big agencies that now rule the roost. Most comics still start off as their own agent, working up through doing open-mic. spots to build up the number of venues that will offer them door-split bookings, but eventually, most end up working for the big agencies which have grown up to dominate the scene. The biggest are Off the Kerb, set up by Addison Cresswell in 1983, which represents acts like Jack Dee and Lee Evans; and Avalon, set up by John Thoday in 1988, which boasts Frank Skinner and Harry Hill amongst its ranks.

Along with smaller agencies, Off the Kerb and Avalon wield enormous power, because being picked up by them can mean regular high-paid work and a way into television. Avalon has set up the National Comedy Network, a college-based comedy circuit running four hundred shows a year. This gives them the ability to pluck fresh open-mic.-level comics, put them out on tour around the Network, and turn them into a viable act without having to go through the rigmarole of working their way up through the clubs on the regular London circuit.

The amount of cash flying about in the modern, big-business style altcom scene is far higher than it was back in 1979. Some door-split gigs in London can still yield as little as forty to fifty pounds, but bigger gigs can pay over a hundred. Then there are the clubs that book acts for two shows in one night on both Fridays and Saturdays, offering the possibility of clearing a good four hundred pounds over a weekend. Outside of London, the comedy clubs pay a guaranteed fee instead of a door split, and this can be as much as a couple of hundred pounds. With fees like these, a comic working an average of five gigs a week would have no problem clearing twenty to thirty thousand pounds a year. Once a career expands into television, the earning potential rockets. A comedian who's comparatively new to television can command a thousand-pound fee to appear on a big panel game, and big names can ask for ten times that amount. Working for the big agencies is also extremely lucrative. In 1992, Avalon estimated that it was earning the ten acts on its roster a spanking two million pounds between them, and the agency's total annual turnover in 1995 was reported to be in excess of five million.

A second reason for the loss of radicalism is the interest of television. The media was quick to pick up on altcom when it first exploded into life. From the very beginning, there were articles about it in the newspapers and the music press, and, as early as 1982, the alternative sitcom *The Young Ones* turned key members of the Comic Strip contingent, like Rik

Mayall, Ade Edmondson, Nigel Planer and Alexei Sayle, into household names. Soon, more of that first generation broke into television. Ben Elton made it big on *Saturday Live*. French and Saunders starred in a sitcom called *Girls on Top* and then had huge success with their own show.

Then the path from altcom circuit to TV stardom seemed to close up. The finest comics from the time in the 1980s when altcom was spreading out through London didn't get the same breaks as their predecessors had. The Jeremy Hardys and Arnold Browns had series on Radio 4, and popped up in the odd guest spot on *The Jasper Carrott Show*, but remained in the ranks of the semi-famous. This logjam broke at the dawn of the 1990s, as a new generation of comics were snapped up by eager television executives and hip independent companies like Hat Trick. Comedians like Vic Reeves, Sean Hughes and Jack Dee were given their own shows and became every bit as huge as the *Young Ones* generation had been. Since then, there's been a regular parade of Frank Skinners, Mark Lamarrs, and Jo Brands making the leap from live stand-up to TV stardom.

Increasing money and media attention mean that the comedians who work the altcom circuit today have a very different set of priorities from the ones their predecessors had. It's hardly surprising that comics tell gags which reflect the lifestyle and prejudices of the ambitious young professional, given that that's exactly what they are. Becoming an alternative comedian is a career move, with a career structure clearly laid down. You start off doing open-mic. spots for a few months, you build up the number of clubs that will book you, you get spotted and signed up by one of the agencies, which gives you gigs all around the country, then you move onto radio and television and reap fame and fortune.

You might start off with artistic or political ambitions for your comedy, but if you want to get ahead, these must take second place to an impressive laughs-per-minute rate. Pleasing the audience is far more important than being

224

original or inventive, because a high laughter rate is best for ensuring rebookings, and catching the eye of any television producers who might happen to be in the audience. Sticking to tried and tested subjects and structures is the best way of keeping the laughs rolling in consistently. By definition, experimentation involves the risk of failure, and few are prepared to take that risk. Political gags involve the risk of alienating people, so they tend to take second place to jokes about shopping or whatever. Radical aspirations have to compete with worrying about getting enough gigs to cover the cost of the mortgage.

I remember talking to somebody who ran a small chain of comedy clubs in London a few years ago about an act he'd put on the previous week. This comic was a veteran of the circuit who'd acquired a bad reputation for taking too many risks and failing too often. At the club in question, he'd done a very tight set, starting with a series of one-liners before moving into more philosophical territory, and had gone down well. Afterwards, a punter went up to the promoter and said, 'Yeah, I can see he's very good and everything, but when I get home from work on a Friday night, I don't want that, I just want jokes.' The promoter said he wouldn't be booking him again.

Nothing has symbolised the triumph of marketing over the altcom circuit better than the meteoric rise of David Baddiel and Rob Newman. At the beginning of the '90s, they were both established circuit acts, Baddiel a stand-up, Newman an impressionist. Neither was generating the kind of buzz that surrounded, say, Jack Dee or Eddie Izzard before they broke through. Their path to stardom started with a hit comedy show on Radio 1, *The Mary Whitehouse Experience*, which transferred onto television. It was the second series of the TV show that caught the public's imagination with its repeated character sketches, particularly 'History Today' in which two crusty old academics endlessly traded infantile insults. Baddiel and Newman became household names, along with their co-stars Punt and Dennis.

From there, the frenzied media hype that propelled them into the firmament was unprecedented. It had started in the music press when *The Mary Whitehouse Experience* first hit the TV schedules. In April 1991, *Vox* magazine declared: '*Monty Python* was to the late '60s and early '70s what *The Young Ones* were to the 1980s and what *The Mary Whitehouse Experience* could be for this decade.' The music press had helped hype comedians to the big time before, notably absurdist variety show impresario Vic Reeves. In the week that *Vic Reeves' Big Night Out* first took to the airwaves, the *NME* plastered his photo across its cover with the caption 'Not many people know this yet but Vic Reeves is Britain's funniest man.'

The fuss about Baddiel and Newman soon outgrew the music press, and reached the dailies. Broadsheets like the *Guardian* and the *Observer* waxed lyrical about these glamorous, young rock'n'roll comedians with their army of teenage female fans. The momentum ballooned alarmingly, and the duo's popularity reached the extraordinary height of a sellout show at the twelve-thousand-capacity Wembley Arena on 10 December 1993. Inevitably, the show was fanfared by another round of articles marvelling at the coming of the stadium comedy gig.

Looking at the video of that show in the cold light of day, what is striking is the very ordinariness of the comedy. Much of the material is standard fare, the kind of thing you might hear from any jobbing comedian working the circuit. What transforms it is merely the context, the fact that it is received with the kind of rapturous excitement that you might expect to see at a concert by teenybopper bands like Take That. Common-or-garden-variety penis-size jokes get huge gales of laughter, explosions of whoops and whistles. Observational routines about picking somebody up at a nightclub are punctuated by deafening guffaws. Rob Newman's material is slightly more unusual, if only because it's almost exclusively about pop music, but again, the response is quite out of proportion to the material. There's an almost unending torrent of teenage whistles as he skateboards onto the stage.

It's almost eerie watching the footage of these two ordinary, decent stand-ups telling their ordinary, decent jokes in the middle of a massive bowl packed with hyped-up fans laughing and screaming their love at every opportunity. The zigzagging follow-spots and the blaring indie music that accompany them onto the stage are a million miles from the sweaty intimacy of an alternative comedy gig in a small pub function room, but the actual comedy is exactly the sort of thing you might see in a London club any night of the week.

Another thing that stands out is that the comics don't quite fit the brilliant marketing image. They were sold as good-looking young rock'n'roll comedians who would appeal to the teenage market, and they did look the part. Baddiel has a kind of well-dressed student look, with gelled hair, designer stubble and little round glasses, whereas Newman could be the frontman of an indie band, darkly handsome with long, flowing locks. They also dress to look young and fashionable, in T-shirts and leathers, suede jackets and jeans. The awkward fact, though, is that they were actually Cambridge graduates in their late twenties, a generation older than their target audience.

The image only jars when their age or their university roots show through. There are references which don't quite make it across the generation gap. The obvious example is that when Rob Newman tells the story of how he was arrested as a teenager after going to see the cult early-'80s anarchist punk band Crass, he has to pause to explain who they were to an audience too young to remember them.

The Cambridge-graduate factor becomes visible in the occasional pseudo-intellectual sentences which they use. Their highfalutin talk seems inappropriate for the screaming teenage fans that Baddiel refers to as 'foetuses'. It's rather

227

like watching a student trying to hold a conversation with a friend's fourteen-year-old sister, who is only listening because she's got a crush on him. This kind of mismatch came to a head with Newman's first solo tour in 1994. A weirdly apologetic review in the *Guardian* ('Very little of this set actually made me laugh out loud. All the better') described how his 'hesitant manner and tangential material' failed to satisfy an audience which greeted his appearance with 'whoops and applause'.

In spite of the fact that the cap didn't exactly fit, the sales pitch was good enough to transform them from circuit comics into megastars in just three short years. It's a testament to the muscle that the big agencies are endowed with, and the extent to which altcom has become a lucrative product. As for the comics at the centre of this marketing triumph, both have moved away from stand-up since the Wembley Arena extravaganza. Baddiel co-presents the lager-fuelled late-night TV show *Fantasy Football League* with Frank Skinner, and Newman had his first novel, *Dependence Day*, published in 1994.

Altcom Now!

In spite of all the changes alternative comedy has been through in its short life, the political backlash, the increasing commercialism, the dominance of formulaic middle-class lifestyle comedy, there are still exciting things going on, glimmers of the crazy anarchy of the early days. There are certainly comics who turn jokes inside-out, and find wild new ways of getting audiences to laugh. There's Eddie Izzard, for instance, the transvestite comic who's made his name largely without the help of television. His hallmark is a carelessly woven string of whimsical fibs put together into an improvisational ramble. Perhaps looking upward distractedly, or showing his street-theatre roots by loosely bouncing about to illustrate an idea, he churns out his tall tales in a lovably posh voice, giving the impression that he's just messing about to amuse himself. One of the things that propelled him into the national consciousness was an appearance on a big televised charity event called *Hysteria 3*, in which he told the story of how he was raised by wolves, wolves which fish with fishing rods and hunt antelope in a small, red hatchback car. At one point, he fluffs a line, saying the wolves had four legs *between them* instead of four legs *each*, and without missing a beat, he uses this to improvise a situation in which one wolf would have to hop along on one leg, dragging the others behind him on a piece of string.

Then there's Lee Evans, winner of the 1993 Perrier Award, who has built a whole act on panic. If stand-up is a confidence trick, Evans plays the trick in reverse, coming on with an epileptic burst of nervous energy, stuttering, apologising and producing enough sweat to soak through his suit and threaten to drown him. His voice softly betrays his West Country upbringing, and it's so pre-pubescently high-pitched that it seems in constant danger of going off the audible scale. He might start his act by wrestling with the mike stand, disconnecting the mike, pretending to get an electric shock from it and starting to call bingo numbers before suddenly shouting 'Wrong night!' What follows is a virtuoso display of grotesque characterisations, monkey walks and funny noises, frantically driven forward by intense, hyperactive nervousness. He's often been dubbed 'a Norman Wisdom for the '90s', but he's far darker and stranger than Wisdom. He might assure the audience that he was never hit by his father as a child, for example. He then slips in that he was occasionally stabbed, though.

Another innovator is Harry Hill, a silly surrealist comic with a quirky, blinking, lip-licking delivery. Oddly dressed in beetle-crusher shoes and drainpipe trousers, his head sticking out over his outsized collar like a balding, bespectacled boiled egg, he presents a collage of popular culture references and strange advice in an avuncular manner that suggests Ronnie Corbett possessed by the ghost of Salvador Dali. Hill's biggest innovation is the reinvention of the reincorporation gag. Usually, this involves the comic setting up a funny idea and getting a laugh with it, then referring back to it several routines down the line. The audience laughs, and often claps, at the comedian's cleverness. The reincorporation shows that the material is structured and honed, that the jokes aren't just coming off the top of the comic's head. It's a trick, a gimmick, the stand-up's version of pulling a rabbit out of a hat.

Hill has reinvented this technique by using it obsessively, setting up more and more running gags, then bringing them all back in one great lump at the end of his act. What is more, they are less running jokes, more running obsessions. He might complain that variety packs of cereals have more than one packet of Coco Pops in them, for instance. Then, several minutes later, without warning or explanation, he'll say he doesn't like them because they make the milk go brown, leaving it up to the audience to work out what he's referring back to. They laugh at their own cleverness in working out what he's talking about, and at the insanity of going on repeatedly about something so trivial.

There are more acts who match funniness with inventiveness a few rungs further down the ladder of fame. One such is Tim Vine, whose big idea is to ignore sophisticated political satire or sexual-taboo-breaking, and concentrate on the kind of simple gags that might be more at home in a Christmas cracker. He doesn't tell old jokes so much as his own original jokes using crusty old formats. Ninety per cent of his comic output comes in the form of infantile puns: 'So I went down the local casino. I said, "My girlfriend's just fallen asleep in the middle of a game of cards." He said, "Poker?" I said, "Good idea." (*Laughter*) He said, "Do you fancy a game of solitaire?" I said, "All right then," and 'e walked off. (*Laughter*) And this policeman came up to me and 'e gave me a thin piece of paper and a pencil. I said. "What's that for?" 'E said, "I want you to help me trace somebody." (*Laughter*) And then a really handsome bloke sprinted past, and I thought. "He's dashing." *(Laughter)* And there was this bloke lying on the ground, snogging a shrimp. I said. "What're you doing?" he said, 'I think I've pulled a mussel.'" *(Laughter)*

He gets away with this kind of thing by being completely brazen. He's like a seaside entertainer, perhaps wearing a blazer, his well-kept blond hair setting off his boy-next-door looks. He looks like he's having a whale of a time on stage, and his sense of fun is infectious, transforming his audience into a sea of smiles even when they're not in the actual process of laughing. What makes him unusual is that he is absolutely relentless: the corny gags come thick and fast, and they just don't stop. A half-hour set might contain a couple of hundred. It's a uniquely purist approach to the pun, taking no more than a couple of sentences to set up the unlikely premise, and discarding any superfluous waffle.

Comedy without politics

The biggest difference between the alternative comedy circuit of today and the slapdash scene of 1979 is that nowadays, the radical political comedian is an endangered species. There are plenty of comics on the circuit who do topical material, but there is rarely any guiding passion or underlying opinion behind the personal jibes about MPs, the once-ubiquitous silly John Major voices or the royal family gags. The leftist comedians who are around, people like Mark Thomas, Kevin Day or stand-up songster Steve Gribbin, tend to be veterans of the 1980s. The dearth of new politicos on the circuit can largely be explained by the mixed nature of modern altcom audiences. Striking a socialist pose in front of an audience of Labour voters is an easy crowd pleaser, but as the social worker contingent moved out over the second half of the '80s, things got more dangerous. I remember being on with a left-wing comic at a major London comedy club a few years ago, and when he started doing gags about the Conservative Party, a couple of lads at the back started heckling him on purely political grounds.

The most outstanding radical comic currently working the circuit must be Mark Thomas. While he holds the microphone in one hand, his free hand prods and points and gesticulates, giving him the air of a trade union speaker or even a preacher. What softens the image is a gentle Cockney accent and a cuddly smile. He tackles the political comedy question head-on, telling people who find politics boring, 'The ruling class love you,' and driving the point home by miming a disgusting aristocrat sexually violating the apathetic punter.

Thomas' comic hunting ground is the entire range of politics, from the personal to the parliamentary. Sex jokes rub shoulders with gags about revolution. His speciality is the political fantasy sequence, in which he takes a leap of logic and runs with it. In a 1988 routine, he suggested starting a revolution by swapping the muzak in supermarkets for punk rock to inspire the customers to riot, then piping the muzak into police cars to sedate them into not intervening. The election of a former porn star to the Italian parliament in the early '90s was the starting point for a similar flight of fancy. He congratulates the Italians on electing a woman from the sex industry ('all *we* do is elect the clients') then fantasises about legalised prostitutes forming a trade union and going on strike: 'They're all there on the picket line linking arms, "Can't fuck won't fuck! Can't fuck won't fuck! Can't fuck . . ." *(Laughter) (Imitating loudhailer:)* "OK sisters, no violence, no violence, not unless the police pay for it like everybody else."' *(Laughter and applause)*

What marks Thomas out is not just his anarchistic fantasies, but also that he has a radical approach to class which makes him the spiritual heir of the original wave of alternative comedians. He has no time for the Thatcherite argument that the working class doesn't exist any more, for example: 'If the working class were that scarce, the upper class would hunt them. *(Laughter)* It's true, they would, they would. *(Mad colonel voice:)* "Go on, bait the traps with pie and mash, we'll flush the buggers out! *(Laughter and applause)* Ohh, come on!" *(West Country lackey voice:)* "They're in the area sir, Oi've found scratchcards, they can't be far aweey!"' *(Laughter and applause)*

His TV series, *The Mark Thomas Comedy Product*, is the nearest anybody has got to capturing the original radical spirit of alternative comedy in a televisual format. Instead of padding out the stand-up sections with sketches or guest artists, there are films of pranks played on real-life politicians in the style of the American *Michael Moore's TV Nation*. Thomas persuades a succession of MPs to act like idiots, playing air guitar, dancing to rave records or allowing him to photograph their bottoms. The stand-up itself is filmed in a genuine comedy club, the Banana Cabaret in Balham, in front of a genuine altcom audience, and the expletives are left undeleted, undisguised by bleeps or euphemisms.

Perhaps the biggest change in alternative comedy is the shift in gender politics. The circuit is still dominated by male stand-ups, and, unlike their feminist-friendly 1980s counterparts, they tend to play to the lads in the audience. It is a brazen, boastful, hedonistic style, full of football jokes and leery comments about women that stop just short of outright sexism. A laddish comedian might pick out a woman in the audience and imply that she's one of the 'Fat Slags' from *Viz Comic*, or perhaps come out with the old club joke: 'You come from Liverpool? Liverpool's well known for its football, and its beautiful women. So which team do you play for?'

Sex is still a rich subject for alternative comedians, but now the emphasis is on pure outrageousness rather than sexual politics. Comics like Frank Skinner and Jenny Eclair brilliantly mine the comic potential of sexual outrage, with routines about sexual encounters with tramps or dangling prolapsed uteruses onto pop stars' faces, but there's a tendency with this kind of thing to delve into the genuinely offensive. In amongst the unsavoury sexual misadventures,

233

there are distasteful gags about Anne Frank or the disabled scientist Stephen Hawking.

Female stand-ups are almost as rare in the 1990s as they have ever been, and women who want to be comics still face more problems than men. Gina Ryan is working her way up through the circuit, and she told me about some of the problems she encountered: being pigeonholed ('If you can't be told you're like Jo Brand or like Jenny Eclair or like Hattie Hayridge they sort of get a bit stuck'); audiences expecting her to be unfunny because she's a woman, and being expected to stick to certain subjects: 'When I started, I started doing things about sport, and the audiences didn't really like that particularly. You'd get questioned, because they didn't trust you. They didn't think you knew what you were talking about. 'Cos you're a woman.'

It's not just audiences that present women comics with problems. When talking to promoters, Ryan says she often gets told to smile more onstage, and dress more glamorously: 'I get more advice about what I look like onstage than I do about my material.' Perhaps not surprisingly, the women who do break through rarely take on the kind of feminist angle that Jenny Lecoat started out with, opting instead for the same blend of lifestyle-based observational material, cynicism and ginger-hair jokes as the male comics.

Opening up

The gender imbalance might still stand, but one way in which the altcom circuit has opened up in the 1990s is that there are more working-class performers on it than ever before. With important exceptions, becoming an alternative comedian was something of a middle-class pursuit in the 1980s, but now the circuit is strewn with working-class acts. There's Keith Dover, for example, who worked for the Ford Motor Company for fourteen years, and kept his day job there long after he'd started doing stand-up. Then there's Nick Wilty, an ex-soldier who fought in the

Falklands. It might seem a long way from the anti-Falklands War jokes of the early 1980s, to the point when Falklands veterans play the circuit, but Wilty's view of the conflict isn't what you might expect: 'My ideal would've been to be taken prisoner, uninjured, and escape in the mainland of South America, and then work my way up to America or somewhere pretending to be Spanish.' There's also Kevin McCarthy (AKA The Man with the Beard), who is the very antithesis of the stereotype of the alternative comedian as a middle-class youth, fresh out of university. He's a middle-aged, big-bellied Cockney with a gruff, growly voice, and he combines his stand-up career with a truck-driving business. Often, he delivers a load on the way up to a gig, then picks up another on the way back home.

There are also working-class comics who have moved over to altcom from the working men's club circuit. Terry Alderton, for example, started out on a talent show on Sky TV at the tender age of eighteen, then spent a couple of years going down badly on the club circuit and in Butlin's holiday camps. Then a friend introduced him to the London alternative comedy circuit. He defected immediately. The working men's clubs had been appalling: the compere would get his name wrong, announce the bingo in the middle of his act, and, on a bad night, pay him off on stage. The altcom circuit offered more artistic freedom as well as better working conditions. He started out as a mimic, and in the clubs they only wanted to hear impressions of characters from 1970s sitcoms. Anybody more modern, like Julian Clary, and they wouldn't know who it was supposed to be. Having moved over, he was able to do more up-to-date impressions, and eventually develop into more of a straight stand-up, playing heavily on his Essex Boy image.

Another sign of increasing diversity in altcom is the growing number of black, Irish and Jewish comics. Irish and Jewish comics play the main circuit, as well as organising their own ethnically exclusive gigs. Ian Stone has described how different it is for him to play special Jewish comedy nights: 'In general you're talking about an older, more middle-class, straighter theatre audience. And so the parameters are different really, the swearing is not really on, the talking about sex and drugs too much, you can't really do that . . . I tend to play the good Jewish boy, really.'

A separate black comedy circuit has grown up over the first half of the '90s, producing its own stars like Leo Chester and Curtis Walker. Black comedy nights at venues like the Hackney Empire draw big crowds, and the scene has transferred to television via the sketch and stand-up show *The Real McCoy*. Comedians like Junior Simpson and Miles Crawford play both black gigs and the altcom circuit, but the longest-serving black alternative comedian (not including Lenny Henry, who never actually worked in altcom clubs) is Felix Dexter, who has played the circuit since the mid-'80s. Cool, collected and well-dressed, Dexter often lowers his eyebrows in a puzzled frown as he skilfully milks the laughs out of his experience of being black. He specialises in middle-class black characters, who ridiculously try to cling onto a kind of ethnic street credibility in spite of their plummy accents, and the fact that they fail to recognise the prejudice that surrounds them. This strand of his comedy is rooted in his own middle-class origins. Before taking up stand-up, he was studying to be a barrister at University College, London.

Beyond London

Alternative comedy was born in London, grew up in London and, possibly because it was the only city big enough to support such a network of performers and venues, didn't leave home for some time. Its metropolitan identity ran through the material like the lettering in seaside rock. There were jokes about particular areas of the capital, like the jibes about Hampstead being a haven for trendy middle-class lefties. Even more popular were the jokes about the London Underground, about the famed unreliability of the Northern Line, or the fact that the chocolate machines on the platforms never seem to work.

Then, as the '80s wore on, little offshoots of the circuit started growing up in cities all over the country. In Glasgow, a riotous gong show led to a meeting of like minds and the Funny Farm was born, running gigs and starting the careers of acts like Bruce Morton, Stu Who?, Parrot and Fred McCauley. Within a couple of years the Funny Farm had its own series on Scottish television. In Birmingham two college lecturers, Malcolm Bailey and Chris Collins, started running comedy nights in various pubs. Bailey was the administrator and Collins was the compere, later adopting the stage name Frank Skinner. Gigs of all shapes and sizes started springing up in North East towns like Newcastle, Middlesbrough and Stockton, and the growing band of Geordie comics formed themselves into a collective called Near the Knuckle. In Bradford, a couple of anarchists called Nick Toczek and Wild Willie Beckett ran a club called Stereo Graffiti, putting on London acts like Jo Brand alongside regional performers like Manchester's Henry Normal, tying each show to some political cause.

All over England, in towns and cities large and small, people caught onto the idea of running comedy shows in pubs: there was the Buzz in Manchester, Spotz in Nottingham, Jokespace in Leicester, the TICTOC Club in Coventry, and the Madhouse, which ran in the Labour Club in Rotherham. Venues came and went, but when a city lost its altcom club, sooner or later another would rise up to take its place. Across the water in Ireland, the same thing started to happen. First there was the Comedy Cellar in Dublin, then venues started to spring up in Galway, Cork and Waterford, and in Belfast and Derry in the North. Native Irish comics like Dylan Moran, Ardal O'Hanlon, Dermot Carmody, Kevin Gildea and Ed Byrne cut their performing teeth by regularly working their own miniature circuit. Then, in the early '90s, they started flocking over to London, where they quickly found great success.

237

At one stage, it seemed that every town or city in Britain would eventually have its own little version of the London circuit, with its own set of clubs and comics. In 1990, *City Limits'* comedy critic John Connor called the non-London scene 'the beginning of a whole new comedy wave'. Sadly, the wave has turned out to be more of a dribble. Many provincial comedy clubs are little more than offshoots of the metropolitan scene, populated by London acts and booked by London agencies. Even comedians who are based elsewhere still tend to find themselves going down to London for most of their work. I once found myself in the ridiculous position of having to be seen by an agent in London before I could get a gig at Sheffield Hallam University, even though it's only half an hour away from where I live.

In spite of this, the provincial comedy circuit has produced an impressive array of acts who lack the joke-a-like uniformity of London comics. This is partly because provincial comics are less swayed by the fads and fashions that sweep through the capital's comedy community, and partly because they tend to find strange routes into stand-up. Comic poet Henry Normal, for example, started out in rock venues supporting punk bands, and Newcastle's Anvil Springstien began his career as a Marxist street act having concrete paving slabs put across his chest and smashed with a sledgehammer. The provincial scene harks back to the London circuit of the early '80s, because it isn't dominated by straight stand-up. Provincial comics often blend patter with poetry, or perhaps throw in songs on the guitar. To give an idea of the variety that exists, here's a taste of just some of the acts.

Originally hailing from York, Rory Motion got his first taste of stand-up at a Labour Party benefit in a room above the Co-op in the tiny North East town of Acomb. In an act that can involve guitar-backed songs, a giant spliff, and a xylophone played with a stick attached to his forehead, the key to his comedy is the clash between being a Yorkshireman and being a hippy. He talks about belonging to a hippy football team called Leyton Disorientated, with a holistic trainer who gives you 'salad and counselling' if you get injured. His dad is a fundamentalist Yorkshireman who plays 'a coal-fired Fender Doncaster', smokes coal instead of marijuana ('Look son, I know it's not very good stuff, but it's only eighty quid a ton') and believes that Geoffrey Boycott is an advanced soul from Atlantis: 'And according to me Dad, he came out of the sea off Bridlington on a golden chariot pulled by seven golden whippets. *(Laughter)* From there, he made his way to Guiseley – the home of Harry Ramsden's fish and chip shop – now . . . made his way by Yorkshire ley line. If you join cricket pitches, pubs and ancient fish and chip shops . . . *(Laughter)* they form these mysterious alignments across the landscape. And er, he believes, well he believes that when you die – you go to *Emmerdale Farm. (Laughter)* Which is fair enough. But he also believes that fish and chips are deeply symbolic. He believes that the fish – represents the Piscean age. And that the chips – are to fill y'up.' *(Laughter)*

Manchester's Bob Dillinger also plays the guitar, but his speciality is to rescue gags from the old joke's home and bring them back to life, often by setting them to music in folksy, Dylanesque songs. Under a spiky brush of hair, he has the kind of face that suggests the lovechild of Rod Stewart and '70s footballer Denis Law. Instead of hammering the punchlines home, he delivers the gags in a quietly amused voice, and patiently waits for the audience to fill the gaps with laughter. They nearly always do. Most of his jokes have an ancient lineage – I've traced one of them back to a sketch recorded by variety comic Albert Burdon in 1933. Here's a sample of the style: 'Went to a pub last night, I met a girl who'd lived in Sellafield all 'er life. Said, "Hey, haven't I seen yer face somewhere else?" She said, "Yeah, it used to be on the front of me 'ead." *(Laughter)* Staggered in after a good few pints, mother didn't find it funny, she said. "Why 'ave you come 'ome half-pissed?" I said, "Cos I ran

239

out o' money." *(Laughter)* Then I went out the next night, a policeman followed me around for four hours. I said, "Ey, what's the score. I've not done anything." 'E said, "I know, you're under arrest for wasting police time."' *(Laughter)* It's a testament to Dillinger's soft-voiced Mancunian charisma that while these gags might look stale on the page, when he delivers them in the flesh they sound fresh minted.

Fellow Mancunian Tony Burgess couldn't be more different. His comedy springs from the modern image of Manchester as a city raddled with crime and gun-toting drug gangs. Still in his early twenties, he comes over like the comedy wing of the Ladchester indie rock scene that started with the Happy Mondays in the late '80s and continues today with Oasis. Head on one side, face screwed up, Burgess totters about the stage occasionally rubbing the top of his head in confusion, telling deceptively sharp gags. He has a seemingly drug-induced, high-pitched Larry the Lamb-style wobble in his voice, and the kind of industrial-strength accent that replaces the 'er' sound at the end of a word with the 'o' that comes in the middle of 'knock' – 'Manchester' becomes 'Manchestohh'. In Burgess's hands, the crime and drugs that afflict his home town aren't just social problems, they're also a source of jokes: 'Obviously raises the question, "What d'you do with criminals?" Michael Howard said, "Prison works," but no it doesn't, 'cos there's so many drugs in prison, isn't there, it's strange, they send drug dealers to prison, I mean, that's not punishment, that's business expansion, for God's sake. *(Laughter)* I should know, 'cos I'm takin' stuff at the moment ter help me heroin addiction. Videos, TVs, stereos, stuff like that, you know. *(Laughter)* But you gotta be careful 'aven't you, talkin' about heroin, 'cos I, I got heckled last gig off a social workohh: "That's awful, that's terrible, have you seen what heroin does to young kids? Well erm . . . have you seen what *social workers* do to young kids, you know? *(Laughter)* At least with heroin you get a bit of a buzz before it takes you away from family and friends, I don't know.' *(Laughter)*

Streetwise political gags are the trademark of fast-talking Liverpudlian Anvil Springstien. Like a Butlin's Redcoat with a Molotov cocktail, he somehow manages to be aggressive and jolly at the same time, getting the audience to shout things at him, cajoling a response out of them, and hardly stopping for breath. Flying in the face of the trend of user-friendly comedy aimed at the young professional, he introduces himself as 'Anvil Springstien – champion of the oppressed, defender of the meek – the only unemployed superhero in the North of England.' With his thick Scouse accent gearing up into full throttle and his hair shaved at the sides and spiked on top, he tells tales of his adopted home town, Newcastle, looking and sounding like the voice of the unemployed subculture. Here's a slice of his comic invective: 'But d'you know – getting back to Thatcher – the last thing that that woman did before she left power? She signed a piece of paper giving her £40,000 a year for life – just for not being Prime Minister! Yeah! At first, when I found out about this I this, I thought, "Cheeky fucker." But then I thought about it for a bit and thought, "Hold on, that's money well spent that is – £40,000 a year just for not being Prime Minister!" Hey, she could've held out for more if you ask me! Margaret, here's £80,000, now fuck off!' (no audience)

Vive la révolution!

Variety comedy lasted for sixty years without much change. The themes, the jokes, the basic approach stayed pretty much the same over the years. A stand-up on the working men's club circuit in the '90s isn't much different from a club comic of the early '70s. In comparison, alternative comedy has evolved at lightning speed, like going from primitive biplanes to Concorde in a fortnight. It's turned the job of being a stand-up upside-down and inside-out. It's been through revolution and counter-revolution, trends have come and gone, and it's still only been around for less than twenty years.

Greater popularity means more punters and more money, and that inevitably means that the average alternative comedian will worry more about career prospects. The money that swills around the circuit puts pound signs in the eyes of everybody from the people who run the clubs to the comics who work for them. The days of people getting into the game through amateurish enthusiasm are all but gone. What's remarkable though, is that even now, when comedy is controlled by commerce, there are still people prepared to push back the boundaries and expand the possibilities of what you can do with a microphone and an audience in search of a laugh. There are still Mark Thomases cracking scabrous gags about the government, Jo Brands having a laugh about punching men in the face, Eddie Izzards daring to go out in front of hundreds of paying punters and just mess about.

It may well be that there's a glut of thirtysomething comics, kitted out in the latest fashions from Next or the Gap, with expert stage skills and no imagination, able to mould the audience like putty but without a single original idea. On the other hand, in amongst the comedy clones there are also different viewpoints and new voices. The Christmas cracker jokers, the laughing lorry drivers, the lesbians, the drug-fazed Mancunians, the Afro-Caribbeans and the lyrical Irishmen all help to keep the original spirit of the scene alive and stop the circuit turning out standardised fast-food Kentucky Fried Comedy. What is remarkable is not so much that business interests have dragged alternative comedy away from its radical roots, but that even after it has become a multi-million pound industry, it still produces a handful of comics who can provoke, shock, amaze and puzzle as well as just get the laughs.

Chapter Nine

What's the Secret of Great Comedy?

Q. What's the secret of great comedy?
A. Jokes.

It's as simple as that. No big secret. Just jokes, you know. That's what makes people laugh. Funnily enough, it was only when I started looking into comedy that I found that out. My idea was that you could just kind of *be* funny, and people would laugh. I'd go on stage with what I thought was a pretty funny idea, like 'Wouldn't it be great to launch a terrorist campaign against dogs?', and I'd just launch into it without bothering to think about gags or punchlines. Sometimes they'd laugh. Sometimes their eyes would glaze over and turn into little LED noticeboards like you get in the post office, and the message would flash across them: 'What is this bloke on about?'

See, what I hadn't realised was that you do need jokes. Even if you don't do 'This bloke walks into a pub . . .' -type packaged gags, you still need punchlines. Even in the most conversational, anecdotal, observational routine in the world, where there's no obvious split between build-up and punchline, where it all seems to be part of a seamless flow of thoughts, there are still punchlines. You can have as many funny ideas as you like, but you need something to puncture them with to cause an explosion of laughter. The audience needs some sort of cue to let them know it's time to laugh.

243

That's a punchline. However well the comic has disguised the process, every comedy routine is nothing more than a series of these laughter-cues, strung together with words and gestures. It's just a series of gags.

Here's an analogy. Before I could drive, I never took any notice whatsoever of what the driver was doing. I knew I wouldn't be learning to drive for quite some time, so I didn't want to use up spare mental capacity by thinking about driving. There were much more useful things to do when I was a passenger. Staring distractedly out of the window for example, that was much more useful. As a consequence, when I took my first driving lesson, I didn't even know what the foot pedals were for. I didn't even know there were supposed to be three of them. I thought that driving was just about getting in the car, starting it, driving somewhere, and stopping. I didn't realise that it was more about going through a series of smaller manoeuvres: turning corners, overtaking, stopping at traffic lights, going round roundabouts, going into service stations and having a go on one of those novelty photo machines that makes it look like you've had your photo taken with Arnold Schwarzenegger. The journey is like a comedy routine, and just as it's made up of individual manoeuvres, so the routine's made up of individual gags. If you don't realise that, you're not going to pass your driving test. It'd be like: funny idea funny idea funny idea funny idea oh dear here comes a T-junction I don't know what to do I don't know how to take a corner whoops I've hit the opposite kerb. Let's go back to the test centre Mr Double, and I suggest you don't take your test again until you've learnt some punchlines.

Let's take the analogy further. Whether you tell packaged gags or unfolding comic routines, part of what makes it work for you is looking relaxed and natural onstage. So rehearsing is a bit of a problem. You need to know what you're going to say, you need to know your punchlines, but if you over-rehearse you'll look stiff and wooden and nobody'll laugh. I've seen it with too many open-mike spots and I've done it myself: the comedian has a glazed expression and goes through every word and gesture in exactly the same way as he or she has done a hundred times before in his or her bedroom. The audience winces and fidgets. Again, that's because stand-up's a bit like driving. You can practise handling the car all you want on a private road but what you can't prepare for is dealing with other vehicles. The heckles, the background chatter and the microphone that breaks in half when you take it out of the stand are the stand-up equivalent of other traffic on the road. It's like: oh yeah I'm all right I've practised all this turning a corner no problem 'Get off you're not funny!' what was that? Whoops, I've just smacked into the side of a milk float. Well, that wasn't there when I rehearsed, what's going on?

Test the theories

Here are some simple experiments you can try yourself:

1. *Aggression theory* states that making a joke is about directing aggression at a third party so that you and the second party can laugh at them together. Try this theory out next time you're on a crowded train. Bide your time. Then, suddenly and without warning, start shouting at the person sitting next to you at the top of your voice: 'I HATE YOU!!! YOU'RE SCUM!!! I'M GOING TO KILL YOU!!! YOU'RE A ROTTEN LITTLE PUDDLE OF SICK!!!!' See if any of the other passengers laugh.

    Predicted result: Horrified silence, faces disappearing behind newspapers, guard comes along and warns you that if you do that again, he'll put you off the train at the next station.

2. *Incongruity theory* states that making a joke is about deviating from expected patterns. Try this out by getting on the train in a giant lobster costume with a bunch of

daffodils tied round your head, a photograph of the Queen sellotaped to your tummy, and carry a big sign saying, 'Hey everybody, I'm a loony.' Sit there and read a newspaper, occasionally making sudden, high-pitched squeaking noises.

Predicted result: Puzzled silence, occasional hidden sniggers, guard has a bit of a joke with you and acts all matey.

3. *Release theory* states that jokes work by giving voice to anti-social urges, thus releasing the tension of repressing those urges. Try this out by announcing to the other passengers in your carriage in a loud voice: 'Hey I know picking your nose isn't very nice, but check this out for a stonking big bogie,' then pick your nose and wave your finger in front of people's faces, saying, 'Look how big and green that one is, eh?' See if the other passengers laugh.

Predicted result: Irritated silence, occasional tuts of annoyance, guard says, 'Yes that is a big bogie, but you should've seen the one I had last week.'

The point of all this is that comedy is too complicated and mysterious to be tied down by a simple formula. It's easy to disprove any of the big theories. All you have to do is fulfil the criteria they lay down for joking to exist – be aggressive to a third party, act weird, or do something anti-social – and not get a laugh. This is easy, because not getting a laugh is child's play.

The experiments I've suggested might sound stupid, but next to some of the real experiments that psychologists have done, they're really quite rational. People have been trying to work out what comedy's all about for thousands of years, but it's only in this century that they've tried to test their theories in the science lab. Ha! What a waste of time! Experimental psychologists have assumed that it's as easy to create laughter in a laboratory as it is to generate electricity. Wrong! One of the fundamental rules of scientific investigation is that experiments should be carried out under controlled conditions, without extraneous variables. But extraneous variables are the very stuff of what makes people laugh: where you happen to be, what sort of mood you're in, whether you've had a few beers, the company you find yourself in, all these things are going to determine whether you find a joke funny or not. If you don't agree they're important, try getting up and launching into a stand-up comedy routine in the middle of a funeral and see how many laughs you get.

That's one of the problems with a psychology lab. It doesn't provide the ideal surroundings for a bloody good laugh. And as if that wasn't bad enough, once you're in the lab, the experimenters do weird things to you. Stanley Schachter and Ladd Wheeler had a little test in which they injected subjects with epinephrine (adrenaline), chlorpromazine or a saline solution before showing them clips from comedy films. Schachter and Wheeler had edited the clips together themselves, obviously believing that psychologists have an innate grasp of the delicate art of comedy cinematography. The thing about experiments like this is, injecting somebody with an unnamed substance isn't an ideal way of getting them in the mood for a good chuckle. I've certainly been desperate for a laugh on occasion, but I've never thought of improving my chances by injecting members of the audience with chlorpromazine. The most extreme example that I've come across of doing weird stuff to the subjects is an experiment by Ronald Langevin and H.I. Day: 'Beckman electrodes with electrode paste were placed on the palm and back of the left hand for Galvanic Skin Response measures, and others were placed just below the elbow on the inside of each arm for Heart Rate measures. An ear clip was also used to ground the subject to the shielded room in which the experiment took place.'

I love that bit about using an ear clip to 'ground the subject to the shielded room', you know, the idea that they're making sure that once they've got you in their lab, you can't escape. I have this image of a cartoon mad scientist: 'Zo, Meester Bond, you are in my power! I have attached ze electrodes to your skin so zat I can convert your laughter power into energy to power my giant laughter gun which is at zis very moment in orbit around ze earth and pointing at London!! Crack ze merest smile and you will generate enough power to destroy civilisation as we know it in one gigantic explosion and ze whole world will be in my grasp ah ha ha ha ha ha haaaa!!!!'

Given all this injecting with stimulants and wiring up to electrodes, it's no surprise that experimental psychologists Pollio, Mers and Lucchesi have admitted that, 'No one has ever reported the occurrence of an explosive, full-bodied belly-laugh under laboratory conditions.' Having said this, I did once read a paper, and sadly I've lost track of where I saw it, in which the experimenters did manage to make the subjects laugh. The experiment was trying to work out exactly which bit of a joke makes you laugh, which precise word it is that acts as the laughter trigger. To find this out, they'd got hold of some jokes, and written them out in big letters on a long strip of paper. Then they'd cut a hole in the wall and wound each end of the strip to a roll either side of this hole. The subjects were taken into the lab, and the joke was wound from one roll to the other so that only one word showed through the hole at a time. The subjects howled with laughter not at the joke itself, but at the sight of this wacky piece of apparatus, the spools creaking as the carefully lettered joke juddered jerkily past. The scientists had tried to set up a psychology experiment, but what they'd actually created was a superb piece of Dadaist cabaret.

Freud's ideas on comedy weren't based on nutty experiments like this, but on his own casual observations. He split jokes into two categories, 'innocent' and 'tendentious'. Innocent jokes are just a harmless bit of fun, but tendentious jokes are about giving voice to repressed aggressive and sexual urges. So far so good, but ultimately, a lot of Freud's analysis doesn't stand the test of time, because it's so obviously rooted in the values and social habits of his day. Here's his angle on sex jokes: man wants sex with woman . . . man starts talking sexy to turn woman on . . . woman blushes with embarrassment and fends man off, which is just a manifestation of her repressed desire (i.e. she says No but she means Yes – nice to know that Freud had something in common with high court judges) . . . man starts talking smut to another man who's in the room to try and break down woman's 'resistance' . . . in polite society, this sort of smutty talk isn't thought respectable, so it has to be disguised in the form of jokes.

So there it is: men crack dirty jokes to their friends to try and persuade women to go to bed with them. The reason they have to do this in the first place is 'women's incapacity to tolerate undisguised sexuality, an incapacity correspondingly increased with a rise in the educational and social level.' What Freud would've made of the modern-day lager-swigging, barman de-bagging, dirty-talking hen party, cackling with pissed-up glee as one of them pretends to fellate to a wine bottle, is anybody's guess.

I think it was Ken Dodd who said that Freud's all very well, but he never had to play second house on a Friday night at the Glasgow Empire. Personally, I prefer the idea of the Father of Psychoanalysis having a go at an open-mic. spot at an alternative comedy club:

(A balding, bespectacled figure with a snowy-white beard shuffles nervously about near the side of the stage, occasionally sipping from a half of bitter-shandy. The compere is squeezing out a few laughs between acts. Then:)
COMPERE: He's just doing a short set for you this evening, and it's his first time at Cheap Laughs Comedy Club, so be nice to him. And remember, the more you laugh, the funnier he'll be, so here he is, er, forgotten his name there for a minute – Mr Sigmund Freud!

(Applause. Freud nervously struts across to the micro-phone stand, cautiously prods at it in a vain attempt to adjust it.)

FREUD: Good evening. Two neurotics were talking one day. One said to the other. 'I don't understand it. Previously, my psychoanalyst has told me that my emotional problems stem from being orally fixated.' 'What of it?' replied the second. 'Well today,' said the first. 'I told him I was unable to pay the fee and he told me to shove it up my arse. Thus implying that I am not orally fixated, but am in fact anally retentive!' *(He pauses. No response. One person giggles. Chit chat breaks out at the back. He continues, more nervously:)* Er . . . that then was my first joke, and it was of the tendentious variety. Erm . . . er . . . Perhaps something a little more observational would be more to your taste? You know what it's like er, when you've repressed your infantile sexual desire towards your mother, and . . . ?

HECKLER: Get off, you're shit!

FREUD: Ah! Non-sublimated aggressive urges. Perhaps you are not aware that aggressive tendentious jokes succeed best in people in whose sexuality a powerful sadistic component is demonstrable?

HECKLER: Bollocks! *(A smattering of laughter ripples across the audience.)*

FREUD: Er . . . Perhaps it would be best if I finished there.

SECOND HECKLER: Baldie!

FREUD: Erm . . . yes, erm, well . . . thank you and goodnight. *(He shuffles off the stage to muted applause and restive muttering.)*

COMPERE: Right, that was Sigmund Freud there. Anyway, back to comedy now . . . *(Loud laughter) (Freud goes up to the man running the club and asks. 'Well, how did I do?')*

Another favourite comic theorist of mine is Henri Bergson.

Bergson's idea was that comedy is a way of staving off the mechanisation of life. He thought that we were all in danger of losing our capacity to think, becoming like robots, filling our lives with repetitive tasks without engaging the brain. Jokes are a form of social control, designed to ridicule people who are getting a bit too robot-like. That is to say we laugh when people start acting like machines or when machines start acting like people. If his theory's correct, here are two top-quality jokes:

1. 'Look everybody. I'm a toaster! *(Laughter)* Look, I'm putting two slices of bread into my head *(laughter and applause)* . . . and pushing them down *(laughter and whistles)* . . . wait a couple of minutes *(laughter, cheers and whistles)* . . . and look, there's some toast popping out the top of my head. *(Applause, cheers, whoops, whistles, people falling off their chairs with laughter)*

2. There's a vacuum cleaner on the market with a cute little cartoon face printed on his little round red body. Put him behind the mic.-stand at a comedy club, and switch him on. Pretty soon he'll have his own series, Friday nights on Channel 4.

Austrian zoologist Konrad Lorenz argued that laughter is just one manifestation of human beings' natural aggression, and that it strongly resembles the triumph ceremony in geese. So next time you see a goose coming towards you with a custard pie under its wing – run for it!

Some common myths about comedy

'What's The Secret of Great Comedy? . . . . Timing . . .'
If you ask somebody what they like about their favourite comic, they'll probably say. 'Ooh, well you see it's his

timing, he's got wonderful timing.' They say that because timing is the only aspect of the art of stand-up comedy that they've heard of. Saying, 'Ooh, well you see it's his jokes, he's got wonderful jokes,' would make them sound a bit stupid, because it's too obvious. Instead they refer to the mysterious skill of timing, to make it sound as if they know what they're talking about. As far as I'm concerned, saying that good stand-up is about timing is like saying that driving a car is about making the wheels turn round. They do have to turn, but when you're driving you're not thinking about that, you're thinking about the pedals, the gear-stick, the steering wheel and all that.

People seem to think that the masterful control and presence that a good comic exudes onstage is created by standing there concentrating on getting the timing right. As if all comedians have a little joke-clock inside their heads, and all the time they're onstage it's ticking away: one two three, build-up two three four, bit more build-up two three, last bit of build-up two three four and punchline, pause for laughs two three, milk it a bit more two three four five six seven eight, start next joke two three . . .

There are, of course, some jokes in which timing is important. Sometimes, the comic leaves a pause to give the audience time to think ahead and work out what he's going to say next. Here's Tommy Cooper to show you what I mean: 'And I found this old violin. *(Giggle)* This ha ha, old violin. *(Giggle)* And this painting, oil painting. So . . . I took 'em to a . . . an expert. An' 'e said to me, "What you've got there," 'e said. "You've got a Stradivarius. And a Rembrandt. Unfortunately . . . *(growing laugh)* Stradivarius was a terrible painter . . . *(Loud laughter)* . . . and Rembrandt made rotten violins.' *(Laughter and applause)*

By pausing after the word 'unfortunately', he gives them time to work out what the joke's going to be, and the laugh grows as they catch on. He pauses after the first half of the punchline, and they laugh again, as the joke does indeed pan out as they had anticipated. That gives him the chance of getting another laugh when he finishes the punchline. Three laughs for the price of one, milking every last chortle out of the gag just by pausing a couple of times. Now that's timing. Even so, the skill is more about communication than the simple passing of seconds. His gift is having the daring to wait and see if they'll laugh, to see if he's got his idea across. It's not about a little in-head joke-clock ticking away: 'unfortunately' pause two three four five, now hit 'em with the punchline.

Another kind of comic whose use of timing is very evident is the offbeat surrealist. People like Arnold Brown, Kevin McAleer and Michael Redmond, who deal in quirky twists of logic, always seem to glue their ideas together with pauses. I think this is because saying weird things in a normal, everyday sort of voice can lead people to say, 'That's not a joke, that's just stupid.' Somehow, the pauses seem to give the wacky reasoning depth and meaning. The stop-start delivery makes the comedians seem a bit deranged, or perhaps gives the impression that they're from some strange parallel universe with different patterns of speech. Either way, it makes sense that they'd be saying stupid things, because they're a bit weird, a bit removed from reality. Or possibly, the punters are just thinking, 'Well, I've waited long enough for this joke, so I might as well enjoy it while it's here.'

'Comedy's very subjective. I mean everybody's got a different sense of humour, haven't they?'
If sense of humour was so individualised, stand-up comedy would be a very different game. There'd be no big, unified audience laughs. You'd tell your first joke, and maybe a couple of people would laugh. You'd tell your second, and two or three different people would laugh. Your third would get a laugh from yet another handful of people, and so on. Each punter would have to sit there patiently, waiting for the next gag that'd appeal to his or her own personal sense

253

of humour. When it came along, they'd laugh and wait for the next one. On a good night, you might laugh at two or three of the jokes. A great comedian would be one who got each and every member of the audience to laugh at least once, and maybe got as many as ten people laughing at any one joke.

Different people do find different things funny, but the sense of humour doesn't differ so much from person to person that it can't be overridden by the skill and charisma of a comedian. Laughter isn't just about individuals. It's about community. You might laugh loudly at a comic when you're surrounded by hundreds of other laughing people in a theatre, but not as much when you see that same comic on telly when you're alone in your living room.

'There's a sad face behind the clown's happy mask.'
Tony Hancock drinking himself to a lonely death in Australia is the best-known version of a beautiful myth. The comedian can coax gales of laughter out of everybody else, but can't find happiness himself. Poor comedian. He has the rare gift of being able to spread laughter to all around, but the gift carries a terrible price: unhappiness. In another version of the same kind of myth, the comic's career starts at school. He is the outsider, picked on or ignored by everybody else. He starts joking to avoid being bullied.

Personally, I think this tragic tale survives more because it appeals to people's romantic instincts than because it rings true. Without wishing to play down Hancock's unhappy fate, people from all walks of life commit suicide. Deciding to put an end to all your cares and woes by guzzling down a couple of bottles of pills isn't just a comedian's thing, but when, say, a bricklayer kills himself, nobody says, 'Well there you go – it was the sad face behind the bricklayer's happy mask, you see.' What's enticing about the myth of the tragic comedian is the idea that behind the outward show is a reality which is the very opposite. It has the same kind of appeal as the Conservative MP who preaches family values then gets caught with a prostitute. The other thing is that the tragic comedian story is a curiously male tale. Nobody seems to suspect Beryl Reid or Victoria Wood of nursing secret woes.

All of this is not to say that comedians don't have any stress or tension in their lives. Like any creative job, being a stand-up has its difficulties. Inspiration comes and goes, it refuses to be caged or tied down. There is always the worry that one day, the ideas will just dry up. The stress of doing a job which involves getting a given response out of a bunch of strangers night after night is all too obvious. Your successes are in public, but so are your failures. You get caught up in silly little ego battles, jealousy and rivalry. You can fall out of public favour. In the late 1950s, Frankie Howerd fell so low that he almost jacked the whole thing in to run a pub, having been one of the most successful comedians in the country just months before. To be honest, there are no occupations without hazards, and working with other comedians hasn't led me to think that they're the hidden glum brigade that the tears-behind-the-mask myth suggests. Certainly, I'd rather be doing this than cleaning out the sewers.

Having a laugh

Dipping into my own past to find out why I might've been drawn to the world of comedy. I think it all started when I was about seven. On the other side of the playing field, there was a little strip of trees which us kids used to call Dobbin's Wood. According to local kiddie-lore, if you got caught in there by the mythical 'Farmer', he'd lock you up and never let you go. I was in there looking for conkers with my friend and his dad, and I got thinking. Just recently, I'd been messing about a bit and being silly to try and get attention and as I searched the twig-and-leaf floor for conkers, I clearly remember thinking to myself, 'I can go two ways now. I can either be a sensible person and give up the messing about, or I can be a bit of a nutter and be as silly as I want to be.' Even though I was still a young kid. I remember consciously deciding to go for the silly option.

At about the same time, I remember other kids would say things like 'You're stupid,' when I messed about, and at the age of seven it's very hard not to get tearful when somebody says that. One day, a kid said, 'You're stupid,' and I just turned right round and said, 'I know.' It was terrific. He was completely stumped. I'd taken away his power to hurt me with a single swipe. After that, just about anything that couldn't have the label 'sensible' attached to it made me really excited. As I grew up I went through *The Goodies*, *Monty Python*, punk rock, *The Young Ones*, anything that was strange and funny. The nearest I got to using jokes to fend off the school bullies was mucking about so people didn't think I was a swot. I went to a comprehensive school and all the middle-class kids were automatically branded snobs and swots. I wasn't happy about being seen as part of some haughty, hoity-toity elite, so I used to act a bit daft between lessons to try and escape the stereotype. I'd wear punk badges and do impressions of Basil Fawlty in the dinner hour. It didn't always work. I remember making fun of a girl for the benefit of some hard kids who were hanging around in the classroom, only to find out one of them was her brother. I had to do some pretty sharp backtracking to save myself from a good kicking.

Psychological approaches to comedy tend to concentrate on its darker side: its aggression, its taboo-smashing, its roots in repressed psychological urges. The tears behind the smile. I think it's more about play. One of Freud's finest thoughts on laughter was that wordplay harks back to the childhood tendency to play with language. Children make up their own words, they say things just for the very sound of the words, enjoying and exploring the possibilities of the pure noise of language. As they get older, this is forbidden. After all, when you're an adult, you can't say things like, 'Can I 'ave a bing-bong billy banana-ana-wana please?' or people think you're a bit mad. Freud's idea was that puns, double meanings and any kind of jokes that involve twisting language are a way of returning to the childhood freedom to enjoy words for their own sake.

I think all joking is like that. Our lives are ordered and controlled by jobs, time, money, taxes, bills, schedules and responsibilities. Humour gives us a break from all that, because it's about disorder. When you're joking, logic goes haywire and language gets torn apart and glued back together again the wrong way. For a few moments it gives adults a chance to say, 'Hooray, it's playtime!' It's a chance to get away from the world of, 'Oh God, I've got a really heavy day at work tomorrow,' and go back to the world of, 'Last one down to the bottom of the garden is a smelly old bottom!'

Jokes are about incongruity, broken rules, surprising meanings. The build-up leads you to expect a certain outcome, then BAM!, the punchline overturns your expectation. That's why comedy can't always cross cultural barriers. It's all about deviation from the expected order of things, but the expected order of things differs from country to country, from era to era. Listening to comedy from a bygone age, it's tempting to think, 'Oo dear me, they didn't have much of a sense of humour in those days. Listen to the rubbish they used to laugh at.' There are two reasons why former greats like Dan Leno and Max Miller don't have the power to make subsequent generations laugh. One is because the modern listener doesn't share the faith that the original audiences had that these big stars were actually funny. Somehow the confidence trick can't bridge the generation gap. The other reason is that the expectations and values which the comedy heroes of the past were overturning have changed as the world has moved on. Max Miller's 'fan dancer' gag might've been pretty racy in 1957, but in a world in which Ben Elton can go on television and talk about nude sunbathing with Technicolor genital explicitness it's become all but redundant.

Because they deviate from the expected order of things, there's something intrinsically subversive about jokes. With their broken language and mad logic, they suggest the possibility that things might be different. At times, jokes have even been used as a deliberate form of political subversion. During the second world war, in Czechoslovakia, the Czech people told jokes to try and undermine the Nazis who occupied their country. Told amongst themselves, these helped to keep up the spirits of the Czechs and let them believe that one day their country would be free. They were of such symbolic importance that some people even collected them, writing them on pieces of paper, and burying them in jars in their back gardens. They also turned the jokes into graffiti, scrawled across walls and fences to laugh openly in the face of their oppressors. The Nazis felt threatened enough by the gags to arrest and imprison anybody who told them, and immediately and fanatically remove the graffiti.

The subversive strangeness of comedy can make being a stand-up truly dangerous. Reversing expectations can make you laugh, but it can also just leave you puzzled. There's nothing like the panicky, unpleasant feeling you get when somebody's told a joke and you just don't get it. You feel alienated and cheated. You might get cross and petulantly blurt out, 'That's just not funny.'

I think that's often why, traditionally, stand-up comics have tended to plump for old jokes, familiar comic structures and stereotypes. You know where you are with an old joke. You know you're going to understand it. Stereotype jokes let you know exactly what kind of unexpectedness to expect. You're on safe ground. Comedians who try to get laughs in new ways, who avoid the tried and tested approaches, who genuinely deviate from the expected order of things, sometimes find themselves facing the 'That's just not funny' response. That's probably why audiences broke out into fights at Alexei Sayle's early gigs: 'What's all this supposed to be about, I don't get it, this just isn't funny, hey what're *you* looking at, right, take that,' WHAM! SMACK! BIFF!

That's the problem of turning comedy into commodity. When you're selling laughter, you want the audience to laugh, have a few drinks, go away happy and come back next week. You don't want them to start punching each other. You don't want puzzled, sullen silences. You don't want people saying, 'I just don't get it.' The more ramshackle and informal a comedy scene is, the more likely it is to produce subversive comedy. The grassroots working men's club scene of the '30s and '40s produced laid-back proletarian comics like Bobby Thompson. But as the cash stakes got higher and the club circuit was augmented by the big, money-making variety clubs, it started turning out the kind of stand-up joke machines who popped up on *The Comedians*. In its anarchic, amateurish early days, the altcom circuit brought some genuinely mad comedy into the world, but as it got more businesslike the rough edges started getting knocked off and it became more about putting across neat little user-friendly comedy packages.

Once upon a time, stand-up comics could get away with doing less than is expected of them now. When Dan Leno strutted the stages of the murky London halls, jabbering away between the verses of 'Mrs Kelly', dressed in a full dame constume, there was no sense that he was doing anything other than a theatrical turn. He was perfectly free to hide behind characters and costumes and sing songs written by somebody else. When Frank Carson belts out the gags in his fun-filled Ulster bark from the stages of working men's clubs up and down the country, he isn't expected to be anything more than a simple joke-teller. Nobody minds if he hasn't written the gags himself or if they've heard one or two of them before.

Since alternative comedy, though, comics have aspired to a higher aim. It started in pre-alternative times with the originality of comedians like Dave Allen and Billy Connolly. As the altcom circuit produced generation after generation of Alexei Sayles, Jeremy Hardys, and Eddie Izzards, the idea that comedians could hide behind theatrical costumes and old gags was smashed apart. It has become enshrined in comedy law that stand-ups should appear simply as themselves, making their audiences laugh by sharing their own unique slant on the world with them. Outside of the working men's club circuit, gags with previous owners just aren't good enough any more.

This has made stand-up into the perfect medium for self-expression, but that opportunity carries a price tag: the risk of failure. How is it possible to be innovative and individual, to be yourself, and at the same time to get to the essential anarchy of the incongruity that lies at the centre of every joke, without the risk that the audience will just say, 'I don't get it it's just not funny'? The temptation is to avoid pushing back the boundaries, not only because the it's-just-not-funny response is bad for the bank balance, but also because of the sometimes devastating ego-damage that a bad gig can inflict.

For me, that's what being a comedian is all about: refereeing a three-way wrestling match between artistic ambition, ego and the need to get paid at the end of the evening. If I'm so new and different that nobody laughs, my ego and my need-for-money will gang up on my artistic ambition and crush its testicles. Stick too rigidly to tried and tested material and my artistic ambition will start thumping my ego and telling me I'll never think up another new joke in my life, my need-for-money looking on with distant amusement. The only sane approach is to try and satisfy all three, keep them happy, and keep the punters laughing.

I started out by taking you onstage, with a description of the perfect gig. I'd like to finish the way I began, and the perfect end to the perfect gig is a big laugh which builds to deafening applause, drowning out my goodbyes. With that in mind, it'd be nice to end with something really, really funny. So . . . er . . . um . . . Well, like I said, it'd be nice.

My name's Oliver Double, thank you very much, and goodnight. Showbusiness . . . is my life.

Bibliography

John Connor, *Comics*, Papermac, 1990

William Cook, *Ha Bloody Ha*, Fourth Estate, 1994

Hunter Davies, *The Grades*, Weidenfeld & Nicolson, 1981

Les Dawson, *A Card for the Clubs*, Sphere, 1974

Les Dawson, *A Clown Too Many*, Fontana, 1985

Florence Desmond, *Florence Desmond by Herself*, George G. Harrap, 1953

John Fisher, *Funny Way To Be A Hero*, Frederick Muller, 1973

Sigmund Freud, *Jokes and Their Relation to the Unconscious*, Penguin, 1976

Jeffrey H. Goldstein and Paul E. McGhee (eds), *The Psychology of Humour*, Academic Press, 1972

William Hall, *Titter Ye Not*, Grafton, 1992

Leslie Halliwell, *Double Take and Fade Away*, Grafton, 1987

Peter Honri, *Working the Halls*, Saxon House, 1973

David Housham and John Frank-Keyes, *Funny Business*, Boxtree, 1992

Frankie Howerd, *On The Way I Lost it*, Star, 1976

Paul E. McGhee, *Humour: Its Origin and Development*, W.H. Freeman, 1979

Geoff J. Mellor, *They Made Us Laugh*, George Kelsall, 1982

Eric Midwinter, *Make 'Em Laugh*, George Allen and Unwin, 1979

Eric Morecambe and Ernie Wise, *Eric and Ernie*, Star, 1972

Jimmy Tarbuck, *Tarbuck on Showbiz*, Fontana, 1985

John Taylor, *From Self Help to Glamour*, Oxford University Press, 1972

Barry Took, *Laughter in the Air*, Robson/BBC, 1981
Barry Took, *Star Turns*, Weidenfeld & Nicolson, 1992
Charlie Williams, *Ee, I've Had Some Laughs*, Wolfe, 1973
Roger Wilmut, *Kindly Leave the Stage*, Methuen, 1985
Roger Wilmut and Peter Rosengard, *Didn't You Kill My Mother-in-Law?*, Methuen, 1989